BASSO CANTANTE

Frontispiece   The author, as Rocco in *Fidelio*.

DAVID FRANKLIN

Basso Cantante

AN AUTOBIOGRAPHY

GERALD DUCKWORTH

LONDON

First published in 1969 by
Gerald Duckworth & Co. Ltd.,
3, Henrietta Street, London, WC2

© 1969, DAVID FRANKLIN

SBN 7156 0416 3

Printed in Great Britain by
The Camelot Press Ltd., London and Southampton

For Mary, Janet and Susan,
who had to live through all this

CONTENTS

ILLUSTRATIONS

ONE

On Being Discovered

CURIOUSLY ENOUGH it wasn't a romantic magazine story of a long, hard, bitter struggle for recognition. It just happened to me, almost around me, without any conscious effort, and it took only a few months.

I had been a Choral Exhibitioner at Cambridge, but not at King's, or John's, or Trinity. At the time, I wished I was a member of one of those fashionable choirs, with people queueing overnight to hear *me*—and the others, of course—sing the Christmas Eve Carol Service. I privately thought my voice was just about the best bass in the University. At any rate, I sang leads in the University opera, and I was in great demand for my low D in the Madrigal Society, for concerts at the University Music Club, and at colleges all round Cambridge. Once, I remember to my pride, my reputation had spread and I was asked to sing as far away as Girton. During one Christmas vac, I even sang in London. Not, I ought to add, in the Queen's Hall, or the Wigmore Hall. The Archway Hall is not quite as central, but it was certainly in London. There was at my college a man called Soper, a year senior to me, with whom I was friendly, and his elder brother Don, a bustling young Methodist minister at Archway, who asked me to sing at one of his Saturday Night People's Concerts. Don billed me, to my astonishment, as 'Harold C. Franklin, the Popular Young

Baritone'. I should perhaps explain that David is a name that
I appropriated later when I turned pro, for, not realising that
the infant they had bred was an opera-singer, my parents
thoughtlessly gave me two names that would have been impossible in the billings. Don knew my initials were H.C., but had
no idea what my Christian names were. The printer urgently
needed the text of the posters, and Don took a chance, a long
chance as it turned out, on what I was called. I sent him an
indignant letter—'I am not Harold,' I wrote, 'and I am not a
baritone.' 'And Heaven knows,' Don replied with his Hyde
Park wit, 'you are not popular.' But I actually sang in London.
I was now free to have myself billed as 'Bass—Leading London
and Provincial Concerts'. I was getting on.

Possibly I could have held my own in one of the big Cambridge choirs. But instead, I served my time in a small choir
in a college not remarkable for its music. It was male-voices-
only, and we sang Evensong on Thursdays and Saturdays, and
Matins and Evensong on Sundays. When I went up, we sang
early Communion too on alternate Sundays, but soon I went
plaintively to my tutor, who was also the College Chaplain,
and pleaded that Merbecke in D, in unison, at 7.30 a.m., was
much too high and sheer torture for a young bass voice.
Successive generations of exhibitioners owe me gratitude for
relieving them of this heavy burden. Early Merbecke in D
disappeared suddenly from our list of duties, and our weekly
stint fell to no more than three Evensongs and a Matins. After
a laborious calculation, during an inaudible sermon by a distinguished visiting theologian, I decided that my Exhibition
worked out at twopence per line for every hymn that we sang.
'Onward Christian Soldiers' I sang, and mentally my private
taximeter clocked up another twopence—it was reassuring to
hear it clicking away, line after line. 'Marching as to war'—
fourpence up. Later I realised that having to sing as little as
this each week during the years when my voice was growing
was invaluable for a professional career. Most singers in
England begin too young, before the voice is firm enough to

take the strain of performance, and my unfashionable choir with its small repertoire spared me from having to overwork the voice. In the end I knew that it was a merciful Providence that had kept me from ever offering myself as a candidate at King's, or John's, or Trinity. I might have got in.

Though the pleasures of belonging to one of these choirs are great, there are, to my mind, two big disadvantages. One is that you spend so much time at choir practices that you simply cannot be available for whatever you want to do in the afternoons—and the afternoons were half the fun of Cambridge; the other is that you acquire what I have always thought of, perhaps unkindly, as the 'King's hoot'. To make the most of the acoustics of King's Chapel, the tone of the choir must be smooth, round, warm, dark—*cupo*, the Italians would call it. There must be a uniformity of tone so that the voices blend. So that they match the male altos, they all have to sing like male altos, even the tenors and the basses. They are drilled until individuality of voice is ironed out, and only the perfection of the King's blend is left. But a professional must live by his individuality, by the unmistakable quality of his voice. He cannot establish himself until audiences have come to recognise his voice among many—and are then willing to pay to hear it. If I had been at King's, the betting is, I think, that I would never have become a pro.

There is proof enough. King's had the pick of the best voices from the schools for years and years and years—the best voices, with musicianship and intelligence thrown in for good measure. But you can count on the fingers of one hand the names of King's Choral Scholars in my time who turned themselves into good pros. (It is only fair to add that there has been an obvious development in King's voices in recent years. The choir have the same polish, the same blending of tone, but the tenors and basses now have far more bite than their predecessors had in the past.)

I had always wanted to be a singer. During my last year in the sixth form at a grammar school in London, my headmaster had taken me to the four nights of the *Ring*. I sat in the gallery at Covent Garden, intoxicated by the heavy, rich wine of Wagner's music. I had been to opera regularly at the Old Vic, and at Sadler's Wells, and had first been to an opera—*Maritana*—when I was only eleven; but opera on the grand scale, and in the international season at Covent Garden, tremendously excited me. I had sung this-and-that at school, and, by school standards, I had a good voice. I was arrogant enough, when I heard singers on the radio and in the theatre, to feel instinctively that my voice could do what they were doing with theirs.

I had day-dreaming fantasies of singing at Covent Garden. Mostly they were full of the glory and the excitement of taking solo calls in front of the red-and-gold curtains, with an adoring audience cheering me. I knew nothing of the tensions of performance, of the endless work of rehearsal. I was content to dream about the adoring audience. But one thing I did know, young and innocent as I was. I wanted to do the thing properly. Not for me the concert party on the Pier in the open air ('in the Town Hall if wet') in a pierrot's costume with bobbles dangling down the front. I did not fancy singing 'The Trumpeter' and 'Up from Zummerset' all through the summer, and acting as the feed to the comedian, with a winter spent bellowing 'Ho! jolly Jenkins', at five guineas a time to Masonic dinner audiences fuddled with drink. I wanted to sing properly, or not at all. I had no idea how it could be done, well or badly. In the middle of my time at Cambridge, my sixth-form master from school, whom I met during one vac in London, urged me to go into the Church. 'With your voice and presence,' he said earnestly, 'you'd be a minor canon at St. Paul's in no time!' Even this giddy prospect somehow did not sufficiently attract me and, when I left Cambridge with a degree in English and History, I played safe, for the first and last time in my life, and got a job as a schoolmaster.

I taught at Sutton Valence. One of the staff greeted me with the information—his stock introduction to new men as they arrived—that Sutton Valence was 'one of the more important of our lesser public schools'. Certainly its pay was above the average. I remember I felt passing rich on £210 a year plus free board and lodging during term-time. I taught English, History, Latin (working each night to keep a step ahead of my form, for I had done no Latin after matriculation) and Divinity. The Divinity bit surprised me. It happened that Form IVb had a Divinity lesson at 9 a.m. every Monday morning, and I was the only man on the staff who had a gap in his timetable at that time. So I taught Divinity. The intellectual standard of the school was not then particularly high. I remember one boy who had written an essay for me on 'The intellectual correspondence between French and English political philosophers in the eighteenth century'. I had talked about the genesis of the French Revolution one afternoon, and, I thought, had talked rather well, and set that essay for preparation that night. Cooper minor produced two pages of badly written incoherence in which his first sentence shone brilliantly like a beacon, and has continued to shine across the years, as an unequalled exhibition of English prose at its most singular. 'The English potictical thinkers,' he wrote, 'were great friends of the French pololical men.' It was a privilege to play my part in educating the future leaders of the country.

There were relaxations from the hard grind of teaching the lower half of each year (and new men always had the lower half). I helped to produce plays, I took charge of school shooting, served in the O.T.C., and took my turn at supervising Sunday walks, and the boys' meals. And I sang. The school music master greeted me suspiciously when I arrived. He said: 'I hear you've got a voice. I expect you sing muck, like everyone else.' 'Yes,' I said, cheerfully, 'muck like the B minor Mass and the *Messiah* and rubbish by people like Schubert, and Brahms.' 'Do you?' he said, interested in spite of his first suspicion; and for the five years I was to be at Sutton Valence I regularly sang the leading bass parts in the oratorios and the concerts which the school produced.

Sometimes I sang outside the school—my fame spread as far as Langley, a village four miles away. One morning the postman, instead of dropping our letters through the hole as he usually did, thundered on our door at 7.15, until I dragged myself from bed and went down in a dressing-gown. 'I'm sorry to bring you out of bed, Sir, but might I 'ave a word with you?' I conceded that he might. 'We're 'aving a little Passion in our church come Easter, and I 'ave been deputed to ask you if you would care to join us in our Passion.' It was bitterly cold on the doorstep in a thin dressing-gown, and I quickly agreed that I was ripe for his Passion, a decision that afterwards I bitterly regretted.

I had two pupils who were afterwards to become famous. One was Sidney Wooderson, the runner, who took the world record for the mile down to a few seconds over four minutes. I like to think that my teaching of English and History had some slight influence on his speed on the track. The other was Groves, C. G. (Westminster House). At the end of one after-noon the form beat it the moment the bell rang, but Groves came to my desk, and said, with grave dignity, 'Are you ready, Sir?' I agreed that I was, and he led me off to a music practice room where he began coaching me in the part of the Christus in Bach's St. John Passion.

I can boast that I recognised talent then when I saw it. The school orchestra—all of twelve players—lacked a viola, so the Director of Music took over the job himself, and allowed Groves, C. G. to conduct. I watched this boy, who had never had a lesson in conducting, and had never stood on the box before. He had the air, the manner, and the confidence of an experienced pro. He gave tremendous leads to little boys struggling at the back desks with awkward instruments. And I nudged my wife, and whispered, 'There, in thirty years' time, stands the next Sir Henry J. Wood.' It was, though I say it myself, pretty sound judgment. For Groves, C. G. is now Charles Groves, who was to conduct the B.B.C. Northern, the Bournemouth, and the Royal Liverpool Philharmonic Orches-

1a. Beginning of an opera house, Glyndebourne, about 1936, before John Christie had had time to pull his theatre down and rebuild it.

1b. Beginning of a career. Mary and D.F. on a night off at Glyndebourne in 1936.

11a. *Macbeth*, 1938. D.F., Hans Peter Busch (son of Fritz, and assistant producer), with Carl Ebert at a stage rehearsal.

11b. The Hallé *Messiah* in the circus ring at Belle Vue, Manchester, 1947. D.F. singing, and, sitting to the right, the other soloists—Kathleen Ferrier, Isabel Baillie, and Heddle Nash. (The conductor, out of the picture, was Malcolm Sargent.)

tras, and has always sworn that in the preparation for life which he received at school all he remembers of the History I taught him are the dirty bits.

For several years, I went in the summer to a Music Camp. This may seem a strange sort of organisation, and a strange way to spend a holiday. It was. We lived under canvas, ate heartily but simply, and made music from morning till night in a barn big enough to hold orchestra and chorus. It was started by a Cambridge physicist, and most of the campers were scientists, teachers, university lecturers, surgeons, accountants, with a sprinkling of young professional orchestral musicians. There was a good deal of talent knocking about and a number of experienced pros were there to give professional leadership and expertness to our eager amateur enthusiasts. One year Steuart Wilson came, then nearly at the end of his singing career, and I sang Hunding to his Siegmund in a concert performance of Act I of *Die Walküre*. It was heady music for a young man—and a splendid, cheap, exciting holiday.

Each Christmas there was a camp reunion in London, when we met, and ate, and drank, and sang through the B minor Mass just for the fun of making music together. One year, I sang the 'Quoniam'. Gertrude Lampson, who had been a professional pianist and accompanist, and was a power in Sussex amateur music, was invited to our performance by a camper friend, heard me sing, and I was introduced to her afterwards by another camper, Ursula Nettleship. Ursula was a teacher of singing, and a woman of tremendous energy and enthusiasm for music. She had discovered me at an earlier camp, and was giving me occasional lessons, to try to help me to get my big voice under control. She whispered to me, before she took me to meet Mrs. Lampson, that I was going to be asked to sing in a Nativity pageant at a church in Chelsea. My first reaction was to say 'Like hell I will', but Ursula sternly told me to say 'Yes'. Astonished at myself, when Gertrude asked me to sing for her, I said, 'Yes.'

This is the way in which promising voices become professional singers. A chain reaction starts, and the reaction that started that night was to take me within eighteen months from an amateur music camp to an international cast at Glyndebourne. No one who saw the performance of the pageant at Gertrude's church in Chelsea would have suspected for a moment that it would have any importance in building a career. The curate had once walked on at the Old Vic, and had never got over it. He had written what I remember as a rather corny and sentimental series of Nativity scenes. My own part in the proceedings was relatively small. I sang a Nunc Dimittis, in pitch darkness, behind the scenes, in a fishy smell of glue and size. I did my stuff on a cue from the stage manager, but it was not until afterwards that the curate told me reproachfully that I had taken the wrong cue. Afterwards, I dined at Gertrude's house, and in the middle of dinner she turned to me and said, 'Mr. Franklin, you have such a good voice. Why don't you do something about it?' I was outraged. I was then in the stage when I knew, because so many people had told me, and because I sensed it myself, that I had a voice. But I would never admit even to myself that I had a lot to learn, and defensively I told myself that I knew about singing. So, coldly, I changed the subject.

A few weeks later Gertrude asked me to sing four small bass parts—Peter, Pilate, the High Priest, and Judas—in the Matthew Passion at the annual music festival of the East Sussex Federation of Women's Institutes. I was to receive an 'expense fee' of two guineas, and to a young schoolmaster, earning by then six pounds a week, this was riches indeed. Later still, Gertrude wrote to warn me not to book a hotel room in Lewes. 'Good,' I thought, 'two guineas—all for me!' She went on to add that Mr. and Mrs. Christie of Glyndebourne had offered artists in the festival hospitality for the weekend. 'Christie,' I said to my wife, 'Christie? Christie. I've read that name somewhere. It was in the *Telegraph* yesterday. Where is it? Yes—here it is. It's that fellow who has built an opera house in his back garden! Very odd. It might be fun to see what it's all about.' She agreed it might be fun, and when the time came I went proudly down to Lewes where I was to sing with famous professional singers, on the very same platform, for the first time. They were Elsie Suddaby, Mary Jarred, Eric Greene, and George Parker, who sang the Christus most beautifully and sensitively, much to my disappointment, because I had decided that this was to be My Big Chance.

I had learnt not only the twenty-four bars that covered my four little parts but every note of the part of Christ. Well, there was always the chance—wasn't there?—that George Parker would collapse on the platform. (I did not wish him permanent ill. A broken leg would be a bit cruel perhaps, but I was prepared to settle for a fainting attack.) There would be chaos, and panic on the stage, and sensation amongst the audience. With a calm but confident little smile playing round the corners of my lips, I should take charge of the situation. 'I will sing the Christus,' I would say, and there would be a murmur of admiration from the audience, and the conductor would silently press my hand. 'Just take Mr. Parker to hospital, and make the poor fellow comfortable,' I'd say, quietly, 'and then we can begin.' And, in a breathless hush of approval, this new, fresh young voice would pour out over the Town Hall at Lewes, and next morning the national press would be full of the rise of a great new star, who had sung a sensational performance. And I could at least have sung the right notes. Unfortunately, Mr. Parker remained obstinately fit, and I was much more nervous in my four little parts than I had ever thought I should be, but shakily managed to get through them somehow. It was not, after all, My Big Chance.

So I thought. But I had the weekend in front of me at Glyndebourne, and, though I could not know it at the time, My Big Chance was after all waiting there for me. Not that there was any sign of it on that Saturday night. We had gone straight to the Town Hall from the station for the afternoon rehearsal, and had changed there into tails for the evening performance. So my first sight of Glyndebourne came in the darkness and the rain as we were driven there from Lewes. We stood around in the front hall—a very big room, with a great log fire, deep armchairs, even deeper settees, books and family portraits, and a feeling of comfort and tradition. I was introduced to John Christie, and to Audrey, and there were sandwiches and drinks and cigarettes. A dark, saturnine man, with pointed ears, wearing a black coat, a winged collar and a black tie, with black and grey striped trousers, wheeled the drink trolley up to me and asked me what I would like to drink. I knew nothing of Le Highlife, and took him for a butler. (Did butlers dress like that? I had no idea.) I was devilish off-hand and poised, and said, casually, 'Whisky and soda, please.' He poured and handed me the drink and then added—damn his impertinence!—'I liked your woice.' I bridled at once and said '. . . which means you didn't like the way I sang?' 'I did not say so,' he said, 'but it is true.' That was my first meeting with the redoubtable Jani Strasser, to whose Svengali I was to play a shy and sometimes reluctant Trilby for over five years.

Jani came from a wealthy family in Budapest. He was brought up in a very musical home. His brother Istvan became a conductor in Russia, his sister is a teacher of singing still in Budapest. There was a family tradition of music and as a boy Jani had sung the leading soprano parts in performances of works like the Verdi *Requiem* round the piano at home. He once told me that by the time his voice broke his repertory included all the major lyric soprano parts in both oratorio and opera. As a young man, he threw up his job in the family firm—they were wheat merchants—and went to study singing in Vienna with Leherhammer. He became Leherhammer's pet pupil, but never made a career as a performer. But, as a teacher, he is knowledgeable about voices, and has an astonishing insight into style and period and, at the last count, he had five languages, in which he is fluent, and can often be devastating.

When he first came to England, he was dining with friends

of mine, and the conversation turned upon bathrooms. Jani said that he liked a bath that you walk down into, and not one that you must climb over the side of. (He had in fact—I've seen it—such a bath in the family house in Budapest, a magnificent sunken bath of black marble.) His hostess said that she liked a bathroom with a lovely view from the window, and a young soprano—charming, pretty, and very much the English rose—said primly that *she* liked to have a blind for *her* bathroom window. 'Why?' said Jani, coldly, 'Are you deformed?'

When Audrey Christie was accepted by Busch as a member of the Glyndebourne company, she went to Vienna to work on her voice, ready for the opening season. But she did not get on with the teacher with whom lessons had been arranged. She was on the point of leaving for home when she was introduced to Jani. She was taken with his work as a teacher, and asked him to come back to Glyndebourne with her. There he became not only her teacher, but a coach, and one of the original team, working with Oppenheim and Erede, under Busch and Ebert. He dominated my life while I was learning my trade, and I learnt more from him than I can ever acknowledge. He has great charm, stamina, and an insatiable appetite for work, and for the best that he can get out of you; and over and over again he can be quite insufferable.

We had another performance of the Passion to give on the Sunday afternoon, in Chichester Cathedral, and that night, as we went into dinner, Ursula Nettleship, who was also a guest at Glyndebourne that weekend, hissed at me that later in the evening I was going to be asked to sing. The Christies had heard only my bits in the Passion and they were curious to hear more. 'Say yes,' Ursula whispered. (She always seemed to be on hand to tell me to say 'Yes' at what afterwards turned out to be critical moments in my chain reaction.) After dinner, as we drank coffee in the front hall, sure enough Audrey said, casually, they were going to have some music in the Organ Room, and would I care to sing? I said yes. I hadn't got any music with me, but we searched through the music shelves in the library and I sang 'The Refiner's Fire' from the *Messiah*, with Jani playing for me, just about as loud, I think, as it can ever have been sung. 'Thank you,' said Audrey politely, and soon after I went to bed. Next morning another guest for the weekend nudged me, as we helped ourselves to porridge and bacon and eggs from the hot-plate, and whispered, 'They were up half the night arguing about you,' and I felt excited and pretty cocky. But I still did not realise how important the night before had been in my life.

Next morning, I went back home, and a few days later term started. My life was full again of O.T.C. and the school play, and teaching, and supervising school walks, and having boys in to tea on Sunday afternoons. I went on with singing lessons with Ursula in London, as often as I could get up. Six months later, I had a letter from Audrey, who said that she remembered my singing from Easter with so much pleasure that she ventured (ventured!) to offer me an audition with Fritz Busch in December. I was madly excited—singing, here I come! And no end-of-the-pier or Masonic concerts, either. Ursula very unselfishly said that I needed help from an expert in opera, and that I must start work with Jani; so twice a week, after a full day's teaching, I left Kent, in a horrible little old Morris two-seater, drove to London, had a lesson with Jani—sometimes they lasted two-and-a-half hours—then sleepily drove back to Kent.

About 21 December, I underhandedly arranged to switch some of my teaching with friends on the staff, to give myself a clear afternoon, and I went to London without the courtesy of asking the Head. I drove to Swanley Junction. I took a first-class ticket to Holborn—I couldn't really afford it, but I had to have a carriage to myself so that I could sing exercises, and get my voice warmed up en route. I took a taxi to the Wigmore Hall—I couldn't afford that, either, but once I'd got my voice going, I had to keep it warm, and I went on singing along Oxford Street to the open astonishment of the driver. I was shown into the Artists' Room at the Wigmore, and found it full of singers that I recognised from hearing and seeing them in concerts and in opera. This was terrifying. It was an impertinence for an unknown schoolmaster to sing against the competition of big names in English singing.

I was the last to sing. Busch listened at the back of the hall. Then he swept up on to the platform, pushed the pianist away from the keyboard, and started playing himself. 'Come. Sing,' he said, and I did my stuff all over again with Busch watching me like a hawk. I finished, and Bing, Strasser, Christie, Audrey, Oppenheim, all came up on to the platform, and went into a huddle, with me on tiptoe on the fringe, like a scrum-half waiting for the ball to be heeled. I couldn't understand what they were saying. Busch saw me trying to listen, grinned, and said, 'Do you speak German?' 'No,' I said. 'Goot,' he said. 'But I'm damn well going to learn,' I said. 'Also goot,' he said, and plunged back into the scrum. After some minutes, they reached agreement, broke up, shook hands all round, and left the platform. No one said a word to me. I found myself standing alone, ran after Jani, caught him up, and asked plaintively how I'd done, and what was happening? 'You will sing the Commendatore,' he said, 'And you will come to Vienna for three months to study with me. We leave on Monday.' I gathered from this that I had become a professional singer. I went to Vienna that Monday.

For the next four years, I worked with Jani. At first, I had as many as three lessons a day—in Vienna, London, Budapest, Salzburg, wherever he happened to be. I was half frightened, half exhilarated by my sudden change of fortune. I wasn't the only one to be scared. When I got back to London from Vienna, just before we started rehearsals for the season at Glyndebourne, I met my old housemaster by chance in the street.

Poor old Bob Taylor! He was very worried, he said, because he'd heard rumours that I had resigned my job in order to follow this madcap idea of singing. Was it true? I said cheerfully that it was—and that was only the half of it. A couple of months before Christmas, I'd been appointed senior English master at Dulwich College, to start the following September, and I'd resigned that job, too. Two for the price of one, so to speak. Bob winced. 'My dear boy,' he said, 'I do hope that you've not made a mistake. Have you thought it out carefully? Do you realise that you had only thirty-five years to go for your pension?' If ever I had had doubts about the wisdom of throwing my hat over the moon, and becoming a pro, that remark settled them. Whatever was to happen to me in the future, it couldn't be worse than a profession where a man could talk calmly about having only thirty-five years to wait for a pension.

Six months after my audition, at the beginning of the 1936 season, I made my debut as the Commendatore in *Don Giovanni* in a magnificent international cast. Brownlee, Baccaloni, Luise Helletsgrüber, Ina Souez, Koloman von Pataky, Audrey Christie, Roy Henderson—and me. I felt a very new boy. Between them, the others had experience of Covent Garden, of Paris, and Vienna, and Prague, and Budapest, and the Scala in Milan, and Salzburg—you name it, they'd sung there. I hadn't sung anywhere. But there were advantages in being flung in at the deep end with a cast like that. True, it was sink-or-swim. I swam.

At the end of the season, we made a complete recording of *Don Giovanni*, and it became a great success in the 78 version. It was copied on to L.P. records after the war, and it stayed in the catalogues, and was consistently recommended as the 'Best Buy' in the connoisseurs' guides until it was finally withdrawn from the current lists in 1965. We had twenty-nine years 'in the charts'. It was issued on another label in America, and it is to be reissued in Great Britain in 1969, and it goes on and on. Not that we get any more from the extra sales. We got a flat rate at the time of four pounds a side. You sang on twenty-five sides, and you got a cheque for a hundred pounds. I sang on four sides—sixteen pounds. But, very oddly, my cheque was for twenty. I had no idea why, until I realised that I sang on a fifth side—I'd forgotten. It was the duet 'O statua gentilissima' between Don Giovanni and Leporello, in the cemetery scene, in which the Don, in a fit of bravado, asks the statue of the Commendatore to come to supper with him. I sang 'Sì'. One word—two beats—four pounds. That made me, for a blissful moment, the highest-paid singer in the world. Not even Gigli got four pounds a note. The trouble was that I didn't keep it up long enough.

This was the first of four happy and exciting seasons at Glyndebourne before the war. My first contract gave me the Commendatore, a couple of small parts in the *Magic Flute*, and the understudy to Kipnis as Sarastro. This for me was unbelievable. I had worshipped Kipnis for years. He had a wonderful, dark, expressive voice, and was one of the world's greatest basses. He had a great range of colour, great tenderness, and an immaculate line. I had heard all of these in his recitals at the Wigmore Hall, and had listened spellbound to his records. And here I was, his understudy, sitting and talking to him at the side of the stage. 'Come,' he said, 'tell me about yourself.' This I was very ready to do—more than ready, it was a pleasure—and I was just getting warmed up when he was called to rehearse—'Herr Kipnis, bitte auf die Bühne.' 'Excuse,' he said, 'I must go.' He got up, then turned with a delightful smile. 'I go, young man,' he said, 'I go—to make competition for you!' It was a charming thing to say to a young, awkward and ambitious beginner. Not that I had much chance to make competition for him. As the Monastatos, who came from Hamburg, said to me pityingly, 'Poor young man! You may sing Sarastro next year, but not this year. Kipnis *always* sings. Even if—Even if—' he struggled for the right phrase, and found it. 'Even if he is *dead*, he will still sing!'

I did sing Sarastro next year. It was fun, singing. I had a big, strong voice. And I poured it out recklessly, and the critics wrote about the power and the dignity of my performances. I thought this was all there was to singing. Then, in 1938, we did the first production in England of Verdi's *Macbeth*, and I sang Banco. *The Times* said something about 'Mr. Franklin's *moving* performance of Banco'—and it was as if I had been slapped in the face. For the first time, I realised that I could move people, could actually move them to tears—and it was one of the biggest shocks that I had ever had. I began to *think* about singing.

In April 1939, I sang in a Mozart Festival at the Flemish Theatre in Antwerp and the Théâtre Royale de la Monnaie in Brussels. I made, in this short season, two interesting discoveries. The first was that when a Flemish stage-hand drops a hammer on his toe, he uses exactly the same four-letter words that an English stagehand does. The second discovery was a considerable shock. When we lined up for the final calls in *The Marriage of Figaro*, in which I sang Bartolo, I was on the very end of the line-up, and I leant forward and looked along the dozen or so singers, from Paris and Budapest and Rome and Vienna and Hamburg, who were jointly bowing their thanks to the audience. The contract had stipulated that each artist must provide his own costume, and, to my awful fascination, 250 years would not have covered the time-span of the weird collection of costumes that, between us, we had brought. Bernard Shaw, in his days as a music critic, once wrote this about productions of opera in England.

There is only one period—'The Past'; only two sets—'An Exterior' and 'An Interior'. In *Martha* I had seen Queen Anne alive, with her ladies in Victorian dress, her retinue Plantagenet, the buffo bass in eighteenth-century full-bottomed wig, and the chorus in tights from *Trovatore*.

I thought this funny when I first read it, and innocently I imagined that those were the bad old days and that they couldn't happen to me. I was wrong. It was a shock to find that not every theatre was prepared to pay the same attention to detail as Glyndebourne. It is, in several respects, a remarkable theatre.

TWO

Glyndebourne

IMMEDIATELY PAST Ringmer village, there is an A.A. sign that points to the left. At last you can leave the main road, and you drive up a long and narrow lane, with high hedges on each side, and a very steep climb it is. Over the top of the hill, the descent is even steeper, but there is still nothing to see, for on the left the trees are much too thick. But soon there is a gap and you turn into the drive, which runs between wide, elegant lawns. And there it is—a great house, with the Sussex downs rising behind it to make a frame for its beauty. There is no time to admire it because, on the left, standing in a position of obvious authority at the top of a little grass rise, is a man in a crumpled brown tweed suit, and an even more battered tweed hat. One arm, and the battered hat, sport official-looking green and gold bands, and you immediately obey when you are firmly waved on underneath the arch to the car park, set in a meadow behind the house.

The car park always looks busy. There are men in evening dress, getting ice cubes out of big thermos flasks, and lovingly tucking up a bottle of wine in an ice-bucket in the boot of the car. There are cushions and rugs and picnic baskets to be collected and counted. Some hurry off to the head waiter to book a good table for dinner. Others send their wives on a quick tactical dash through the gardens to leave a basket, a cushion, and a rug under a favourite tree, or on a familiar seat, to claim a comfortable place for the interval picnic. Then they can relax and enjoy the first of the many pleasures of the evening— the social parade on the lawns—and it is pleasant enough, to see men well turned-out in formal black-and-white, and women in brilliantly-coloured gowns, against the background of the house and the gardens.

The house looks well in the early evening sun, which warms the soft red brick, the creepers clinging to the walls, windows set in grey stone, the great lawns which sweep away from the house, and the old English flower-beds set around the lawns and inside formal yew hedges. A lake with a thousand water lilies curves away from the edge of the lawn. There is the scent of flowers and wood-smoke in the air. Behind those hedges is a croquet-lawn, and, strangely enough, the players are wearing evening dress. But they are not visitors. They work here. They are the orchestra. Turn away from the game towards the house, and you pass a grey building, which looks almost like a college court, with a row of cypresses standing guard. These are the dressing-rooms. You can hear from the open windows voices in scales, arpeggios, phrases from familiar arias. There, rising high above the buildings that have grown behind the house, is an enormous square tower. This is the home of a country gentleman, but a unique one, for that tower belongs to a theatre, and this is Glyndebourne.

Walk over the lawn towards the house, past the mulberry tree on the right, and go up the steps on to the flagged path that runs beside the house. Cross the path, and go through that small doorway, and you find yourself in a passage, with, on the left, a handsome ironwork gate, which keeps you from the private part of the house, and, on the right, an arched door into the Organ Room.

It is a big, handsome room. There is an organ at one end, and a sort of minstrels' gallery at the other. There are big bay windows, deep armchairs, and huge settees, from the depths of which it is pleasant to lie on your back and stare at the high vaulted roof. There are big oak tables, with bowls of dried lavender, and rose petals—very pleasant on a hot day, to plunge your hands deep into them. And this room was where it all started.

John Christie, who owned Glyndebourne and founded the Opera, was a fascinating, often bewildering, character. He looked like Mr. Pickwick, with round, beaming face, eyes that twinkled behind gold-rimmed glasses, and a thin fringe of hair that framed a shining bald pate. Perhaps, a Pickwick from the Tirol, for, when I first knew him, *Lederhosen* were his favourite workaday wear. He had been born to wealth. The Glynde-bourne estate had been in the family for 700 years, and in that time, he once told me, the succession had descended 'five times through the female line'. He was given the conventional up-bringing that could be expected for one of his class. He was sent away to a private school at the tender age of six, and was regularly beaten as part of his education. Later, he went to a prep school, a bigger one, and there he received bigger and better beatings, to encourage him towards higher academic standards. Then came Eton, where, in the normal course of events, he was flogged. He used to tell the story of a flogging he took from the vigorous hand of the Headmaster. In spite of his place within the Establishment—or perhaps because of it?—Christie had an irreverent mind, and finding himself bending over a chair, with his trousers in a heap at his ankles, and offering his bare backside to the Headmaster's birch, he stretched a hand to pick up a broken twig from the floor as a memento of the occasion. The Headmaster was astonished and angered at this breach of the code of stoicism, and Christie very nearly suffered an immediate repeat flogging for his levity.

From Eton, he went to the Royal Military Academy at Woolwich, but two physical handicaps prevented him from becoming a regular soldier. The sight of one eye was bad, and in the course of his training in the riding-school, he fell awkwardly when jumping his horse over a difficult fence, and smashed an ankle. So he abandoned the idea of an army career, and went to Cambridge. He read Natural Sciences, and went back to Eton as an assistant master. During the First World War, he was accepted into the army, in spite of his eyesight, and served in France. Back at Eton after the war, he was offered a housemaster's job. But it would have meant staying on for ten years, and Christie was not prepared to spend so large a slice of his life in an Eton house—there were other things to do. So he went back to Glyndebourne and lived the life of a country gentleman and a landowner. But not an ordinary one—not an ordinary one at all.

He lived his life well, and always a little larger than life-size. In the trenches in France, he slept in his dugout on a brass bedstead that somehow he had contrived to bring with him from Glyndebourne. He had etchings on the damp, earth walls, and a couple of days after the first grouse of the season had been shot in Scotland, two brace arrived in the trenches, to be cooked over a coke brazier, and to supplement army rations. The first time I dined at Glyndebourne, I sat at the right-hand of his wife. The room was lit only by subdued lighting on the family portraits around the room—and they all looked, even the women, exactly like John Christie—and by candles on the table. Each of us had a candlestick to himself. The shades were enamelled black on the outside, and red inside, and there was a gentle and attractive glow of light that shone on the silver and the brilliantly polished table. The candlesticks themselves were an unusual deep bronze and, though it is true that my experience of candlesticks was limited, I had never seen anything like these. I asked Audrey Christie what they were made of, and where they had come from. She told me that they had been made by Wedgwood, and were copies of a pair of Elizabethan silver candlesticks that had always been in the family. When John had asked the firm to copy them for him, Wedgwood had replied that it would not be an economic proposition, nor could they set a realistic price, unless they made at least a gross. 'All right,' said John, 'make me a gross.' I was fascinated by this unexpected glimpse into the way the upper classes lived, and asked Audrey, in some awe, what she did with a hundred and forty-four candlesticks? Audrey said that they could seat up to twenty-five people, and it was pleasant for everyone to have a separate candle, and the rest were in one of the attics. 'And when any of our friends get married,' she added, 'we give them half a dozen.' For me, this was the ultimate in gracious living, but for Christie it was quite ordinary. It is more convenient to make a gross? Go ahead—make them.

The same ruthless common sense dominated the way in which he ran his estate. Glyndebourne made money for him. At first, he had two men and a lad who did odd jobs round the estate, and repair work on the cottages and farm buildings, put up fences, cut down trees, and built new barns. Christie called them the Ringmer Building Works, and by the year before the Second World War, their turnover was a quarter of a million pounds. He owned the Ringmer Motor Works (which, incidentally, provided the taxi service in the seasons before the war, to take principal singers to and from rehearsals and performances), and the Ringmer Water Works as well.

He inherited from his mother a large lump of the coast of North Devon. There was another family house there, which for some years Christie ran successfully as a hotel. Some miles to the north, on a strip of sand dunes, he built, I think in 1935, another hotel, which offered on the coast the comfort and the luxury of the West End. Besides a cinema, ballroom, and squash courts, it had its own golf course. Christie had another eighteen holes constructed, and, very soon after the hotel was opened, the English Amateur Championship was played on his courses. The hotel stayed open all the year round through the years of the war, and was comfortably full of refugees from bombs.

Everything he put his hand to went well—building, garage, hotels, golf-courses and his opera house. How did a man with this conventional upbringing, beaten at prep school, flogged at

Eton, who had fallen off a horse at Woolwich, got a degree at
Cambridge, taught at Eton, and come into control of a country
gentleman's estate—how did such a man do anything so
extraordinary as putting an opera house in his garden?

For years he had spent his holidays fishing, but one summer,
at the end of the 1920s, he made a change in his routine. He
went with friends to Munich and Salzburg, heard concerts,
and was taken to the opera. Through his friends, he met some
of the performers, and, though he was not himself a musician,
and had had no academic or technical training in music, he
began to get interested in musicians and their work. Back in
England this new interest grew, and he decided that he must
have a room for music. So he built the Organ Room, which
almost from the first seemed part of the original house, though
that was hundreds of years older. I was once told that when
the organ had been installed in the new room, he bought up
the firm in charge of the work and reorganised them, so that
his organ works became a flourishing member of his team.

Then there was organ music for his friends, and chamber
music, too. They sang scenes from operas, with Christie himself
singing Osmin in *Entführung*, and Beckmesser in bits of
Meistersinger. I shall always be sorry that I never saw these
performances. Then Christie got more ambitious, and began to
hire professionals to come down to Glyndebourne to stiffen
the amateur casts of these private little performances. For one,
he engaged a young soprano, Audrey Mildmay, who was a
principal with the Carl Rosa Company. He married her, and
between them the idea of an opera house began to grow. 'My
wife was a genius,' Christie said over and over again after her
death, and always maintained that it was Audrey who was
essentially responsible for starting Glyndebourne Opera.

So they began to build their theatre, with the deliberate
intention of producing performances of a standard never seen
in this country. It was an arrogant and astonishing project.
For a private gentleman to dare to think that he could rival
the standards of Covent Garden, and Vienna, and Salzburg—

extraordinary. His friends were astonished. An opera house? In the garden? Fifty miles from London?

'We were thought to be utterly, utterly cracked,' said Christie. The first night they had something over forty people in the theatre, which then could seat 200. The second night was a little bit better—there were fifty-four. They had arranged a special train to take people back to London after the performance from Lewes, and on that second night seven people travelled in the train. But since that beginning in 1934, when two ladies settled themselves in the front row at the first performance of *Cosi fan tutte*, and one opened her programme and said to the other, 'Let me see, dear—is this *music*?', the house has been packed night after night, season after season.

In its first few performances, Glyndebourne took a giant stride into the front rank of the world's opera houses. And, to its credit, the press recognised its quality from the very beginning. The *Daily Telegraph*, in its notice of the first performance, said it had never seen a performance like it in any other country, or at any other time. Very quickly, Glyndebourne became a cult for musicians, not only for those who had the money for what, even in those days, was a very expensive evening. Young people saved a bob here and there all the year, so that they might share in this new experience.

A friend of mine was in 1934 a young schoolmaster in Eastbourne. He was determined that he and his wife should see *Figaro* at Glyndebourne, no matter what. There were two difficulties—they had a young baby, but no baby-sitter, and they could afford only one seat. So they found an ingenious and practical solution. The child's feed, for which mother's presence was essential (I put this as delicately as I can), was due soon after the curtain went up. So mother sat in their battered car in the car park and fed Junior in Act I, while father sat in their seat. Then he returned to the car, mother dumped the child in his arms, and went to the theatre for Act II. Just as father was settling down to his vigil, John Christie came bustling past and saw father out of the corner of his eye, stopped, came back to the car, opened the door and said sharply 'Come on! If you aren't quick, you'll be too late for the second Act.' Father said he could not go into the theatre, because he had a baby to look after—and to prove it he lifted the child and showed it to Christie. 'I'll fix that,' said John, 'Come with me, and hurry.' They ran to a cottage, where one of Christie's gardeners lived. Christie banged the door knocker, and asked the gardener's wife to look after the baby. She made little cooing noises, declared it was a lovely baby, and that she would have great pleasure in the baby's company. Christie turned away: 'There you are!' he said, 'all arranged.' Father, cornered and embarrassed, stood on one leg and blushed and muttered. 'Can't hear you,' said Christie, 'What's up now?' and father finally managed to say that they were very poor and had been able to buy only one seat, and it was his wife's turn to have it for Act II. 'Soon settle that,' said Christie briskly, took hold of father's arm, and ran him at a vigorous trot down the path, towards the theatre, and into his private box. And there father sat in luxurious, if bewildered, state with Christie's other guests for the rest of the performance.

This was typical of John Christie. He was delighted with the success of his theatre and wanted everyone else to share his pleasure. But there was another side to Christie. From the beginning, it was made very clear that audiences were expected to wear evening dress. This brought to Glyndebourne audiences who knew nothing about music, and came because it was the thing to see and be seen at Glyndebourne. I wrote a script about Glyndebourne in the early 1950s for the B.B.C. Overseas Service, and during the programme interviewed Christie. I asked him what he would reply to the complaint—it was often made—that Glyndebourne was trading on its snob value. Characteristically, he was delighted. 'Excellent!' he said. 'My answer is quite simple. We are doing the work better than other people. We insist that the audience wear evening dress, even if it means leaving London at three in the afternoon. We want to make the audience take trouble, so that they will respect our work. They must touch their hats—not of course to us—but *to the work*.'

'Doing the work better than other people' . . . Christie had remarkable powers of concentration on what was needed to do the work better than the others. I know a man who was shot in the back of the head during the war—which left him with a band of vision four inches wide and that only straight ahead. Things to his right or his left he simply did not see. It was not necessary to shoot Christie in the back of the head, for he had, by nature, a narrow, restricted vision. He thought about one thing at a time, his builders or his hotels or his garage or his theatre, and he focused his attention so fiercely on that one thing that he never saw what other people said were difficulties. He added to his concentration a simple conviction that whatever interested him was equally interesting to everyone else. This was often comic, sometimes bewildering.

On three separate occasions I heard John Christie talk to music conferences. Each time he was flatteringly introduced by the chairman who ended up with this kind of formula— 'Mr. John Christie, the founder of the world-famous Glyndebourne Opera, who is now going to talk to us about his work. Mr. Christie.' The first time, he began: 'The size and the scope of our work grows from year to year.' I saw the audience hugging itself in anticipation, wriggling comfortably into its seat, nudging its neighbours and whispering, 'This is going to be good.' He went on, 'In each of the last two years, we have had to double the size of our car parks in Devon. This means that, inside two years, their capacity has been quadrupled.' He talked for forty-five minutes, only about the economics of car parks and hotels in Devon, and sat down again without once having mentioned the opera house.

On the second occasion, he fixed the audience with beaming enthusiasm and began, 'I owe more to Eton than I can ever acknowledge.' This time, we had his setpiece on the eccentricities of the masters who taught him when he was a boy, and, to the astonishment of the audience, again he never even mentioned the opera house.

The third occasion was at a weekend course on opera at Glyndebourne. I had been asked to give a lecture, but was told when I arrived in time to begin, that I must start twenty-five minutes later than announced. The chairman said that they had persuaded Mr. Christie to come to talk to the audience and he was sure that I would not mind waiting. I said that I did not mind in the least—I should be most interested to hear what Christie would talk about. The chairman look puzzled. 'Well,' I told him, 'you might get the bit about car parks in Devon. Or it might be schooldays at Eton. . . .' The chairman, now in a panic, said that I must be joking. 'Or you might get the bit about Somebody-or-Other's match at Lords,' I said, thoughtfully. 'I've not heard it myself, but I believe it is a star turn in his repertory.' 'Good gracious!' said the chairman. I was right.

Christie came on to the stage, was enthusiastically received by the audience and nervously introduced by the chairman. He started dramatically: 'Somebody-or-Other's match at Lords was one of the greatest cricket games that has ever been played.' (The chairman looked at me in horror. I winked at him.) It was an Eton and Harrow match, and Eton—or perhaps it was Harrow—won with a couple of runs to spare, off the last ball but one of the very last over. And Christie gave a vivid ball-by-ball account of the day's play, demonstrating with enormous enthusiasm the googly action of the bowler who won—or perhaps lost?—the game; he then retired from the meeting, quite convinced that he had told the audience what they had been longing to hear, and having achieved the remarkable feat of talking for twenty-five minutes to 700 members of a weekend course on opera, without mentioning the theatre in which they all sat.

This change of subject, from one thing which interested him to another which interested him more, could happen almost at a moment's notice. When I was to interview him for that radio programme, I arranged beforehand the line that our conversation would take: my half of the conversation would be edited out of the tape, and we should broadcast what would appear to be a connected statement from him. The questions which I was to ask him would merely be paragraph headings, to set him off on the right line. For instance, I had asked him, in rehearsal, 'What do you think is the most important factor in Glyndebourne's success?' He said, slowly and earnestly and with great emphasis: 'This season, we have scheduled 220 three-hour rehearsals for our five operas. This is much more rehearsal-time than any other opera house in the world gives to the work.' 'That's fine, John,' I said. 'That's just what I want.' We started recording. All went well until we came to the bit about what had brought Glyndebourne its considerable success? He said, slowly and earnestly and with great emphasis: 'My wife was a genius . . .' 'Stop the recording,' I said to the engineers. 'John, this is where you were going to give me those rehearsal statistics. Two hundred and twenty three-hour rehearsals—remember?' And we had to do it all again, while I gingerly herded John into the line we wanted.

Christie could be like this whether his audience was one of hundreds or just one man. He still said what came into his mind, innocently and directly. And often his innocence had devastating results. One season before the war, we had all been waiting very expectantly to hear a famous coloratura soprano working for the first time with the company. Her first orchestral rehearsal in one of the dining-rooms brought pretty well all the chorus there, all the music staff, and all the singers who were not due to rehearse somewhere else. Christie wandered in with his pug-dog, Tuppy. (There always has been a pug-dog at Glyndebourne.) Christie climbed on to the tea-bar, and sat with his back against the wall, Tuppy sitting interestedly beside him, and together they listened to the rehearsal. I'd heard this soprano in Budapest some months before, and I thought then that she was very good. That day, there was no doubt about it. She was very good indeed.

John Christie never took his eyes off her, fascinated and absorbed. She finished her first big aria and the orchestra discreetly rattled bows on their music-stands, and the brass and woodwind tapped their feet on the floor, and there was a murmur of pleasure and congratulation from all round the room. I was sitting within a couple of feet of John Christie and asked, 'What do you think?' John shook himself out of his trance, and said, in a perfectly normal voice, and with great enthusiasm, 'I think she looks just like Tuppy!' Though it had not struck me before, Christie was right. She *did* look exactly like Tuppy. But it was scarcely the right occasion to say so publicly.

I met him one day, soon after the start of rehearsals in my first season, and he asked me how things were going.

'Fine,' I said.

'Enjoying yourself?' he asked.

'Enormously,' I said. 'I was terrified at first, but everyone's very helpful and now I feel quite at home. I'm mostly with Brownlee and Baccaloni, and they are very kind.'

'Brownlee—very nice man,' said Christie, 'but I've not met Baccaloni. What's he like?'

'Very funny,' I said, 'and what a voice!'

Next day, Christie wandered in to a rehearsal, and someone introduced Baccaloni, one of the great buffo basses, to him. 'Signor Baccaloni,' said John earnestly, 'welcome to Glyndebourne. Franklin tells me you have a good voice!'

This may seem strange. But it was Christie's ability to concentrate on one thing at a time, and his directness in saying whatever happened to be in his mind at the moment, that brought the opera house into life. It was so impossible a scheme that no one with a conventional mind would ever have brought it off, would ever even have started it. But Christie, seeing one thing at a time very intensely and clearly, and blindly ignoring everything else, triumphantly created an opera house after everyone had assured him that it was a dotty idea—it couldn't be done.

His aim was simple. He often said to me 'For us, nothing less than superb will do.' Arrogant? Well—yes. But he had a clear vision of what he wanted, *and* his simple, direct mind. He had been introduced to Adolf Busch after a concert in London, and asked him who was the best conductor of Mozart in the world. Adolf said, simply, 'My brother Fritz.' Fritz had been conducting at Dresden, but was at loggerheads with the Nazis in Germany, and had left to work in Denmark. So Christie wrote to him, told him he had plans for a new opera house and asked him to come to Glyndebourne. Busch worked a lot with Carl Ebert, a brilliant German actor, whom he had brought into the opera house, and who had become the outstanding producer of his time. They arrived at Glyndebourne. Christie showed them the plans for the new theatre, and told them that he wanted performances of the very highest standard. They would have a free hand in the artistic direction—what about it? Busch and Ebert were astonished. To work in such surroundings, miles away from town distractions, to have adequate rehearsal time, to be able to search for perfection in performances—this was what every artist longed for. But fifty-odd miles from London? A small theatre, which would seat only 200 people? This was impossible. They told Christie regretfully that it was a wonderful idea, something they had always wanted but had never managed to achieve, and they would give anything to be able to direct his theatre for him— but. 'But what?' asked Christie. 'But it could never pay,' they said. 'In Germany every opera house is supported by subsidy. How can one man run an opera house out of his own purse? It won't go. Impossible!' Christie said, 'That is nothing to do with you. Money is my business. Yours is only the artistic direction.' So they accepted, and Glyndebourne Opera began.

This decentralisation was typical. Christie had great imagination and enormous energy. He never stopped working on the theatre, always planning more space, more comfort, more facilities. The first time I met him, he took me on a tour of the theatre, then less than two years old, and made me scramble with him through the ruins of the part which he had just pulled down in order to rebuild it. He was always at it. Actual performances were an unwelcome interruption to his permanent occupation of pulling his theatre down and putting it up again. But though his restless search for the best led him to endless extension of the theatre buildings, in every other part of the work he picked the men who could do the job, and let them do it without interference. This was how he worked.

There was no doubt about who was the boss in the theatre. Busch and Ebert, both of them big men of imposing appearance, with natural authority, had strong clear views about what they wanted. But if ever there was a clash between the two, it was quickly settled. 'Ne, Carl, das geht nicht,' Busch would say—and it did not go. Busch added to his formidable power the knack of managing people. He knew how to get the best, and most, out of them. There's a famous story of the very first rehearsal of the orchestra back in 1934. The players of the L.S.O. who were engaged for the festival knew Fritz's brother Adolf, and his other brother, Herrmann, both first-rate players of chamber music, but who was this Fritz? 'Never heard of him,' they said to themselves. Fritz came in, stepped on to the box, gave a stiff Prussian bow to the orchestra, and, in the little English that he then knew, made a polite speech, hoping they would be friends, and make good music together. The orchestra muttered something, as orchestras do, and politely rattled their bows on the back of their fiddles. So, said Busch, briskly, to work. They would start with the overture to *The Marriage of Figaro*. The problem for the orchestra is that it goes very fast but it has got to be pianissimo—and it is very difficult to do that at speed. 'Now, gentlemen,' said Busch, and raised his baton. The orchestra was poised, ready to play, and then— 'No,' he said, 'Already too loud!' The orchestra laughed, and Busch from that moment had them in the palm of his hand.

Tall, heavy, with a typical German head, close-cropped hair, eyes rather close together, Busch could be quite terrifying; but behind this impressive appearance there was a child-like sense of humour. Busch loved little jokes, and he often used his stern appearance to get a rise out of an unsuspecting singer. Geraint Evans, in his first season, was working with John Pritchard in the Organ Room one morning when Busch came in. Geraint had not met him up to then, but guessed it was the boss. Pritchard went on playing, and Geraint went on singing. Busch walked straight to the piano, leant over Pritchard from one side, and took over, playing on without a break. Pritchard slipped out of his chair, and Busch slipped into it, played until the end of the aria, then without a word got up and walked away to the door. Geraint felt crushed. Busch had given no advice, had made no comment. 'God!' Geraint thought, 'I must have been awful.' Then, just as Busch reached the door, he stopped and turned round. 'I think we'll get on together,' he said, mildly, and went out.

I remember a night when he frightened the life out of me, too. It was in my second season, and I was singing Sarastro in *The Magic Flute*. I sang seven of the eight performances but the last performance was to be sung by a bass from Vienna, who had come to do four performances of Osmin, and had complained that he wasn't getting enough money from his four Osmins to make it worth his while. So they took away one of my performances—and one of my fees—and gave it to this other chap. I was a bit worried. I had no idea how good he was —and singing is such a cut-throat business that you hate to have anyone who might be good taking over one of your own parts. I had a seat in the house for that performance and, very much on edge, I met Busch on my way into the house. 'To-night, my boy,' he said, 'you shall hear a *real* Sarastro!' This depressed me greatly. I might have been even more depressed if I had known that Busch had gone to the band-room, and told the orchestra with great delight that he had got me worried.

I listened gloomily to the first act. The other Sarastro had a fine stage presence, and much more experience as an actor than I. He had a good voice—too good for my peace of mind. I began to feel a bit happier when, in his second aria, he sang lines 1 to 4 of verse one, and then suddenly lines 7 and 8 of verse two, panicked, lost himself completely, and to finish verse one sang lines 3 and 4 from verse two. I was very relieved. '*That*'s more like it!' I thought. I met Busch on the way out. 'What did I tell you?' he said. 'A real Sarastro! He sings both verses at once'—and he gave me an enormous wink. All was well, and I could stop worrying.

When he was working, Busch was thorough and practical. John Pritchard, who started in opera as a coach at Glyndebourne, was astonished one day at an ensemble rehearsal when Busch walked round the singers and rather rudely, he thought, snatched the spectacles from those who wore them. Busch saw Pritchard's surprise. 'I want to know *now*,' he explained, 'who isn't going to be able to see the beat from the stage!' Practical—yes. And human. I once had to sing with a very heavy cold, and I was worried about my top notes. He came to find me on the stage before he went down into the pit to start the act. 'Don't worry,' he said, 'I'll have the trombones play fortissimo—no one will hear whether you are singing or not!' He did, and they didn't.

Busch's command of men, and women too, was easy and complete. One morning, he began his rehearsal with the overture to *Don Pasquale*. It was still a bit early and some of the orchestra weren't as alert as they might have been. They missed the first few bars, and straggled in one by one. Some conductors would have shouted. Some would have ostentatiously crossed themselves. Some would have been heavily sarcastic. Busch said, quietly, 'Eferyvyn in this vonderful orchestra is infited to play!' There was a general laugh, the stragglers blushed and shook themselves awake, and there was no more trouble.

In the four years in which I worked for him, I only once saw Busch not completely in command in the pit. On one occasion we were singing *Don Giovanni*, the B.B.C. were broadcasting from the theatre, and Busch was eager to have a first-rate performance. All went splendidly until Anna's long and very difficult aria towards the end of the second act—'Non mi dir'. The Anna that night was a marvellous singer, but somehow she got lost in the middle. Immediately—this was the drill when anything went wrong—Busch's left hand went up like a traffic cop's while the right went on beating four-in-a-bar. If you missed an entry you waited, with his left hand, until your next entry, when it came down with the lead. You came in, Busch smiled, and all was well again. But not that night. Anna thought she knew where she was, and experimentally tried an entry where none existed. Busch was horrified, and his left hand shot up even higher in the air. It gave her the proper lead, but she missed it. She floundered on, hoping that miraculously she would find herself safely back with the orchestra. But she never did find them again. Busch tried two or three times more —left hand up, and at the next entry an enormous lead right in her face. But, frightened and almost hysterical, she went on singing rubbish to the end of the aria, when Busch, to every-one's horror, looked straight at her and put out his tongue.

He was quick to handle emergencies. I remember in 1939 a performance of *Figaro* in Brussels. It was part of a Mozart Festival, held there and in Antwerp. I was not singing that night, and was in the house. As usual in short festivals, with singers assembled from all over Europe, we were under-rehearsed. So was the orchestra, and in the long finale of Act II, they suddenly got at sixes and sevens. I held my breath. It did not seem possible Busch could rescue them, and it looked certain that he would have to stop them and start again —the crowning humiliation for an orchestra and conductor. Some conductors would have gone berserk, stamping, shouting at the bewildered players; but that night I saw Busch do some-thing I had never seen before or since. His right hand went on calmly beating four-in-a-bar, and his left hand did a slow 'come to father' gesture over the heads of all the players. It started with the first violins on the left, went gently round the seconds, the woodwind, and finished over the violas and cellos. It looked as if he was gathering them up and, miraculously, by the time his left hand finished its sweep, the orchestra were safely together and once again under control. It was an uncanny demonstration of command.

Busch was not a Svengali. His greatness as a conductor was firmly based upon detailed and complete rehearsal. This was what surprised and fascinated me, when, a complete innocent, I first arrived at Glyndebourne. The principals came knowing their parts by heart. There was no time to learn a part at Glyndebourne. We arrived four weeks, five weeks at the most, before the first performance, and some parts will take a singer months to memorise, and to work into the voice. So our sessions with the music staff were only for coaching, to mould our prefabricated parts into the style, the tempi, that Busch and Ebert had planned. You could spend hours on a couple of bars.

My first part at Glyndebourne was the Commendatore. When, as the statue miraculously come back to life, he clumps into Don Giovanni's palace, after the Don has cynically asked him to supper, he begins with the words 'Don Giovanni!' It is a difficult entry for a young bass. The top D on the second syllable of 'Giovanni' is high and awkward, and in 1936, before my top notes were set, Jani Strasser, for years Head of the Music Staff, worked and worked on me. 'Don Giovanni', I sang. Too shallow. 'Don Giovanni', I sang. Too dark—bring the tone forward. 'Don Giovanni', I sang. Too open—dangerous for the voice. 'Don Giovanni', I sang. Too 'covered'—it would never ride the orchestra. 'Don Giovanni', I sang. That was overdone—the tone was too thin—this time keep the back open, to add warmth to the edge of the tone. 'Don Giovanni', I sang and, just at that moment, the head of Rudi Bing, the General Manager at Glyndebourne (now at the Metropolitan, New York), appeared at the window of the small room where we were working. 'That Don Giovanni! What a rude man!' he said. 'You call him and call him, and he never comes!' He laughed at his joke, and disappeared. I suppose it was funny, though I did not laugh, for working with Jani Strasser was no joke. I know now that when I was prepared for a performance by him, I was prepared far better than by anyone else, but over and over again I would cheerfully have cut his throat. It was some consolation that the other singers, even those more experienced than I, went through the same gruelling ordeal with him. He was insatiable. Nothing escaped him, and he had—he still has—an appetite for detail which fascinated and appalled us.

While the principals were working with individual coaches— in those first years there were Strasser, Hans Oppenheim, and Alberto Erede—the chorus worked separately under their chorus-master. There were technical rehearsals on the stage— fitting the sets together, and designing the lighting. In 1938, Ebert took ten days to light *Macbeth*, working with a full crew of stagehands and electricians from after breakfast each day until one or two next morning. Ten days!

After a week or so of individual rehearsals, on our arias and in our separate lines in the ensembles, the music staff began to put pieces of the jig-saw together. Not that, having been coached in the individual parts of, say, the second finale of *Figaro*, we were suddenly plunged into singing it all together. We still had to be rehearsed in sections. Bartolo, Marcellina and Basilio, who sing as a block in the finale, worked together first as a separate group. So did the Count and Curzio, and so, too, did Figaro, the Countess, and Susanna. In each of these sections the singers were drilled in accuracy, in precision, and colour. Then, when each section was working easily and precisely, the whole ensemble would be brought together for the first time, and the final work of polishing began. Again and again they were relentlessly driven through the music, so that the voices blended, made a good sound, and were balanced, to bring out in turn Figaro, the Count, Susanna, and the Countess, in the bubbling development of the comedy. One of the glories of Glyndebourne was the brilliance of its ensemble. The music swept along, gay, lighthearted, brilliant, and apparently effortless—but the achievement of effortlessness was damned hard work.

By now the orchestra had arrived and started rehearsals by itself, generally, in those days when there were no separate rehearsal rooms, in one of the dining-halls. They were drilled with the same fanaticism as the singers. The players of the L.S.O. said that working with Busch had a magical effect upon their work. All through the winter they had been slogging away in London week after week, always under-rehearsed. Sometimes time was so short, that two conductors would have to share one three-hour rehearsal for two separate concerts.

It was in a rehearsal like this that the affectionate nickname first appeared by which Sir Malcolm Sargent was always known. He and Beecham once had to share a three-hour rehearsal for their two concerts, and Sargent had his half-rehearsal first. Beecham came in after the tea break, began work, and for minutes repeatedly affected to find fault with the playing. Finally, he put down his baton, and looked at the orchestra with concern. 'Tell me, gentlemen,' he said. 'What's the matter? Flash Harry been upsetting you?'

English orchestral players have always been expert sight-readers. They have to be, because they have had to rely on their speed, ingenuity and resourcefulness, to contrive adequate performances out of inadequate rehearsal. But, at Glynde-bourne, there was time to rehearse. Busch took great care over every detail of balance and tone, and after a couple of weeks of the season the orchestra was transformed and found itself playing far better, and more excitingly than it ever had during the winter.

I always enjoyed the moment when the singers joined the orchestra for the first time. It was what the Germans call a *Sitzprobe*—a 'sit rehearsal'. I was always much too eager to sit. Later in the routine of rehearsals, you have so much on your mind—positions on the stage, keeping in your lights, having one eye on the prompter and both eyes on the conductor, doing whatever-it-is with the bottle or the fan or the chair or the sword or the marriage contract exactly on cue—that you have no time to savour the physical pleasure of singing with an orchestra. But, in the *Sitzproben*, that pleasure was at its height. Thoroughly prepared by piano rehearsals, voices fresh at the beginning of the season, comfortably dressed, the women in summer frocks, the men in sports shirts and flannels (and this was bliss compared with the weight and the discomfort of some of the stage costumes which we had to wear in performance), with no tension, no strain, no audience, and no critics ready to tear into us if we put a foot wrong, it was fun just to make music.

At about this time in the routine, the first stage rehearsals would start, and this was when we came under the direction of Ebert. From time to time during individual calls and ensemble and orchestral rehearsals, he would wander in from the stage and listen to an aria, a quartet, a chorus, and make suggestions about dramatic points which must be brought out in the music. But music rehearsals were Busch's—stage calls were Ebert's. And now the really hard work began.

Every single step, each gesture, each grouping had been planned by Ebert, maybe months ahead. He had approved designs for the sets, and had been sent cardboard models. He knew how much space he had to work with, where the stairs would be, where furniture would be set. Ebert himself is no academic musician, and cannot play the piano, or read a score for himself; but, with a pianist to play for him, he worked through the score, finding phrases, moods in the music that suggested movements and stage pictures to his mind. He worked out how many steps would be needed to get a singer on to the stage and into his lights, ready for the beginning of his aria— whether the music, after the aria, gave enough time to get the player off the stage and safely out of the audience's view before the next scene started. He saw in his mind, months beforehand, the stage patterns in which he began to drill us. Ebert had imagination, patience, and, like everyone at Glyndebourne, a relentless eye for detail. In a radio interview he said once that he was never content. 'I am cursed with eyes and ears that are never satisfied with what they see and hear. Always I see things

45

that go wrong. If I say that, well, perhaps tonight it wasn't too bad, then everybody is already happy!'

My first morning on the stage as a pro was typical of the way he worked. We were blocking out the first scene of *Don Giovanni*, in which I was killed. It was not an easy death. The fight had to be carefully planned so that the clashes of our swords came on exactly the right beats of the right bars, where Mozart had written 'sword clash' chords. We fought on a curved stone staircase, and I had to die to within what engineers would call a tolerance of no more than three inches. The set was one of three, stacked one behind the other, so that the time needed to change from one to the next should be cut to a minimum, and this meant there was very little room to spare. I had to die on the steps—and if I got it wrong and the edge of a step cut into my back, I could be in agony in a couple of minutes—dead men cannot wriggle into a more comfortable position. I had to die with room for Donna Anna to manœuvre her panniered skirt around me, between me and the wall of the staircase. I had, of course, to die in my lights—there is no point in dying movingly in the dark, where the audience cannot see you. I had to die so that the four chorus men who, seven minutes later, were to come on and carry off my body, had room to bend and pick me up with some appearance of ease and dignity. Hoarse whispers of, 'Have you got him, George?' 'All mine—*to* me!' 'Pull him a bit your way, Jim— then I can get hold of his leg'—these would not have added to the pathos of the scene. The critical point in my death was the fall after I had received the fatal thrust from Don Giovanni. I turned and fell, and turned and fell, and turned and fell, all morning. I sang very little, but I went home for lunch, at the end of my first morning's work as a professional singer on the stage, with the skin off both my knees, and blood-stained trousers.

Once the act was blocked out painstakingly like this, and sometimes painfully, we then went back to the beginning, and ran through each scene, with a piano, until it began to get fluency and rhythm. Then we ran through an entire act, again with piano, and the tension of rehearsals continually grew.

There was a morning's interlude in those rehearsals of *Don Giovanni*, when we had a dress parade, and for the first time we wore costumes, and displayed them for Ebert and the designer, Hamish Wilson. My Act I costume was approved, and I changed into the Act II outfit, as the statue of the Commendatore. It was very uncomfortable. It was made of heavy canvas, stiffened with size, so that it looked as if the folds were carved in marble. And it smelt to high heaven—people looked at me oddly when I passed. That first day I wore it, Ebert and Hamish were not satisfied with the stone effect. Hamish whispered a suggestion, and Ebert approved. Hamish told a stagehand what he wanted. He led me away and said, 'Stand over there, Mr. F., against that wall.'

'Why?' I asked.

'You'll find out,' he said mysteriously. 'And shut your eyes.'

I did what I was told, while he dipped a whitewash brush into a pail, and flicked it at me from a range of about six feet. 'What the hell was that for?' I asked furiously, wiping a dollop of whitewash from one eye.

'You're a statue, ain't you?' he said.

'All right, I'm a statue,' I said, 'so what?'

'Pigeons,' he said.

Next we did a whole act with the orchestra, but with ordinary clothes and no make-up—then a dress rehearsal with piano and costumes but no lighting—a dress rehearsal with everything—costumes, lighting, make-up and orchestra—act by act. There was a private dress rehearsal with the orchestra 'AS PERFORMANCE', then a public dress rehearsal before an audience and, finally, the first performance. In all this long process of preparation Ebert's concentration never faltered. Every rehearsal was followed by 'notes'. He had one of his assistants taking dictation from him all through the rehearsal, and afterwards, we assembled on the stage, while the notes were read by the assistant and Ebert showed us exactly what had gone

47

wrong, and what he wanted us to do instead. The maddening thing was that, even though he could not sing, he could act any of our parts better than we could. He was a tremendous actor, resourceful, ingenious, and imaginative—he could even act a woman better than the women could. And it was not only on matters of position, and grouping, and colour, that he watched us with endless attention. No technical detail was too small to escape planning.

When we did *Entführung* after the war, for the first time for more than twelve years, there was a note in the prompt-book, that at one point in the action a stagehand was to be sent to a rostrum on the Prompt Side, behind a first-floor window from which Blondchen eloped with Pedrillo, her lover. She climbed from the rostrum through the window on to a ladder and, with her legs straddling it, slid down into the waiting arms of her man. When we came to this bit, Ebert said he could not understand why a stagehand should have been sent on to that rostrum. What did he do? I was the only member of that cast who had sung at Glyndebourne before the war and, playing the Oldest Inhabitant with some relish, said I remembered perfectly well. 'Good, my dear,' said Ebert. 'Please. Come. Tell me.' I reminded him that at one public dress rehearsal Blondchen had climbed on to the rostrum and through the window and spread her legs over the ladder and had let go with her hands to slide down. But the back of her short skirt had caught over the top of the ladder, and she slid only a few inches. And there she hung, with her skirt tight around her waist, and a splendid display of legs and attractive underwear for the delight of the audience. During 'notes' after that rehearsal the decision was taken. A stagehand must accompany Blondchen to her rostrum and make sure that, when she got on the ladder, her skirt was tucked safely under her. It proved a popular assignment.

As another example of Ebert's fantastic eye for detail—on the last night of *Don Giovanni* in July 1939—there occurred a very surprising break in the technical routine. After the Commendatore's stony hand-clasp had sent Don Giovanni riding on a trap-door down into hell, normally I waited for a black-out and then lifted my cloak, turned, and nipped out behind the french-windows on to a high rostrum. When my eyes had got used to the darkness, after minutes of being in the intense glare of spotlights, I carefully made my way down a rather rickety ladder to stage level. But I had only four or five seconds to get out of sight, and I *had* to be out before the final sextet started. On this last night in 1939 the black-out was late. It was only a second or two, but I knew that if I waited until it came, and the lights came up again for the sextet strictly on cue again, and found me still there, it would be disastrous. So, with dignity, I turned and began to stalk off, as if it had been rehearsed like that. A moment after I had turned, the black-out came, and gratefully I picked up my skirts and ran off like Charlie's Aunt into safety. After the final calls, I was taking off my make-up in my dressing-room when Ebert came round with 'notes'. 'Quite right!' he said. 'Quite right to turn round and valk off. But, next time—' (this was the last performance in 1939, and we all knew war was coming, and we had no idea when, or if, we should all work together again)—'next time, make up behind the ears. Tonight they were pink. Make them like a statue. Just in case. . . .!' When I made up for the first post-war performance of the 'Don' at the Edinburgh Festival, I made a point of showing Ebert that the backs of my ears were grey, ready for any emergency.

Ebert even directed the applause. Ringing the changes on the principals, in twos, and threes, or alone in front of the curtains, stimulated the audience to go on clapping. People have a natural curiosity to see who is coming on next, and a hope that their special favourite will appear again and give them a chance to cheer him once more. One night in 1938, just after Neville Chamberlain had come back from Munich with 'peace in our time', he was a guest in the Glyndebourne box. It was a good show, the audience was warm, Ebert expertly drew the applause on and on, and it went on for minutes. At last it died, and we turned to leave the stage. Suddenly, strangely, the cheers broke out again, and Ebert leapt again into action. 'You, and you!' he said quickly, and pushed two of the singers in front of the tabs. 'Stop them!' shouted the stage director—but it was too late. They were already out there, to find the audience standing, but with their backs to the stage, and applauding the Prime Minister, who was taking a call himself from his box. I've always been glad that Ebert didn't send me out then. Very embarrassing.

The strain on singers of measuring up to the standards demanded of them by Busch and Ebert was enormous, and some of them could not face it. From time to time a singer who had found difficulty in rehearsals quietly disappeared, and another would arrive in a hurry. I accepted this pressure, this kind of discipline, without question, because this was my first professional experience and I innocently thought that this was the way all opera companies worked. But some singers who had already made reputations in slap-dash run-of-the-mill performances in the average opera house thought that the Glyndebourne insistence on perfection, on rehearsal after rehearsal after rehearsal, was somehow rather sissy. A very famous English tenor told me one morning at a rehearsal in the Organ Room back in 1936 that he had been rung up the afternoon before, in an emergency, and had rushed up to London, to sing a performance of *Bohème* at Covent Garden without any rehearsal at all. 'Bam!' he said, 'just like that— professional! This lot here—they're just a bunch of bloody amateurs.' On the surface, there was some evidence that he was right. Childs, John Christie's butler, served dinner to Christie's guests in the long interval on nights when we did *Entführung*, and then quietly asked permission to withdraw, went to his dressing-room, and got into costume and make-up for his part of a deaf-mute in the opera. Perhaps it was not strange that the butler should be one of the company, for he was very much a key figure in Christie's household. Childs had been Christie's butler at Eton, his batman in the army, best man at his wedding, and godfather to his children.

One night in 1937, when we were playing *The Magic Flute*, the electricity grid was struck by lightning, and all Sussex and Surrey and Kent were plunged into darkness. Our performance came to a sudden halt in the middle of a bar. We stood around on the stage and asked each other what had happened, the audience chattered with excitement, and the orchestra tentatively tuned and played odd wisps of sound in the pitch-black. Then, from the door leading to the Organ Room, Childs appeared majestically leading a line of maids from the house, each with a handful of candles. They placed and lit a candle on each music-stand in the orchestra, and set a crescent of lighted candles on the front of the stage, while the stage fireman, thinking of the chorus of priests and their long, ankle-length robes, had hysterics in the prompt-corner. In the soft, romantic light of the candles we began the performance again, to the delight of the audience. Childs, in tails and black tie, materialised in the wings beside me, as I stood waiting for my next entrance, and asked me how late we were running. I said I thought it must be about forty-five minutes. 'Dear me!' said the butler, 'I must go and telephone the railway, and ask them to hold up Our Train.'

You might think that a theatre where a butler dealt with special trains was just an amateur romp. Far from it. Busch and Ebert, and their staff, were the most ruthless bunch of pros that I ever met. But their professionalism was concealed behind a sort of country house charade. It was Audrey Christie who was, I think, mainly responsible for the unique blend of professionalism with the atmosphere of an English family house. It was to be tremendously important in the success of Glyndebourne Opera.

Christie always insisted that his wife was a genius. Certainly she was a woman of remarkable gifts. She had great charm and wit. Her good looks were reinforced by her poise and elegance. Not only in real life—she took these qualities with her on to the stage, where her technique and experience projected them to an audience. She was a good pro. As singers say, she was a 'good performer'. She was not in the very top rank of singers, nor would she herself have made any claim to be an international artist. But she was not, as people were eager to sneer in the early days of Glyndebourne, just a rich man's darling who sang because he had built the theatre, and was paying for it. She won her place in the company fair and square.

She had told me that, when Busch agreed to conduct at Glyndebourne, he made one condition. He realised that Christie would want his wife to sing in the festival. This he could understand. But, he added, 'If she sings in my operas, she must be good enough to sing by my standards.' So it was arranged that one day Audrey must sing to Busch. It must have been a considerable ordeal for her, for whether Busch came to Glyndebourne or not depended on this audition. She finished her aria and, without a word, Busch got up from his armchair, walked the length of the Organ Room, took Audrey's hand, bent and kissed it, and turned round to face John Christie. 'I am your musical director,' he said.

She kept her place in the company, and sang as an equal in the international casts that Glyndebourne collected each year, despite the enormous pressures upon her. People were eager to find fault with her. Because she was Mrs. Christie, she had to sing better than they would have expected of one of the hired singers. In between rehearsals and performances, she could never relax as the rest of us did. She was the mistress of a great house, and had always to be the hostess, not only for the nightly parties in Christie's box for performances, not only at a formal dinner in the interval, and not only to the audience who were made to feel that they were guests (they never had to collect litter from the gardens after performances), but to the company centred on Glyndebourne for months at a time each summer.

She charmed us into feeling that we were guests of the house. We had the run of the gardens, we had meals together in the company restaurant, there were staff bars and a big and handsome Green Room, and this comfort and friendliness made us part of the family. It was Audrey who started the charming tradition—as it has become by now—of 'Mrs Christie's champagne'. She left a half-bottle on the dressing table of each principal singer on each first night during the season, with a little note of good wishes. It could be very lonely for a young singer in a dressing-room, waiting to be called on to the stage for a difficult performance. I remember sitting in my room on the ground floor, staring at my make-up in the mirror, my breath coming quicker, feeling sick, and shaking a little, listening to the audience chatting and laughing gaily a few feet away outside on the lawns, and wondering how they could be so heartless, when I was so miserable and so tense. Audrey knew what singers went through on first nights, because it happened to her too. 'Mrs Christie's champagne' was a delicate stroke of man- and woman-management. Someone cared, and it made you feel much less lonely.

Ebert used to talk about the early seasons when rehearsals finished at about six, and the music staff and production staff went to their rooms, changed into evening dress, and dined at leisure. The conversation then, he said, was brilliant and gay and amusing, and Audrey showed herself to be a great English hostess. She was fun to be with. Ian Wallace told me of a party which Audrey gave one night in the middle of a season. They found in the wardrobe a costume for an elderly lady, and an elderly wig, and Ian carefully made himself up as a raddled old bag and was taken into the party by Audrey and introduced to everyone as 'The Duchess of Surrey, a very keen opera-goer'.

There's a splendid story of a weekend party in the winter, in the very early years. As many of the management team as happened to be in England would go to Glyndebourne every weekend, planning, thinking, arguing for the next season. One Sunday the Queen Mother, who was then Duchess of York, called when they were all out for a walk, and Childs, the butler, arranged for her to be taken round the theatre. When they got back from their walk, Childs brought tea to them in front of the enormous log fire. He told Audrey that the Duchess had called and said that he had arranged for her to see the theatre. He hoped this was what Mrs. Christie would have wished? Next weekend they were all at Glyndebourne again and once more they went for a walk in the afternoon, all except for Hamish Wilson, who was too lazy. When they got back they teased him for being idle and he said he had in fact been very busy. He'd been wondering what he would do if he had a Distinguished Caller again. 'What did you decide?' they asked, and he said decisively, 'I'd sit down and knit a red carpet *at once!*' Being with Audrey had this sort of effect on people. She infected people with her own gaiety.

These roles Audrey played with ease and certainty and charm in public. In private her influence in the inner circle of top management was even more important. Her experience, her years of work in the theatre, her judgment, her intimate knowledge of the singers with whom she worked each day, her wit—all of these she used in the never-ending talk of plans, and casting, and singers. When she rehearsed, she was the disciplined pro, and obediently, one of us, she took direction willingly and eagerly. A genius? Perhaps not. But she had a lioness's share in the planning and the unbelievably rapid growth of Glyndebourne.

This was the theatre, and these were the people who made the theatre, where suddenly, in 1936, completely unknown, I found myself to my astonishment singing for the first time in an international cast.

THREE

Turning Pro

I HAD BEEN twice lucky. First, Glyndebourne had offered me a contract and, privately, John Christie helped me with a generous cheque to cover the expense of my going to Vienna to work with Strasser, and to help tide me over the awkward gap between the end of my salary cheques from Sutton Valence, and the opening of my first season at Glyndebourne. Ursula Nettleship organised contributions as well among her friends. I was swimming in luck. Secondly, Glyndebourne made it a condition of their help that I should study with Strasser; so the problem of finding a teacher—and luckily Strasser is a good teacher—was firmly settled for me.

The fact that I had been taken up by Glyndebourne was an invaluable help, too, in opening doors for me. Young singers find it difficult to get agents interested in them. Agents always have as many singers as they need. Established singers get good fees—beginners take what they can get. Agents get a percentage from every engagement that they can secure for their singers, and, obviously enough, what they earn on a beginner's small fee is less than they get from the big fee earned by a well-known singer. So there is no particular attraction for them in young singers who have not yet made themselves known. Instead of having to pester agents to take me on, I found that the biggest agents in the country came to me. On the night of my first performance at Glyndebourne, Monica Nixon, a partner in Ibbs and Tillett, came to my dressing-room after the show, told me who she was, and, bless her, asked me if I was willing to have my name added to their list. I indicated that Franklin was willing. But, even when you do get your name on an agent's books, it is never easy to get into the profession. William Byrd wrote in 1588:

> Since singing is so good a thing
> I wish all men would learne to sing.

It is just as well that all men do not 'learne to sing'. The profession today is small and overcrowded. The mass media and the aeroplane between them have brought wealth and luxury to a handful of singers at the top, but music can support far fewer singers in all than there were, say, sixty years ago. True, there was little opera then in Britain. The Moody Manners company, the Carl Rosa, and one or two other touring companies flogged round the provincial theatres, almost perpetually on tour. There were spasmodic seasons at Covent Garden with international casts. But there was no permanent, resident opera company in Britain.

There was, however, plenty of other work for competent singers, in oratorio and especially in ballad concerts. These brought front-rank singers to popular audiences, audiences that today have been lost to beat groups. The leading singers of the day, singing 'Excelsior' and 'The Trumpeter' and 'Down in the Forest' and hundreds more sentimental songs, were household names. Certainly Ada Crossley, Clara Butt, Edward Lloyd and Robert Radford were much more familiar to the man in the street than Richard Lewis, Janet Baker, or Geraint Evans would be today. It may seem now a waste of good singers, or good voices, that they should sing ballads, but ballads needed *singing*. 'Ah! Moon of my Delight', 'Myself when young', 'I'll sing thee songs of Araby' are all in their way as physically challenging as Italian opera. Singing these ballads, then, brought singers not only big popular audiences, but an invaluable training for the bigger and more exhausting roles in their repertory. Ballads had another advantage for young singers learning their trade. If you get emotionally involved when you sing great music, you find difficulty in singing clearly and easily. But it would have been difficult to have been emotionally involved with, for instance, 'Because' or 'Until'. (I have often toyed with the idea of writing another in this genre—'Nevertheless'.)

There were often tours arranged by agents for four or five artists together. They included big names like John McCormack and, naturally, Clara Butt, and there would always be four singers so that they could finish with the quartet from *Rigoletto*. There would be a violinist, even Kreisler or Elman in their younger days. A good accompanist—for instance, Landon Ronald—would complete the party to accompany everybody and play a group of solos, and they would set off on what became a standard route—Birmingham on Monday, Sheffield on Tuesday, Manchester on Wednesday, Liverpool on Thursday, Newcastle on Friday, Edinburgh on Saturday, and Glasgow on Sunday. They took in six or seven more one-night stands on the way home. These 'packages', with variations in the make-up of the party, left regularly for the well-trodden road.

The content of programmes in those days, not only on these tours, but in concerts at the Queen's Hall or the Albert Hall in London, was a motley rag-bag. I once read an advertisement, dated about 1909, of a concert in which the Queen's Hall Band, conducted by Sir Henry Wood, was to play fourteen opera overtures, one after the other! In 1908 the announcement of that night's Promenade Concert on the front page of the *Daily Telegraph* included the news that a mezzo-soprano was to sing an aria from the Verdi Requiem—the 'Liber Scriptus'. The lady, with an admirable business sense, made her own announcement in the adjoining column that, *as an encore* to the Verdi aria, she proposed to sing the new ballad entitled 'Hey Nonny Nonny'. But, rag-bag or not, this was *work* for singers, and there was plenty of it.

There was still enough to go round in the thirties, when I started, and, after the war, in the first few years of peace, there was even more. The Arts Council, which had begun its work during the war as C.E.M.A. (Council for the Encouragement of Music and Art) to boost morale in small towns and villages by taking good music to the people, was still supporting music clubs and choral societies. Even villages in Wales and the north of England could afford four soloists from London in their annual performances of the *Messiah* in their chapels. You made your name as a singer with the Royal Choral, or the Hallé, or the Huddersfield Choral Society; but your living you made in the small towns and the villages in the provinces. I arrived in a mining town in South Wales to sing in the *Messiah*, and saw the posters on the platform. They announced:

Miss Joan Hammond (soprano)	Mr. Edward Reach (tenor)
Miss Gladys Ripley (contralto)	Mr. David Franklin, M.A. (Cantab), (bass)

In Wales, they have a great respect for anyone who has 'got his letters'—but the important point is that this small town had booked four London singers, with four London fees.

The tendency of the Arts Council since then has been to concentrate subsidies into block grants for Covent Garden, Sadler's Wells, and the major orchestras. Some grants are still channelled to music clubs and choirs through the National Federation of Music Societies, but there is nothing like as much concert work today as there was at the end of the war and after, when music was still part of the government's apparatus for reinforcing morale.

Sometimes, one did the reinforcing in odd places. I sang in 1944 for C.E.M.A. in a village hostel for land-girls in Hertfordshire. A few weeks before, the house had been hit by a flying-bomb, and the corner of the building had been ripped off. Before they could get a tarpaulin into position rain had poured in, and the action of the battered old upright piano had been gravely affected by the damp. When our accompanist played the first chord of the evening, she discovered with fascinated horror that the keys which she had struck stayed down, and she could not go on with the phrase until they had come up again. So the front of the piano was taken off, and Ursula Nettleship (she turned up again, this time as one of the C.E.M.A. regional representatives) stood over the pianist, improvising a kind of mad harpist technique, pulling back the hammers as soon as they had been played, so that the pianist could play them again. This was by no means the only difficulty one met in C.E.M.A. concerts. At another, the piano had been tuned— but a semitone sharp. The violinist, who was to play the César Franck sonata, got very excited. If he tuned his strings up to the pitch of the piano, they would certainly break under the strain. The pianist said that he would cope—he would put it down, and, in effect, he played it in A flat. It was an extra-ordinary intellectual feat, to transpose a vigorous and complex work and simultaneously re-finger it, *from memory* in per-formance.

Since those pioneering days of C.E.M.A., radio and the long-playing gramophone record have enormously widened the catchment area of good music. They have between them made it available, almost constantly on tap, over the whole country. Oddly enough, the modern provision of 'instant music' has had a striking side-effect on the field of psychological medicine. Doctors have long known that music therapy is valuable in forms of mental illness. But, even if you knew this in the nine-teenth century, where did you get your music? The answer is that you made it yourself. I found during research for a radio series, even as late as the years before the First World War, surprising advertisements in the Public Appointments columns in the national dailies. 'SUCH-AND-SUCH ASYLUM. Male Ward Nurses required—second clarinet and first trombone (doubling cello) preferred.' The young Elgar's first job as a conductor was as bandmaster of the big asylum in Powick, near Worcester. He trained his nurses' band, wrote music for them, and led them for patients' dances on Saturday nights. It was a do-it-yourself music-therapy. But not now, for asylum bands are a thing of the past. Music? Turn on the radio.

In recent years, television has added its ration—a small one, but still something—to that generously given by radio and the gramophone. But on balance the effect of television has been most damaging to concerts of live music, for it hypnotises people into staying by their own firesides at night. Music clubs tend to plan their concerts for nights when the big-audience shows are not being transmitted. (Some years ago, I was engaged three years running to give recitals at a music club in Dolgelley, in North Wales. Each year, I had capacity audiences. The hall seated 600 and, in a town of a population of only 2,000 plus, this was a very high figure. Roughly, one person in three in that town heard my concerts. I felt very flattered—until I realised the reason. Dolgelley lies in a fold of the mountains, and at that time TV reception was impossible. Only on the outskirts of the northern half of the town, and then only in houses high in the mountains, was it possible to get a picture at all. So the rest of the town still kept, willy-nilly, the old-fashioned concert-going habits of the 1930s and the 1940s.)

There is another factor that has reduced the total number of singers who can find sufficient work to make a living, and concentrated what work there is amongst the small number at the top. Up to the 1930s a singer could make a comfortable living in the concert hall with no more than half a dozen oratorios, and a couple of dozen songs in his bag. But now that the mass media have widened the audience's experience, he is required to sing much more music, and much more difficult music. The singer has had to learn to cope with new and sophisticated modern idioms, and those who had relied merely upon the quality of their voices and a competence in old-fashioned, well-known material, have fallen out of the race. Schönberg, Alban Berg, Britten, and Stravinsky have sorted out the sheep from those goats who could not read or memorise modern music. But television, which has reduced the number of audiences for live music, and reduced the total number of singers in the profession, has made it easier and quicker for successful singers—those who can handle difficult music, who have good microphone voices, and have good looks as well—to reach the top. A successful first appearance in a popular TV programme has brought young singers immediately to the notice of societies and music clubs and orchestras all over the country and has done for them in five minutes what would have taken five years and more in the days when I started. There is room for only a few at the top, but for them there are big rewards. There are hundreds who do the round of auditions, and competition for the few big prizes has become much more fierce.

It has been made fiercer by a steady influx of voices from Australia and America. These have three great advantages. By and large they have a superb natural physique—and singing is a form of athleticism. Secondly, they have grown up in a warm, sunny climate, in which voices can bloom. Thirdly, Australia and America are wealthy countries, with oil tycoons or sheep tycoons, and thick cheque-books, ready to give scholarships or subsidies to promising youngsters.

Though the problems have been intensified by modern conditions, for the young singer there are still basically three questions. Is my voice good enough? How do I get it trained? How can I get my foot in? To begin, very properly, with the first of these questions, there are hundreds of good voices in this country. They can be heard in music festivals, in male voice choirs, in choral societies, in Sacred Concerts and Grand Popular Concerts in church halls and chapels. But a good voice by itself is not enough. There are no natural song-birds. I once read in an American book about singing:

Mother Nature knows better than we do what to do with our voices.

I'd like to hear Mother Nature cast as Brünnhilde, or Tosca, or Turandot. The author wrote, about Schubert's 'Du bist die Ruh':

If deeply felt, these moods should be unerringly communicated to the listener.

Alas, this is not true. Singing is not a sentimental telepathy, but a deliberately and carefully organised physical process. Amateur actors can occasionally give good *single* performances, relying on their intelligence and imagination; being a professional actor, doing it night after night after night, demands training and technique. But amateur singers cannot rely on their intelligence and imagination to give even one performance of taxing music. Intelligence and imagination cannot by themselves bring into the voice the top C that crowns the aria. It must be drilled physically into the singer's instrument, and that means training like a pro. Unless his voice is trained, a singer is like a pianist trying to play a concerto on a public-house piano. And more than that. A pianist playing on a bad piano can damage his technique, but the instrument itself would remain unaffected. Imagine that, as the pianist plays his concerto on a bad piano, the tone of the instrument itself deteriorates—and then you have a complete parallel with the singer. For that is what happens to a singer who tries to sing seriously without proper training. The voice disintegrates.

The pianist, the violinist, the cellist, the oboist—they are lucky. They can buy their instruments ready-made, and they have only to learn to play them. The singer must first build his instrument. Then he must learn how to play it, and finally, he must acquire musicianship enough to use it with taste. Building the instrument is not easy, for standards of voice-training in England have mostly been and still are, in a word, awful. Singers are vain. Singers are ambitious. Singers are suckers for the charlatans—heaven knows there are enough of them in business, and there always have been. Round about 1908, there was a famous lawsuit about The Natural Voice Academy. The self-styled Professor who owned it advertised regularly in the national press:

The Essentials of an Aesthetic Tone in ONLY Six Lessons

—and BY POST! After this Initial Instruction, the Intelligent Pupil can do the Rest—UNAIDED.

This was admirable bait. Every singer is convinced that he has a magnificent voice, and that he could make an outstanding career, that lessons—just a few—could put on the final polish and put Success—and money, lots of lovely, lovely money— within his reach. Students are poor, and impatient to begin cashing in on their singing. The idea that six lessons, and only six, could put them on the right track, and that then they manage on their own—it must have brought them in by dozens. And then, when they found that they could not 'do the Rest— UNAIDED', as certainly they could not, the Academy could regretfully point out that they couldn't have been intelligent enough. Easy.

W. H. Cummings, who was Principal of the Guildhall School of Music, went gunning for the Natural Voice Academy. At an annual conference of the Incorporated Society of Musicians, he deliberately called its Professor a quack, and sat back to wait for action. The Professor sued him, as Cummings had hoped, and he sued, too, all the papers that had carried a report of the speech. It was arranged that the case against the *Daily Telegraph* should be heard first, as a test for all the other actions that were pending. There was great public interest, and the dailies carried long reports of each of the four days that they spent in court. The Professor gave evidence about the anatomical discovery he had made, apparently overlooked by the medical profession, that the hinge of the jaw is not a ball-and-socket design, but a kind of sliding stud. It can open, he found, not only up-and-down but backwards and forwards. More than that, this forward sliding motion was essential, he said, for good voice production. He put several of his pupils in the witness box, and one after the other they demonstrated the results of his teaching, dutifully sliding lower jaws forward until they protruded below and in front of the upper jaw, and, in this uncomfortable position, singing exercises for the information of the court. 'Pat-a-wat-away, pat-a-wat-away' they sang, for the amusement of the spectators, and to the satisfaction of counsel for the defence.

His star witness was Sir Charles Santley—the Gladstone, the W. G. Grace, of English singing. He led Sir Charles deferentially through his achievements and distinctions as a singer, and finally came to the question on which the case was poised. How much value did Sir Charles attach to the Professor's system of teaching? In the ringing baritone voice that had thrilled the Royal Albert Hall and the Royal Opera House, for which Gounod had especially written 'Even bravest heart' in *Faust*, and that now bounced resonantly around the court, he said 'No value whatever!' The oracle had spoken, there was loud applause in court, and Darling J., who was trying the case, sternly demanded silence in court, and then, with a little bob towards the famous singer to acknowledge his standing and reputation, he reminded those in court that this was the one public occasion on which Sir Charles might *not* be applauded. This was the end for the Professor. He lost both case and reputation. His costs made him bankrupt, and the quacks in music had to be more careful in their advertising.

There were many of them. Some teachers in the north hit on the happy idea of calling themselves Schools of Music, or Colleges of Music, and of granting their own degrees. Teachers taught and then examined their pupils, announced that they had passed, and presented their diplomas. They had working arrangements with the photographer round the corner, who kept gown and hood and mortar-board handy in the studio, so that successful pupils could have their pictures taken in academic finery clutching a roll of parchment, so that Mum could boast that her Elsie had 'got her letters'—and at thirteen, too. Rival teachers would then start granting their degrees to twelve-year-olds—anything to get business. There was one self-styled College of Music in London that offered the degree of Mus. Doc. The only test for candidates was that they should play a single chant not a double chant, mark you—in not more than two sharps or flats. Whether it had to be played at sight was not specified. The college had gown and brilliantly coloured hood specially designed for this doctorate, and available to successful candidates at a cost of three guineas. The college prospectus prudently added the reminder that male candidates should provide their own trousers.

The Incorporated Society of Musicians campaigned against these fake schools, and eventually official registration became obligatory, and they had to stop giving their own degrees. But nothing could stop them teaching, and the flood of pupils swept on. Singing, playing the piano, or the fiddle or the harmonium —these were social accomplishments of which families were proud, and on which they relied for their home entertainment. I counted, in one issue of the *Sheffield Telegraph* in 1908, thirty-six advertisements by teachers of piano, singing, stringed instruments, organ and harmonium, elementary theory, harmony and counterpoint, anything that Sheffield wanted to learn. There has today been a great change in our social habits. Now, in the *Sheffield Telegraph* and other provincial dailies, you will find no more than two or three teachers offering their services. The great days of teaching music are over. Nevertheless, there are literally thousands of would-be singers taking lessons all over the country. Not all of them would admit that they have an eye on a professional career. They want to sing well enough to take solos in their church choirs. They want to compete in music festivals, or to sing in the local amateur operatic society's annual assault upon Gilbert and Sullivan. They have the itch to sing, they all believe privately that their voices are exceptional, and they long for the applause of an audience—on an amateur basis, of course. But they dream of being discovered, and, if they were offered a professional contract, nothing would stop them.

So even today, the vanity of singers makes them still vulnerable to advertisements. There was just before the war an Italian teacher in London who announced in the concert columns that he was to hold a pupils' concert at the Wigmore

Hall. The feature of this occasion was given star billing.

A tenor will die on top C from fff to ppp—
WITHOUT FALSETTO!

I was curious to see and hear this feat. He did nothing of the sort, poor boy, though, in the effort of making his decrescendo from fff to ppp, he did nearly strangle himself.

How can a good voice find the right teacher? In small towns, the church organist is the court musician of the area. He plays for services, he trains the choir, he accompanies at concerts, and he teaches. On the strength of his choir-training, he often teaches singing to adults, as if this were the same as teaching a group of boy trebles. Some organists are good voice-teachers— Kathleen Ferrier's first teacher was one—but this is only a matter of chance. There are perhaps—who knows?—good singing teachers to be found amongst butchers, or carpenters, or blacksmiths. There is no special quality in organists that makes them, *as organists*, qualified to teach singing. Thirty years ago at Glyndebourne John Brownlee said to me: 'Learning to sing is imitation', and you cannot imitate anyone who cannot do it himself. In general, it is difficult to find a good teacher who is not a singer.

Though I think it impossible for a non-singer to teach, it is equally impossible to guarantee that singers themselves can make good teachers. Singers must work on *sensation*, what the voice feels like in the head. Many singers sing by instinct and find it impossible to isolate and identify a sensation, and describe in *words* what it is that they do. Without words, how can you teach? A piano teacher can tell a pupil to lift his wrist, or drop it, to do this and that with the weight of the arm, and the pupil can watch himself and check that he is doing what he has been told to do. But the muscles that are used in singing are hidden in the head and in the body. We cannot see them, we cannot touch them, and some of them we cannot directly control. Without words to describe and communicate a sensation, how can a singer be taught? It is commonly accepted that every voice, to give it brilliance and carrying power, needs head resonance. Getting this head resonance—that is the problem. Some teachers approach it—or rather avoid it—by telling their pupils to 'think it up'. You can 'think it up' like mad, and nothing will happen, because this is a physical problem, and, however difficult it is, it has a physical solution. But, if the pupil has 'thought it up' and the voice still remains obstinately in the throat, the teacher is blameless. The fault is the pupil's— obviously he has not been thinking correctly. Maybe it is frustrating for the pupil, but it is comforting for his teacher. And convenient, too.

The difficulty of communication, the singer's defenceless reliance on the honesty of his teacher, and sheer vanity make the singer very vulnerable. Item—I once heard a friend, a good teacher, working with a girl who was quite awful. When she had finished her lesson, and had gone, I asked him how he could bear to listen to the noise she made. He said she paid him two guineas a time, three days a week, and in cash. If he forgot to declare these amounts, and so paid no tax on them, it made him a sizeable sum in the year and he said that it takes a lot of courage to tell the equivalent of £600 to get the hell out of that door. Item—a young tenor, who had never had a lesson in his life, enrolled at a School of Music, and was allotted to a teacher whose only qualification for teaching singing was that he played the organ. The boy's very first lesson was on 'Che gelida manina', one of the most difficult of all arias, even for experienced and competent professionals. Item—another young tenor came to me about the same time to ask my advice. His teacher was ruining his voice, and this young man had the sense to realise it. I said that, obviously, he must leave his teacher at once. He was sure that the Principal would refuse to transfer him to another teacher. Then, I said, he must leave the School. 'But,' he said, in genuine dismay, 'that means I shall lose my grant!' It took me some time to persuade him that there was little point in having a training grant of £300 or £400 a year from his local authority, if its final result was that his voice was wrecked. Over and over again, teachers who know nothing of voice production set their pupils to bang away at aria after aria, with no technical preparation, when the voices are much too young and immature to take the strains of big singing. The teachers enjoy playing the music, it passes the time, and an aria a week gives the pupil an illusion of progess. But his voice is destroyed.

Assume that the young singer has found a good, honest teacher who knows what he is about, and has built the voice into a reasonable and reliable instrument. Now the second phase begins—the pupil must learn to play the instrument. Most youngsters are eager to cut their singing teeth on opera, and opera has its attractions, because, if they are successful, they may land a full-time contract. But there are dangers. The self-interest, the personal ambition, and the vanity of conductors and producers at schools of music sometimes lead them to produce works that are downright harmful to the development of young voices. It is common practice to accept singers straight from school with instrumentalists, and though instrumentalists at school-leaving age may be ready to start working on an adult repertory, singers mature much later. Is *Die Meistersinger* a student work? Or *Falstaff*? Or *Don Giovanni*? Yet each of these works has been done by one or other of the London schools of music.

Some years ago, I went to a student performance of *Don Giovanni* at a London school of music. Donna Anna, I was told, was singing that part for the second time in her school career. They did in turn each of the four major Mozart operas—*Don Giovanni*, *Figaro*, *Cosi*, and the *Flute*—and this year *Don Giovanni* was back again. 'But,' I said, 'her course lasts four years?' 'Yes.' 'This is her last year?' 'Yes.' 'Then she must have sung the part for the first time in her *first year*?' 'In her first *term* actually.' 'Before she had had any voice training?' I asked, horrified. 'Yes,' said the Principal's wife. 'It's extraordinary, isn't it?' I replied tactfully that it was at any rate unusual. She then said that it was odd—common opinion round the school was that Anna wasn't singing nearly as well that year as she had done four years before, as a beginner. This was the triumphant result of four years' teaching. In that same production the running order was altered because the conductor dearly loved the exquisite Mask Trio in Act I, which is sung in front of the curtains. Normally, the set for the final scene of the act is built behind the curtain during the Trio. They had little stage machinery, but a lot of student stagehands, and they made a great deal of noise. So the Trio was sung with absolute stillness behind the curtain, and the three singers—Anna, Elvira, and Ottavio—made their exit. Then back came Ottavio, alone, and astonished me by singing 'Il mio tesoro', the second of his great arias, from Act II. The set was changed during this aria, and he sang to an accompaniment of bangs and rattles and squeaks from the stage. During the interval I protested to the conductor, who was an old friend, that this revision of the running order put an intolerable burden on a young voice. Ottavio is difficult enough for a student, God knows, but Mozart's spacing of his arias and ensembles through the opera does give him some chance to rest and to relax between his ordeals. But this new order had given him, in quick succession, his long and taxing opening scene with Anna, the quartet, and then his scene with Anna and his aria 'Dalla sua pace', the arrival at Don Giovanni's party, the difficult Mask Trio, and, immediately, 'Il mio tesoro', and then the vigorous first finale. The boy was on his knees by the end of the act, and the voice went to pieces, and cracked over and over again. I said bluntly this was cruelty to a young singer for whom the Principal was responsible. He said obstinately that he was not going to have the Mask Trio interfered with. I said, 'What about interfering with a young tenor voice?' He said, 'There are always more tenors.'

Opera, then, is a tempting but dangerous field for students to train in. Oratorio in its way is just as difficult as opera, as physically exhausting as opera. It is possible to argue—and I often have argued—that oratorio is even more challenging than opera. Standing on the stage at the Royal Albert Hall, with a symphony orchestra all round you, in the open, is much tougher work than singing on a stage, with the orchestra shielded by being sunk in the pit and partly covered by the apron of the stage.

When I first started singing oratorio, and sang it with keen physical enjoyment, I came up against older singers who took a different view. Oratorio, they said, is sacred, and therefore it must be sung with reverence and discretion. In fact it was, and still is, sung as a relic of Victorian ham sentimentality. This attitude ignores history. Oratorio was often in its early days staged as opera. Handel's *Saul* and *Belshazzar* make magnificent stage productions. Even *Messiah* itself has been played as an opera in Sheffield. One of the Philharmonic chorus there once told me of the production—'Aye, there were 'oondreds of angels all round t'organ, draped in black. It were loovely!'

If, then, the student must be warned against both opera and oratorio, what is there left to sing? Lieder? Yes, but there are one or two facts about Lieder that the young singer should know, and is not always told. Lieder-singing is of limited professional value. Occasionally, if you are really good, you may expect an engagement to sing in the Third Programme, or in the very restricted market of music clubs. Each of these has its own disadvantages. If you broadcast in the Third, your German must be good. (I once shared a Schubert programme with a tenor who sang 'Heidenröslein', which means 'The Little hedgerose', but pronounced it as 'Heidenrosslein'. As the producer acidly pointed out to the embarrassed tenor, he had been singing about 'The Little hedgehorse'—quite different from what Schubert had intended.) But your good German, which is essential in the rarified atmosphere of the Third, is almost completely lost on the average British music club. Very few of our people understand German, and certainly not well enough to cope with the subtleties and the intricate verse patterns of Lieder. You have got either to accept that your delicate changes in colour, your subtle manipulation of the words, your pointing of the metrical accents, will go for nothing, or to try to find a translation which satisfies both the sense of the original and the demands of the music. There is a third alternative, to explain to the audience before each song in your programme just what it is all about. But I never thought that this was a sensible procedure. To interrupt singing with constant spoken explanations is very disturbing both to the concentration of the audience, and to the voice of the singer, for speaking and singing do not easily mix. In any case, very few audiences can remember a long explanation of the nuances of a song, and marry them to a text in an unknown tongue two, three, four minutes later. It is, I think, an insoluble problem, and one which reduces the commercial value of singing Lieder in Britain.

Another fact of life that young singers must accept is that, for the most part, Lieder should be sung only by mature, experienced singers. Some Brahms, for instance, is physically very hard on the voice. Schubert, on paper, looks very much easier, but his songs are so packed with thought, and with subtlety, that only the most experienced and adroit singers can hope to approach them successfully. There was once a distinguished Lieder singer who, when her own career was ended, made another career as a teacher. She adopted the singular tactic of starting her pupils, from the beginning, on Schubert. The theory was that if you could sing Schubert, it developed and trained the voice. I suppose it is true that if you can sing Schubert, you can sing anything. But as a method of training I think this is not even arguable—it is rubbish. The instrument must come first—what you can play on it comes later.

There is a story, which I love, which I think makes a point. A young English soprano went for an audition to a famous foreign teacher of Lieder, with whom she wanted to have lessons. She sang to the great man.

He listened and then said to her, 'Child, you have a nice little voice, a nice little technique. But it is so—so *innocent*. Now I must ask you a qvestion. Tell me, little one, are you a wirgin?'

'Yes,' said the girl, astonished. 'Why?'

'No, child, it is too soon. You must live and loff and suffer. Ven you 'ave lived and loffed and suffered, then you vill come back to me and I vill teach you to sing our great Schubert, Brahms, Wolf. Now go, little one.'

Next morning, promptly at ten o'clock, there was a knock at the door of his studio.

'Komm!' he said.

The door opened, and the girl shyly put her head into the room.

'It's all right now,' she said. 'Can I come in?'

The fourth important field of singing is what is known in the trade as the Art Song. It is a clumsy name, but it is necessary, I suppose, to distinguish songs from sentimental ballads. Some Art Songs are as difficult as Lieder—I know nothing, in any language, more difficult than Vaughan Williams' 'Silent Noon', which demands of a singer every possible quality of controlled and legato singing. To take another example and another kind of difficulty, Roger Quilter's songs, with their syllabic settings, make a sustained line difficult. Singers who are clever with words can use their words to distract the attention of an audience and so avoid the necessity of a good legato as the foundation of their tone. By and large, the Italians are the best singers in the world. They have the best line, and they have the best voices, but it is not that they have the best line because they have the best voices. They have the best voices because they have the best line. Anything that damages or interrupts the line—immaturity, singing big stuff too early, an over-dependence upon words—these can destroy a singer's quality.

The singer who has been lucky enough to find the right teacher, to have developed a voice which he can sell, to have been sensible enough in his training to avoid the big, athletic parts in opera and oratorio, and to have been guarded in his approach to Lieder and to the Art Song, must now equip himself with musicianship enough to handle all his work. It is fashionable to make fun of the musicianship of singers. I do it myself. In the bar with the orchestra after a performance, or at a musical party, I modestly murmur my prefabricated self-deprecation—I suppose as a defence—that it feels strange to find myself amongst real musicians, for I am no musician. I am a singer. God knows that singers themselves have done a great deal to point the distinction.

There was a bass-baritone at the Garden, who had one of the most exciting and glorious voices I ever heard in my life. It had a lovely, dark colour, and was completely even throughout the whole enormous range of three octaves. One night in the dressing-room, when we had been discussing singers' ranges, he sang four Cs one after the other, from a tenor top C to the bass low C two octaves below a piano middle C. If only he could have counted up to four in a bar, and if only he could have remembered his four-in-a-bar once he had counted them, he could have made a fortune as the outstanding Wotan of his time. With Wotan, Sachs, and the Dutchman, possibly Kurwenal, firmly fixed in his mind, he could have travelled the world in luxury and with applause. But counting up to four in a bar was an intellectual feat quite outside his capacity. We came together off the stage one night after a performance of *Rosenkavalier* and walked together down the corridor to our dressing-rooms. He sang the small but important part of the Commissary in the last act. 'Went all right tonight, didn't it, Bill?' he asked. I said, guardedly, that I thought it was a bit adventurous. 'Adventurous?' he said. 'What are you getting at?' I said that sometimes I had had to cut in on the end of his phrases because he was running late, and sometimes I had had to wait a couple of beats, or a whole bar, because he had finished too soon, and, for my money, I'd rather stay with the conductor and with the orchestra. 'Are you trying to tell me it wasn't right tonight? Is that it, Bill?' he asked. 'It was wrong to hell,' I answered. 'God damn it,' he said, genuinely surprised, 'I thought tonight was one night when I *had* got the bloody thing right!' Singers said of him—and this is the ultimate in criticism of musicianship— that he was the sort of man who made mistakes in the *Messiah* when he was singing with the book in his hand.

Many years ago a very great Italian baritone came to Glyndebourne to sing *Figaro*. When he began rehearsals, he was surprised and worried because the running order there included a page of recitative which had always been cut in his performances in Italy. He was a fine singer, and a brilliant actor, but notes on paper meant absolutely nothing to him. It was a week before he had memorised the missing page, and before every performance of *Figaro*, to reassure himself, he went with a pianist to a rehearsal room, just before he went on, and ran through the page two or three times to make sure he had still got it right. He was a superb Falstaff—and every note of that great part he had learnt by ear. Someone said that it must have taken so long that it would have saved him time in the end if he had learnt how to read music first, before tackling the part. Yet, whatever his difficulties in memorising music, he never made a mistake, once he had learned his part, in rehearsing or in performing it. In the way he handled his music, in the grace and the subtlety which he brought to the shaping of a phrase, he was the most *musical* of singers. But he was not, academically, a musician.

Instrumentalists tend to think that the most important function of musicianship is the ability to read at sight; proud of their craft, they tend to despise the singer whose reading is not very good. The truth is that it is not in the least necessary for a singer to be able to read well. It may be convenient for him to be able to learn new music quickly, but how long he takes to learn it in private is his own affair. The audience pay to hear the finished performance, however long it has taken to prepare, and never expect to hear, or want to pay to hear, a singer singing a part at sight.

For the singer, sight reading can be no more than a convenience. I would go further—in some ways, good reading is a disadvantage. A bad musician must sing the stuff so often, to drill it into his memory, that at the same time he sings it into his voice. Time is always short at rehearsals—a good reader is always popular with conductors, particularly in ensemble or small chorus work. A good reader, who will save time and money by learning the notes quickly, often sings with so little technical preparation of the voice that it becomes damaged.

The only academic requirement of a singer, then, is that he shall be able to sing accurately from memory at a performance. But there are other features of his musicianship which contribute greatly to his standards of performance. A historical period affects music and the way it must be sung, just as period costume affects the way you stand, and the way you walk. Knee-breeches, silk stockings, a silver sword at your side, lace cuffs, a powdered wig—all of these affect your carriage on the stage and they should also affect the way in which you phrase the music. So the singer must know something of the historical setting of the work, and of the historical setting in which it was written. Mozart's *Marriage of Figaro* and Strauss's *Rosenkavalier* are both set in the eighteenth century—but Mozart's eighteenth century is quite different from Strauss's.

The singer must have good intonation. Often singing out of tune is a matter of technique, and a perceptive teacher can put it right. There are some people—very few, in fact—who have a physical defect of the ear and as a result simply do not know if they are singing on the note or not. If you have such a defect, you must face it. You must not try to sing professionally and, if you sing as an amateur, it would be a kind act to sing in private, behind closed doors. With the windows shut.

Once, at a music festival, I was adjudicating an ensemble class. There appeared on the platform a very strange septet, whose ranks included a boy treble, a woman soprano, a woman contralto, a male alto, plus tenor, baritone, and a bass. They were scientists, teachers and artists by profession, fair bulging with high I.Q's. Even the small boy looked formidably intellectual. Their singing meant a great deal to them, they took it very seriously, and they sang diabolically out of tune. They knew it, and were bewildered and embarrassed. In amateur music circles to sing out of tune is as shameful as having what in Victorian times used to be called the 'social diseases'. Nice people never mentioned them. Nice adjudicators do not even admit that it is possible to sing out of tune. I am not particularly nice and I said bluntly that they sang diabolically out of tune. But it was

not that they were unmusical (sighs of relief all round) or that
their ears had suddenly ceased to work ('Thank God! Melanine
—the doctor says I'm normal!'). They had the oddest collection
of voices I had ever seen together in one group. They all sang
different vowel-shapes, placed in different parts of the head, and
so they all got different assortments of resonances, with differing
proportions of the upper frequencies. They therefore had the
same difficulty in tuning as piano tuners, who have to find a
pitch which is, for instance, a compromise between F sharp and
G flat. It was impossible for these singers to find a compromise.
Their little boy treble produced his voice quite differently from
the woman soprano—the female and male altos used completely
different production techniques. These technical differences had
produced the unbalanced, untuned sound which was giving
them—and me—such distress. The choir of King's College,
Cambridge, sings marvellously in tune because everything is
geared to the same method of production. The trebles, male
altos, tenors and basses all sing exactly the same way and get the
same mixtures of resonances, and so intonation is perfect.

Occasionally singers are accused by audiences, and by critics,
of developing bad intonation by sliding from one note to
another. This also is referred to in rather embarrassed tones as
if it were another of the 'social diseases'. This one is known as
'scooping'. The criticism is based on a fundamental misconcep-
tion of the way the voice works. Some teachers, some choir
trainers, demand that their singers should attack every note
cleanly and separately, like the detached notes of a piano, or of
an oboe, where the depression of a key brings a clean sharply-
defined new note. String players work differently. By continuing
to bow on the string but lifting or lowering a finger the note is
altered without any interruption of the tone. This means that,
with a continuous stream of sound, there must be a link between
one note and the next.

With all instrumentalists, their object is to build as strong a
line as they can, so that they get out of the phrase every last
ounce of shapeliness and the pleasure of the melody. Pianists and

wood-wind players try to conceal from the audience that, in fact, they play detached notes. The pianist uses the sustaining pedal, and they all use the weight of their fingers and the perfect timing of their action, to bind the notes together in one long pouring line. String players can go even further—with a glissando they can deliberately emphasise the 'scoop'.

Of all instruments, the human voice can best, and most easily, produce the long flowing sustained line which makes a good phrase. If a singer tries mistakenly to detach notes, so that each is a separate entity, beautifully tuned and complete in itself, but having no connection with the note before it or the note after it, the voice rapidly tears itself to pieces with a series of separate attacks. If a singer wants the best quality that is possible from his physical equipment—and who would not want it?—he must sustain the voice from note to note for an important technical reason. The best quality in any voice comes from the use of every possible resonance, and once the singer has all his resources fully employed, he must sustain the flow of air from the diaphragm into the resonances so that the same quality remains throughout the whole passage. It is this that every singer tries to achieve, either consciously or from instinct, and if he does it clumsily, or heavily, he lays himself open to a charge of singing out of tune, of attacking from under, or indeed over, the note. He must use his craftsmanship to conceal these *portamenti*, not so much in Italian opera, where they are accepted not only as legitimate technical devices but as an integral part of the style. But there must also be these same joins between notes—or in other, cruder, words, the singer must 'scoop'— even in Bach. In Bach, the singer's tact must vary the speed of the join, and so hide it from the critic; but it is there, and must be there, nevertheless.

One of the most important factors of the singer's musicianship is that he is required to be sensitive enough to sing both as a soloist and in an ensemble. This is in my mind one of the advantages that the opera has over the straight theatre. In the theatre, if more than one actor speaks at a time, the dialogue

77

becomes incoherent and the ear of the audience cannot separate them. But, in the opera house, two, three, six, seven, a dozen singers can sing together and the audience can hear, not only the pattern of the ensemble as a whole, but any individual voice that it chooses to focus on. Obviously, an audience cannot pick out one individual voice in a chorus, which generally sings in block chords. But it is possible to select solo voices, singing independent lines in an ensemble, and the composer can use them, either to represent in music the next conflict or development of the plot or to reflect upon the situation in which the characters now find themselves. The practical effect upon the singer's musicianship is that he must be able at will to dominate the orchestra, and, again at will, to find a quality that will blend with the other singers and with the orchestra in one shining stream of sound.

Once the singer is prepared to do all these things with his voice, he is ready to think about getting started. Somehow, good singers do not generally have to worry about getting started. You sing as an amateur, for the love of singing. You get the itch to sing. Singing gives you a subtle mixture of pleasures— physical, intellectual, sensuous, emotional, exhibitionist. You sing. You cannot help singing. Someone hears you—and your chain-reaction starts, because people love discovering singers. It gives them a vicarious sense of personal success. I was discovered several times. I had been discovered at least three times before Christie found me and I was discovered again after that several times more. Once you are discovered, you sing your audition, and you get your contract with an opera company. Easy.

But, if it is not a principal's contract that you are offered? Here you must know what you are up against. The notion that you can start in the chorus, and work your way up to be a principal, is one only for romantic novels. Sadler's Wells do ask young singers of promise to begin with a year in the chorus, and some of them are later promoted to principal parts, but the number of principals at Covent Garden who have fought their way out of the chorus since the company was formed in 1947 can be counted on the fingers of one hand.

There are two reasons for this. The first is that the chorus at the Garden, like every chorus, work very hard for their money. They are called for rehearsal every morning. If there is no stage production in hand, it will be a music call, learning a new opera, memorising new music, refreshing their memories of the chorus-work in an opera soon to be taken out of the cupboard and put back into the repertory. There is three hours' singing in the morning. And there is a performance to sing that night. If there is no performance—if, for instance, the ballet are working that night—they will have a second three-hour rehearsal in the afternoon. Six hours' singing in the day, day after day, week after week through the year, will take the shine off any voice, and the sad fact is that, after a few months in the chorus, most voices are fit only for the chorus. Principal parts are physically and technically beyond them.

The second reason is that a chorister is much more valuable to the management as a chorister than he would be as a principal. In the course of a year's work, he gets scores of little jobs to do, that he does each night as a matter of routine. He carries on the veil to put over Tamino's head in Act II of the *Flute*—he moves Musetta's chair at the end of Act II of *Bohème* to make room for the soldiers to march on—he carries round the tray of brimming glasses in the party scene in *Traviata*—he is one of the men who seize Monterone in Act I of *Rigoletto*—he is one of the two men who hold Zuniga at pistol-point in *Carmen*—he carries a flaming torch in the opening of *Don Giovanni* so that Anna can see her murdered father.

Each member of the chorus has a long list of chores like this, that make productions run smoothly and easily. Sir David Webster once told me that the training of a new chorister in his music, and into his production routines, costs roughly £1,500. And if the management have spent that amount of money on a chorister, it is obviously sensible to keep him as a chorister. Even when a principal is suddenly ill, and there is an emergency, it is simpler to telephone, and find an experienced singer from Vienna, or Berlin, or Milan, or Zürich, who can get on a plane and be at the Garden in three or four hours, ready to play a familiar part, even without rehearsal, than it would be to take someone out of the chorus, rehearse him in a hurry, and then find someone else to do all the little jobs he has to do in the show. Once you get a chorus contract, you must expect to have to stay there. So, at your audition, it's a principal contract or nothing.

But what if you have not got the right voice, or enough voice, or you have the wrong physique for opera? The normal repertory opera contract calls for you to undertake parts at the discretion of the management, and to which you are suited 'by reason of voice and physique'. There was a clause in the pre-war contracts at Glyndebourne which tied the artist down a little tighter. It ran: 'The artist hereby agrees to shave beard and moustache daily before performance', for the obvious reason that beard and moustache, or even a bristly chin, could damage the sort of make-up which the producer required you to put on. (In contracts offered to lady artists, this clause was firmly struck out, and initialled by the management. Deliciously tactful!) Having the right physique for your voice is much more important today than it used to be, say, in the Golden Age of Song, before the first world war. Then singers who were, to put it tactfully, substantially built, waddled on to the stage, settled themselves in the nearest spotlight, and stood motionless, with no attempt at acting the part, and spun out an incomparable line. Bernard Shaw, in his days as a music critic, wrote that in English opera houses there was 'sheer carelessness, a lack of artistic conscience, a cynical conviction that nothing matters in opera so long as the singers draw good houses'. And the canaries of the time, whatever they looked like, did attract big audiences. But today, certainly in England because of the influence of Glyndebourne, audiences expect singers not only to sing like, but to look like, the characters that they have to represent. A short and tubby man, no matter how beautiful and noble his voice, cannot hope to sing Sarastro, or Boris Godonov. A tenor, with whom I sang both at Glyndebourne and at the Garden, was eating his heart out to be a lyric tenor. But he was about a foot short of romantic requirements on the stage, and it was pathetic to see the little man, a good singer and a good actor, trying to carry by storm a soprano who towered over him. In one performance of *Rigoletto* at the Garden, I was waiting for my next entry, at the side of the stage, and I saw Edith Coates, as Maddalena, seducing this mini-tenor. It was difficult to get to work on him, and she bent down, got a grip on his arms, and heaved, and lifted him up and sat him on a table, so that she could get near enough physically for the verisimilitude of seduction. He finally accepted that Rudolfo, and José, and Ottavio, and the Duke in *Rigoletto*, were not for him, and reconciled himself to singing, and very successfully, the tenor buffo parts—David in *Meistersinger*, Pedrillo in *Entführung*, and the like.

I know a soprano, and a very good one, who was wrongly built for lyrical parts. She was too short, and too heavy. She used her voice, and her considerable talent and powers as an actress, to make an unseen and outstanding career on radio, both as a singer and as a straight actress. She has not been the only singer to find that the microphone can provide a living. There is a pool of free-lance singers in London, on whom conductors and producers draw for the small choruses and ensembles that they need for radio—for instance 'Friday Night is Music Night', or 'Gala Night at The Opera'—for a chorus in television opera, both in vision and out of vision (there are different rates for the job), for groups in the backing behind the stars who sing on pop records, and for the small groups who record seductive jingles for TV commercials. They are the singers who are employed for 'sessions'.

This is a type of work that has developed in the past few years with the tape-recorder, and has given an opportunity for the journeyman singer—and the journeywoman, too. It has brought a new basis for payment. In the opera house, singers negotiate with the management for a weekly salary, which may specify a maximum number of performances per week. When guest singers visit a company, or when singers are engaged for single performances in the concert-hall, their fees are governed by the singer's price in a competitive market. A beginner could, for instance, be offered fifteen guineas to sing in the *Messiah*—and glad to get it—while, for a front-rank name, his agent might ask, for exactly the same work, fifty, seventy-five, a hundred guineas. But for 'sessions', singers are hired by the hour, and there is a rate laid down for each type of job, which takes into account the number of hours required to do the job. For a radio show, for instance, with a three-hour rehearsal beforehand, which must include an hour's break between rehearsal and broadcast or recording—five guineas. An extra rehearsal of three hours on the same day—two-and-a-half guineas. An extra three-hour rehearsal on the day before—three guineas. If there is a paying audience—three guineas extra. For TV opera, in vision—thirty-six guineas a week, to include all rehearsals. Out of vision—twenty-eight guineas a week, and this for a shorter period of rehearsal, for they have no moves to learn, and have not to memorise the music, but can sing with the music in their hands. If the transmission is recorded, any re-takes are paid for separately—five guineas for fifteen minutes or any lesser period. For classical recordings, in a choir of twenty or more, per three-hour 'session'—five guineas. For a choir of less than twenty—six pounds. For a 'half-session' (i.e. two hours) for a choir of over twenty—three pounds fifteen, and for a choir of under twenty—four pounds ten. For pop 'sessions', for any size of choir—nine pounds for three hours. 'Half-sessions' (again two hours)—six pounds ten. Overtime is paid pro rata. Film 'sessions' carry the same rates as pop 'sessions', with fares to the studios paid on top. Jingles 'sessions' in theory last only one hour, start to finish. Generally, the musicians record first—they work in the studio for only one hour for their fee of twelve guineas. The singers are dubbed on afterwards, and are paid seven pounds for their hour, plus a percentage for a block of repeat transmissions, which varies according to whether the jingle goes out in one region or simultaneously on the whole network.

Obviously, with the whole pay-structure based upon the time taken to do the job, the 'sessions' singer must be a good musician and a first-rate sight-reader. People who are slow to learn the notes, or make mistakes in performance or recording so that re-takes have to be done, waste time and money. They must too, have good technical control of their voices, and good clear words. If you can offer these qualities, and one other—stamina —you can make a useful, perhaps a comfortable living. In general, 'sessions' singers are a mixture of singers who haven't managed to make the grade as established soloists, and promising youngsters who don't make enough as soloists to live on, and fill up with 'sessions' while they are waiting for fame and fortune. You have to be lucky to fit everything in. The B.B.C. usually book a chorus some three months ahead. For pop 'sessions', there can be a phone call just a few hours beforehand —and, if you are out, or already have a job to do that day, bad luck! Jingles, too, are set up just a few hours ahead. You drop what you are doing, push on to the tube, run for a bus, get to the studio, pick up your music, and start singing it crisply and accurately *at sight*. It is a hard life, much tougher than singing in a resident company at an opera house.

The old-fashioned alternative to the opera house, if, for instance, your voice was not big enough for the theatre, or if you weren't the right shape or size for the stage, was to make a concert hall career. It has never been easy. The traditional way to launch yourself was to give a recital at the Wigmore Hall, which you paid for yourself. It was expensive—the hire of the hall, the engagement of a good accompanist (you tried to get Gerald Moore if you could), posters for publicity, the printing of programmes, announcements in the press, a hair-do and a new dress (the men were luckier, because the same old suit of tails would serve). All of this could be set off against tax, if you were lucky enough to have an income on which tax had to be paid. (I know of a soprano who bought herself a couple of bouquets, to be handed up to her on the platform as spontaneous tributes from her delighted audience, who got her Inspector of Taxes to accept them as a necessary professional expense. She was a resourceful woman.) You sang the conventional programme—a group of Arie Antiche, a group of Handel in Italian, a group of Haydn and Mozart, and, after the interval, Schubert, Brahms, and Wolf, with a finisher of a group of English songs, including one or two first performances by composers with whom you happened to have been a student. With luck you would get short notices in *The Times*, the *Morning Post*, the *Telegraph*, the *Daily News*, the *Manchester Guardian*, maybe the Sunday papers, and possibly one or two of the weeklies. I never did a 'Wigmore'. I thought it odd that this kind of programme, and these notices, were expected to get you engagements to sing in the areas where the singer makes his living——doing the *Messiah* in Pudsey, and *Elijah* in Ramsbottom. And, for the most part, they did not get you the work you wanted. The recital at the Wigmore Hall was a status-symbol that was not generally recognised in Pudsey or Ramsbottom.

Nowadays, the only way to make a concert career is to sing whatever you are offered, whenever you are offered it. A *Messiah*, Stainer's *Crucifixion*, a concert in the Parish Hall— you take whatever chances you find, and for whatever fee you can get. It may be a couple of guineas—it may be five. You sing, not for the money, but for the experience, and for the chance that someone will hear you who will like your work, and ask you to sing at another concert a little further afield. Gradually you widen the areas in which you are heard. If you are lucky, if you are to be the one in a thousand who will make the grade, you very very slowly work your way up to more important occasions and bigger fees. When you find that you are singing so much that you are earning enough to live on, and that your work is interfering with your singing, then you give up your work and— hey presto!—you are a professional singer.

It is a long business. Young singers dream of an audition with an agent, whose startled and delighted recognition that here is

84

a new star leads him to pour engagement after engagement into their laps. This does not happen. When you do get your *Messiah* in Pudsey, and your *Elijah* in Ramsbottom—and Aberdare and Dolgelley and Paisley and Aberdeen—they will come to you through an agent. Not because the agent has gone out and found the work for you, but because your chain-reaction has spread so wide that Pudsey and Ramsbottom and Aberdare and Dolgelly and Paisley and Aberdeen have heard of you, have been told that you are good and promising—and not too expensive—and have asked the agent to book you for them.

Agents have two kinds of stock-in-trade. One is a list of telephone numbers and addresses of societies and music-clubs and orchestras that employ singers, and the other is a list of singers, with their telephones and addresses. No agent will offer you work, unless one of his clients has asked for you. Getting them to ask for you is the tricky part. And even if they have asked for you, it is very difficult for you to compete with the established singers, especially if they are on an 'exclusive' contract with the agent. This means that all the singer's work must go through the agent's hands, the agent getting his commission on everything the singer does. It is therefore in the agent's interest to push his 'exclusive' artists.

I once sang a successful audition with a famous conductor. His office wrote to an agent and told him to book me for the bass part in a performance of the *Dream of Gerontius*. Afterwards, the conductor told me that the agent had telephoned him to protest. 'The *Dream*?' he said. 'We always book a baritone for that. It lies very high. Why not have X? He's dependable, and we book him a lot for the part.' (X was one of the agent's 'exclusives'.) The conductor insisted on having his own way. Now that he had found a bass—me—who could sing the part as Elgar had written it, he was going to have me. 'You bloody well book him, and do as you're told,' he said. I got the engagement, but for trying to persuade the conductor to have someone else the agent took ten per cent of my fee.

On a number of occasions, I have gone to perform for choral

societies and music clubs, and have been most enthusiastically greeted. They were delighted to have me at last. They had tried over and over again to get me, and had been told each time that I was already engaged for that particular date. Some of these dates I checked with my diary and sometimes found that I had been in fact free—but the agent had not even tried to find out if I was available. I assumed that one of the 'exclusives' was available, needed the work, and got the job. This is a common experience amongst singers, and it confirms their belief that the only way to get work from an agent is for the people who are organising the concert to *insist* on having the singers they want. Some agents have their two lists of names and addresses and telephone numbers but little knowledge of the works to be performed, for which they supply artists. Redvers Llewellyn was once, before the war, on holiday in Switzerland, and agents sent him a contract to sing, in Birmingham, the bass part in Dvořák's *Stabat Mater* and—since that is not long enough by itself for a full evening's programme—the baritone part in Handel's Sixth Chandos Anthem, as a fill-up. Redvers, who is a fine high baritone, had never sung the Dvořák, and had never even seen a score, but assumed that the agents knew what they were doing, that both parts were in his range, and signed the contract. Back in England after his holiday, he got a copy of the Dvořák, and found to his horror that it went down to a low E. Redvers has not got a low E, nor has any high baritone. Panic. He told the agents, who asked me to take over the engagement from him. The Dvořák was in my repertory. No trouble at all. But I knew the Handel went up to a top G, with a high tessitura into the bargain. No bass has a high G—I certainly hadn't. I said cheerfully they must be joking, for there was no one in the country who had a chance of singing both works, and rang off. If the agents had known the works out of which they earned their bread-and-butter, they should have told the society that they needed not one singer but two, a baritone for the Handel and a bass for Dvořák. That was what they got in the end. They held Redvers to the contract which he had signed, and told him that he must sub-contract a singer to do the Dvořák for him. He rang me, and, I remember, asked me to 'do it cheap'—two fees, and two lots of expenses, cut deeply into Redvers' one fee.

The biggest and most important employer for the singer is the B.B.C. For the youngster, it presents a separate problem. Auditions are scrupulously fair and carefully conducted and assessed. But, to get an audition at all, you must produce evidence of a number of professional concert engagements. Once you get broadcasts, and the publicity that comes from broadcasting (and getting your name into eight million copies of the *Radio Times*) you will get concert engagements. But, without concert engagements to your credit, you will not get the audition that might lead to a broadcast and so to concert engagements that you need. Somehow, you must break the vicious circle. It depends once again on luck, on being heard by someone who will take an interest, and enjoy discovering you, and offer you enough concerts for you to qualify for an audition with the B.B.C.

In fact, the quality that any singer needs more than any other single factor in his success, is *luck*. Luck particularly in finding the right teacher, for standards of English teaching are bad—so bad that, strangely enough, in the end they work to the advantage of the established singer. There are so many good voices in the country that, if they were all properly trained, there would not be enough work to go round. I have always argued that the standards of teaching in the schools and colleges of music have had the same salutory effect as past plagues and floods in the Orient. Millions were killed by disease, or drowning, or starvation, and this alone kept the teeming populations of the East within reasonable limits. British teachers of singing destroy hundreds of good voices every year, and, if they didn't, some of us would never have made a living.

I know now that I was very lucky indeed, for my chain-reaction led me to Glyndebourne, where I found both my teacher, and the beginnings of a career.

FOUR

'A Miscellaneous or a Book?'

BUT VALUABLE though Glyndebourne was at the beginning of my life as a singer, it offered no more than four months' work a year, and in between Glyndebourne seasons I lived the usual life of the English singer. I sang oratorio, concerts, broadcasts, one-night stands wherever work was going, and a large proportion of them was in the north of England. I think it was Harold Williams, the Australian baritone who sang for many years in Britain, who once said that for the professional singer in this country the South Coast ran along the road between Leeds and Manchester. He could have extended the coastline to the south-west to run along the industrial valleys of South Wales. Over and over again singers find themselves working in industrial areas where they dig coal, or spin cotton or wool, and work steel.

I once sang, just after the war, three nights running for the same choir in Llanelly. I seemed to have something of a success on the first night, and, as a mark of favour, next morning I was taken round the steelworks to watch terrifying cauldrons of steel being tipped, white-hot, into moulds. The heat, the noise, the danger, all frightened the wits out of me. I only had to walk for a couple of hours round the works, and this exhausted me, but the men working an eight-hour shift in that atmosphere were men from the chorus with whom I was to sing again that night, and after eight hours in the nearest to Hell I can imagine, they sang the Verdi *Requiem* like lions.

It is strange that men have always sung best where life is toughest. The softer South of England has relatively few choral societies, and in rural areas they are mostly rather 'county', and middle class in towns and cities. The Royal Choral Society, for instance, is a society for men in white-collar jobs—stockbrokers, bank managers, men in the City, schoolmasters. The sopranos and the altos are wives of white-collar men, or women who themselves work in white-collar jobs. But in the North, and in Wales, choirs are classless. Miners and spinners and weavers sing side by side with men from the bank and doctors and schoolmasters. Singing in industrial areas has always been part of the life of the community.

So, almost every week, I caught the 10.15 a.m. from Euston to Manchester, or the 9.15 a.m. from Paddington to South Wales. There were always other singers on the train. 'How's it goin', boy?' they'd ask. 'Busy, are you?' (Free-lances always ask each other if they are busy. Heddle Nash once made a classic reply to another tenor. '*Busy*?' he said. 'Bloody Holy Week, and me without a date, and me the best bloody Messiah in the business!') And then they always added, 'What are you singing? You doin' a miscellaneous or a book?' A 'book' in Wales is a complete work—the *Messiah, Judas Maccabaeus, The Creation, Samson, Elijah* or whatever. A 'miscellaneous' is a concert in which each performer picks where he likes, and God help the audience. Whichever it was, 'book' or 'miscellaneous', you were committed to travel long distances, rehearse, and *sing* on the same day.

Thus our life made a great contrast with that of singers on the Continent, where music has always been centred on the opera house, and it meant a different work-pattern not only for singers but for conductors and orchestras, too. On the Continent, a young conductor began his career in the opera house as a humble rehearsal pianist working with singers. He flogged his way backwards and forwards through the score on a battered old piano, while singers memorised their parts—and incidentally the pianist learned his operas himself. If he was any good, he worked his way up the ladder, standing in the wings with a score to make sure that the singers made their entrances exactly on cue, conducting singers off-stage, being assistant chorus-master, chorus-master, taking sectional rehearsals when the orchestra was working at Wagner or Strauss and split into strings, woodwind, and brass; being allowed to conduct part of an orchestral rehearsal while the boss stood at the back and listened to the balance. Gradually he acquired training, experience, and authority. This kind of training-ground was not available in England until, after the Second World War, opera was at last nationally subsidised. Before then, young conductors had to grab whatever chances they could get, and there weren't many going.

The orchestras of the Continent had a great advantage in their operatic base. In England, before the war, orchestras lived dangerously without subsidy, and there were four—or was it five?—in London alone, competing for audiences, and having to rely on what they took at the box-office. Even now, with support from the government filtered down through the channels of the Arts Council, their position is still precarious. Some of them—for instance, the Royal Liverpool Philharmonic and the Hallé—have city councils with cultural leanings and ambitions, and get substantial financial backing from them, after the annual argument in the council chamber. But this sort of argument is not as common on the Continent, because it has been accepted for over a hundred years that opera must be subsidised by the state or by the city. We know the Vienna Philharmonic Orchestra as a great concert and recording orchestra. But it does not have to depend on its concerts for a living. It makes its bread-and-butter playing five nights a week in the pit for opera, and it shares the theatre's subsidy. Concerts and records are a bonus.

Like orchestras, the singers of Europe are residents in the opera house. They rehearse, study new parts, re-work operas in the current repertory, and sing two or three performances a week. If they are scheduled for more than that they go to the office and start banging the table. There is time to work, time to think about their work, time to prepare the voice, and time to rest it. Free-lances in England had a simple programme—travel, rehearse, sing, travel, rehearse, sing, world without end, amen. One week in 1946 I worked my way through this schedule:

Sunday	Rehearsal of Bach cantata in Broadcasting House, London.
Monday	Second rehearsal and broadcast of Bach cantata.
Tuesday	Early train to Manchester, rehearsal all afternoon with section of Hallé choir, accompanist, and records for lecture-recital I had written on Berlioz' *Faust*, and evening performance.
Wednesday	Early train to London, rehearsal in afternoon, and broadcast in Third Programme of the Michelangelo Lieder of Hugo Wolf (incidentally, the most difficult set of songs I have ever had to sing—and in the middle of a week like this!)
Thursday	Early train to Manchester, three hours' rehearsal with piano of Berlioz' *Faust*, and evening train to Sheffield.
Friday	Morning—three hours' piano rehearsal, afternoon—three hours' orchestra rehearsal, evening performance. (That day's work totalled eight-and-a-half hours.)
Saturday	Train to Manchester.
Sunday	Morning—three hours' rehearsal with orchestra and different choir of Berlioz' *Faust*, afternoon—performance. Evening—train to London.

This was the way that singers had to live in England, if they were to be successful. One famous English soprano, noted both for her stylish singing and iron stamina, sang the *Messiah* over a thousand times during her career, and reckoned to sing it each

Easter twenty times, and each Christmas another twenty. Added to her other work, these performances of the *Messiah* meant that twice a year she travelled almost non-stop for weeks on end. Heddle Nash one week spent six successive nights in a sleeper between London and Glasgow, three nights going north, and three nights south. The British National Opera Company, on tour, were playing a season in Glasgow, and he sang for them on Monday, Wednesday and Friday, while on Tuesday and Thursday he had concerts in London, and on Saturday a broadcast from London. Walter Widdop, the greatest of English Wagnerian tenors, told me towards the end of his career that he had come to realise that he had wasted too much of his energy, and too much of his voice, in night trains. He would have been able to keep his top notes coming more easily, if he had been content to sing only in opera, instead of singing Tristan at the Garden and then rushing north to sing a *Messiah* in Bradford, and sitting up all night in another train to get back to London with a performance of *Lohengrin* to follow.

For English singers the problem was not one of learning to sing beautifully, but of finding stamina enough to travel long distances, hurry through a rehearsal, and still have stamina to sing beautifully. And in this they have been at a disadvantage with foreigners who were members of a resident company. It is true that star singers in Europe today travel even longer distances than we did. I met an Austrian soprano in the wings at the Garden, as we went down ready for our first entrances, and politely asked her how she was. 'Tired,' she said, and yawned. 'I have sung four nights in four different cities—Zürich, Vienna, Paris, and now London.'

I had the same sort of week myself in 1949. I was a member of the company at the Garden, and had permission to sing with Glyndebourne in the Edinburgh Festival. The last week of the Festival was the first of rehearsals at the Garden for the new autumn season, and the Garden made it a condition that I must be in London on my days off in Edinburgh for rehearsals of *Aïda*. So on Monday I sang in *Don Giovanni* in Edinburgh, Tuesday morning I flew to London, rehearsed all day, and caught a sleeper train back to Scotland, Wednesday I sang in *Don Giovanni*, Thursday (this was a variation on the theme) I went by train to Glasgow, because I couldn't get a flight from Edinburgh, flew to London, rehearsed all day, and caught a sleeper back north, sang in *Don Giovanni* on Friday, on Saturday went to the end-of-season party, spent Sunday packing up and caught the night train to King's Cross. I had the garage bring my car to be ready for us, packed my family and luggage into it, drove home, had a bath, breakfast, and a change of clothes, and was on the stage at the Garden by 10 a.m., ready for another *Aïda* call.

This for me—thank God—was exceptional. For the stars of Europe in the last few years, it has become a commonplace to leave after a performance in Cologne and drive in a fast car 250 miles along the Autobahn to Munich, ready for a morning rehearsal—if they manage to keep awake. Indeed, some singers have killed themselves, dropping off for a second as the road went round a bend, and the car went straight on at eighty miles an hour into the trees. But stars who drive themselves like this are people of exceptional qualities of stamina, who are prepared to work and travel like this because of their pride in performance, because of their ambitions, and not infrequently because of their eagerness to cash in on the huge fees that their voices can earn while they last. And their money makes it possible for them to travel in whatever comfort is possible. Nevertheless, their extravagant journeys do not affect the major argument that the ordinary members of a resident company in Europe were, and still are, much more fortunate than the English singer who had to travel tiringly to concert halls all over the country.

This vast difference between their conditions and ours can be accounted for, I think, historically. For the good of English singers, the Wars of the Roses ended much too soon. If we were still divided into White Rose and Red, at least, in the intervals of raiding each other over the Pennines, Lancaster would have built his opera house in Manchester, and a summer theatre in Blackpool—rather, perhaps, Lytham St. Annes. And York would have had his Royal Opera House in his capital city, and another to amuse him, in his summer hols, in Scarborough. These four theatres would be few enough compared with the scores in, say, West Germany today, but at least they would be more than the two permanent theatres we have at the Garden and the Wells. (If loyal citizens should point out that Manchester already has an opera house, the sad truth is that, handsome and attractive though the theatre is, it is an opera house only in name. Whenever the Garden played there on tour, the first thing they did when they got into the theatre was to tear up the first five rows of stalls to make room for the orchestra. No scenery could be kept in the theatre. It was stored in railway-vans, as indeed it had to be for all ten weeks of the tour, and was brought up on lorries from the sidings for each day's work.)

Opera's lack of theatres in England is certainly not due to a lack of public interest in opera. Whenever the Garden tours, when the Wells goes out into the provinces, the box-office does tremendous business. It is not that the English are not interested in singing, either. We have always sung in Britain—in church, in choirs, in pubs on Saturday nights, in sing-songs at parties. In the old music-hall, amongst the acrobats and jugglers and serio-comics and light comedians and male impersonators, there were performers billed as 'chorus singers', and, when they shouted at us 'Now all *together*', we obediently and willingly joined in the second chorus. At the Cup Final at Wembley, or at a rugby match at Cardiff Arms Park, thousands sing excitingly and sometimes movingly before the game begins, and millions of the rest of us, watching and listening at home, envy them for their luck in being there and having the fun and the pleasures of singing. Some of our people, and particularly the Welsh, sing so passionately that it has become a way of life.

Certainly it was an essential part of the social graces of the

Elizabethan gentleman. Thomas Morley in his *Plaine and Easie Introduction to Practicall Musicke* explained in 1597 how he had began to study music:

> Supper being ended and Musicke books (according to the custome) being brought to the table, the mistress of the house presented me with a part, earnestly requesting me to sing; but when, after many excuses, I protested unfainedly that I would not, everyone began to wonder. Yes, some whispered to others, demanding how I was brought up . . .

That famous advertisement for a piano method began 'Everyone Laughed When I Sat Down To Play'. Four hundred years ago, Everyone Laughed When Morley Would Not Sing, and the scorn of his friends worked on him.

> . . . upon shame of my ignorance, I goe now to seeke out mine old friend, Master Gnorimus, to make myself a scholler.

And Morley was so apt a scholler that he was equipped not only to sing other men's madrigals, but to write a good many himself.

This is where one of the threads of the British choral tradition had its beginning, in the singing of madrigals for the entertainment of the family and its friends. Not in every home—you would not have heard the farmers, the blacksmiths, and the ploughmen having a go at 'Now is the month of Maying', 'The Silver Swan', or 'Thule, the Period of Cosmography'. The pleasures of madrigals were reserved for the great houses of England and their noble families, or at least the educated classes. Morley—'Musicke books (according to the custome) being brought to the table'—seems to suggest that the normal practice was to remain at the dining-table, and to sing there, a glass of wine or a flagon of ale at hand to ease the throat and wet the whistle. Sir Steuart Wilson disputed this. He once assured me that he personally invented the legend that the Elizabethans sat for their madrigals. For some years he sang with the English singers, and Steuart, who was always generous to young singers,

was good enough to pass on to me a valuable discovery he had
made about polyphonic music. A programme of two-and-a-half
hours of madrigals is very hard on the feet, he said, and he therefore set about inventing this ancient tradition so that he and his
colleagues could sit comfortably at their work. Sitting or standing, madrigals were sung at first only for the pleasure of the
singers. There were two interlocking interests, the poems that
poured out in that most lyrical period of English poetry, and the
pattern-making of the polyphony.

A hundred and fifty years later, there appeared another kind
of music with which people could entertain themselves. The
glee reached and kept its peak of popularity between 1750 and
1830. It was not polyphonic. There was not a separate melody
for each part. One voice had the tune, and the others accom-
panied it, generally in block chords. Glees could be comic,
dramatic, sentimental, declamatory—sometimes, all of these one
after the other. Properly, they were sung by male voices only—
this kept the convivial after-dinner smoking-concert atmosphere
—and, again like the madrigal sung in the home, with only one
voice to each part. This meant that the glee was still the hobby
of educated men. In 1761, the Noblemen's and Gentlemen's
Catch Club was founded, to sing, and to eat suppers. There was
a third purpose, that of a benevolent friendly society, with rules
designed to ensure that members must at some time break them,
and so incur fines to contribute to the financial well-being of the
Club. On coming into a legacy, a member had to pay the Club
either a flat rate of ten pounds, or a percentage of his windfall.
Marriage carried a fine of twenty pounds. During the singing, a
bottle of sherry was provided for every three members, a bottle
of madeira for every seven, and no coffee or tea was allowed on
the table. If anyone sang out of tune, he was required to drink
another glass of wine—though, if this was regarded as a punish-
ment, it is a sad commentary on the quality of the Club's
wine-list.

The Gentlemen's Glee Club of Manchester was sternly ab-
stemious during singing hours:

Singing to commence at half-past seven: supper to be on the table at ten: the chair to be vacated, and the room quitted, at twelve: no refreshments of any kind to be brought into the Club room before supper.

The Bristol Royal Orpheus Glee Club was equally austere.

An interval of thirty minutes is allowed for social intercourse, over a cup of tea, and then practice is resumed.

It was probably a wise precaution. Some of the glees could be complicated, and a clear head was essential.

Ordinary people were excluded from these diversions—they could not learn the notes. They could not even sing in choirs. Then, in the middle of the eighteenth century, the Methodists started their work. There had always been a religious background to English singing. William Byrd had written in 1588:

There is not any Musicke of Instruments whatsoever, comparable to that which is made of the voyces of Men, where the voyces are good, and the same well sorted and ordered. The better the voyce is, the meeter it is to honour and serve God therewith: and the voyce of man is chiefly to be imployed to that ende.

But, before the man in the street and his wife could honour and serve God with their voyces, they had first of all to be taught how to learn the notes. There was a succession of books on how to sing and how to sing 'from book'. One was Arnold's *Complete Psalmodist*, which first appeared in 1750 and went into many editions. It gave instruction on the singing of the psalms, and practical hints on music theory. There was, for instance, this poem which helped the man in the street to find his way through the dizzy maze of key signatures:

> Whene'er no flat your B does grace,
> Then Mi stands in its line or space.
> But when a flat is found on B,
> That flat is Fa and E is Mi.

If both be flat, your B and E,
Then in A standeth your Mi.
But, if your B, E and A be flat,
Then D is Mi—be sure of that.
If B, E, D, and A all flatted be,
Your Mi is on the letter G.
But, if a flat is in B, E, A, D *and* G,
Then in C you'll find your Mi.
But if a flat is in these six,
Then in E your Mi is fixed.
But if in all seven the flats do come,
They've brought your Mi carefully home.

It is oddly touching that ordinary, simple, working folk should learn this awkward doggerel to signpost a route for them round the complete key-cycle. Arnold added other instructions designed to produce a sort of congregational coloratura:

The first and most principle Grace necessary to be learned is the Trill or Shake; that is, to move or shake your voice distinctly on one syllable the distance of a whole tone.

There was also the 'Grace of Transition':

That is, to slur or break the Note, to sweeten the Roughness of a Leap.

In other words, you filled up an interval by putting in the intervening notes in an organised slur. Though they did not realise it, Arnold's readers were being taught how to perform a *portamento*. If they carried out their instructions to the letter, services must have been very remarkable. Trilling is difficult enough for a soloist. To have an entire congregation moving or shaking their voices the distance of a whole note, or sweetening the Roughness of a Leap with a slurred 'Grace of Transition'— the mind shrinks from what the imagination suggests the sound of the psalms must have been like.

The Methodists were simpler and plainer. In 1765 they published *Select Hymns with Tunes Annexed, Designed Chiefly for the use of the people called Methodists,* and it contained rules for singing the hymns:

> Sing them exactly as they are printed here, without altering them or mending them at all: and, if you have learned to sing them otherwise, unlearn it as soon as you can.
>
> Sing lustily and with a good courage. Beware of singing as though you were half-dead or half-asleep; but lift up your voice with strength.
>
> Sing modestly. Do not baul, so as to be heard above or distinct from the rest of the congregation, that you may not destroy the harmony.
>
> Sing in tune. Whatever time is sung, be sure to keep with it. Do not run before, nor stay behind it, but attend close to the leading singers, and stay therewith as exactly as you can. And take care you sing not too slow.

These were rules laid down for a particular sect, but they define the qualities of all good choral singing. The Methodists were so successful that they began to alarm the Established Church. In 1760 the Archbishop of Canterbury wrote to parish priests:

> Something must be done to put our Psalmody on a better footing: the Methodists gain a multitude of followers by their better singing.

In 1762 a parish clerk, in the preface to a book on parochial music, complained that the parishes' admiration of Methodist singing was so great that their tunes were creeping into the Church, and, what was more, alleged that Anglican congregations

> would pay the Clerk and the Organist to stay away, that two of their people may supply their places; by which means they have every Thing performed in their own way.

In 1805, *A Letter to a Country Gentleman on the Subject of Methodism,*

written by a Suffolk parson, roundly condemned hymn-singing
in the home:

> It is injurious to the domestic economy of the poor. The
> labourer of this class returns from his day's work nearly
> exhausted with it; but, instead of taking the rest so much
> wanted, in the chimney corner, he immediately takes his wife
> and children from the wheel and other useful employments in
> the house; which is not infrequently kept up at the expense of
> fire and candle to an unseasonable hour. I have often heard
> this singing in some of the poorest cottages at so late an hour
> as nine, and sometimes later, of a winter's evening.

The success of the Methodists came from their clear-headed and
practical approach to the problems of getting people to sing
well together. In 1795 the Methodist Conference issued an
instruction that no man was to sing in unison with the women
who had the tune. He must either sing the bass part as har-
monised, or keep quiet. (If you have ever suffered from listening
to the man in the pew behind you trying vainly to find the top
Ds and the E flats with the trebles, and then groping wildly for
the lower octave, you will applaud the wisdom of this ruling.)
There is an interesting comparison here with an edict of the
Council of Laodicea in the year 384, which forbade congregations
to sing at all in the mass, as they disturbed and spoiled the good
singing of the choirs. The Methodists, too, wanted good music
in church, but theirs must come from the congregation, not
from trained, sophisticated choirs. Their Conference looked with
suspicion even upon organs, and in 1808 announced that it
would not approve the provision of new instruments. Much
better, they thought, for the people to learn to sing boldly on
their own, instead of following sheepishly in the wake of the
organist. One organ was surreptitiously introduced into a chapel
in Liverpool—though how the builders could be 'surreptitious'
with anything the size of an organ is not at all clear—and
when this deception was discovered, the Conference ruthlessly
ordered it to be torn out.

Methodist ministers were equally tough with orchestras in church. The famous preacher Bradburn, who once preached for no less than three hours, became impatient with the length of an anthem 'The horse and his rider', scored for trumpets, horns, violins, hautboys, bassoons, bass viols, double bass, and voices. Bradburn stopped it dead with a ringing cry of 'Put that horse into his stable—we've had enough of him for today.' There was excuse for his impatience, for some of that generation of church musicians must have been a bit trying, the Larks of Rossendale, for instance, which is a valley about twenty miles north-west of Manchester. The Larks were artisans who made their own instruments, taught themselves to play them, and wrote their own hymn tunes, to which they gave vivid names like 'Sparkling Roger' and ominous names, too, like 'Grim Death'. Sooner or later, the minister of the church that they were honouring with their presence would grow impatient with the elaboration of the music they played, and, protesting that they were not worshipping God, but using His service as an opportunity to indulge their love for music-making, he would attempt to impose restrictions on them. When this happened, as it did not infrequently, the Larks would leave that church in a body, move to another further up the valley, and dig themselves in there.

Educational work in music, first started by the Methodists, had spread outside the Church, and sight-reading classes were held all over the country, using a textbook called *Singing for the Million*. They were commonly called 'penny singing classes' and, if you had no penny, because of a temporary financial embarrassment or a domestic crisis, you could 'look over' for that week. This educational work amongst the masses, like home sessions of hymn-singing, was not universally approved. There were some who held that teaching young girls to play the pianoforte had led them into a dangerously frivolous way of life, and seriously asked the question whether Christians should encourage classes in singing held in the evening, and so tempt young people to go out at night?

In spite of this moral uncertainty, the sight-reading movement grew, and a surprising number of the great Northern
choirs were born in the 'penny classes'. The Sheffield Amateur
Musical Society was founded in 1864, and, as late as 1909, it was
still referred to by its older members as 'the class'. Its rules made
provision for some occasions of relaxation—within limits:

> On every third practice evening, solos or concerted music
> may be performed by members, due notice having been given
> to the Committee, but it must be distinctly understood that
> these shall be sacred music, the appointment of which is to
> be entirely under the control of the Committee.

At Bungay, in Suffolk, the singing class in 1849 numbered nearly
eighty. The subscription was the usual penny a week, but this
paid not only for the hire of their practice room, with gas and
a fire, but, once a quarter, for what was described as an
'abundant' tea. To one of these feasts, held in that year,
there came nearly 200 visitors. A local paper reported the
occasion:

> Most of them were working-people, servants, apprentices,
> etc., but with a considerable proportion from the classes
> above them, tradespeople, farmers, clergymen and dissenting
> ministers. An excellent and well-supplied tea was served at
> half past five by attendants who made it their business to see
> that none was overlooked and that order was everywhere
> observed. This concluded, the business of the evening com-
> menced.

(The necessity for preserving order may seem surprising, and
perhaps I should add that one Sunday afternoon in the B.B.C.
canteen in Birmingham, I saw a large table set for a knife-and-
fork tea, with a TV producer hovering anxiously over it to see
that all was prepared. 'What's going on?' I asked him. He told
me that he was doing a live religious discussion, and that a
number of parsons were taking part, and he was giving them a
meal to liven them up for the programme. 'Surely a glass or two

of gin would do the job quicker?' I asked. 'You don't know these parsons,' he said. 'A couple of cups of hot, sweet tea, and they come out of their corner fighting mad.')

The 'business of the evening' was a monumental programme of music, three overtures by a dozen instrumentalists, anthems, motets, choruses from favourite oratorios, the odd madrigal, and a lot more food.

Between the pieces, fruit, cake and wine were handed round with the same order that was observed during the tea, and the company then assumed the appearance of a fashionable soirée.

There was great editorial relief that this unconventional and potentially dangerous mixing of classes had passed off successfully and peacefully without any permanent damage to the structure of society.

Not once on this occasion had the semblance of a violation of decorum cast a shadow upon the pleasure of the evening. Nor had one occurred after the close, when the same persons resumed their social relations, as masters and servants, and employers and employed.

There are pleasant and amusing phrases to be found in the histories of our choirs. In 1846 the Oldham Choral Society recorded with smug satisfaction that, in the fourth year of its existence, the Society had shown itself a great improvement on some of the neighbouring music clubs, where up to two-thirds of club funds were spent on liquor instead of music. The Nottingham Sacred Harmonic Society, founded in 1845, included the whole libretto of the oratorios which it performed in its programmes, and made them much more dramatic for the audience by including stage directions.

'Till darkness melts in light.' (*He lies down.*)
'Bless the Lord . . . O . . . my soul . . . bless . . .' (*He falls asleep.*)

'And the Ark—the Ark—the Ark of God, the Ark of God . . .
is taken!' (*Eli falls backwards.*)

The classes have long disappeared, and with them some of the
choirs to which they had given birth, but there are still in existence distinguished choral societies that grew out of the same
humble origins. One of the world's greatest choirs, the Huddersfield Choral Society, began in 1836 as a club. There were
monthly practices, and the original purpose of the club was to
organise enjoyable practices—there was no thought of performances. Club evenings were arranged for nights when there was
a full moon for the convenience of members who had to walk a
distance from their homes, and, I suspect, for the opportunity of
the pleasures of the flesh which was offered to the basses and the
tenors, as they walked the sopranos and the contraltos home.
The men paid a subscription of 2*s*. 6*d*. a year, which included
three gills of ale and a hunk of bread and cheese at each practice. Sopranos and contraltos paid no subscription, but were still
entitled, not only to their singing, but to ale and bread and
cheese. Other rules provided for the government of the Society.

Members in rotation have the privilege of selecting the
Oratorio to be performed at the next meeting, provided that
a majority of the members think that copies can be procured.
Any member is allowed to give his opinion after the performance of any piece of music, provided that he does so in a
respectable, friendly, and becoming manner.

A dangerous provision, I would have thought. There were
other, and surprising rules. No member of a Hall of Science, no
Socialist, could join, and the Librarian, under pain of expulsion,
was forbidden knowingly to lend any music to a Socialist.

In these rather unpromising surroundings, in schoolrooms
and church halls the British choral tradition grew. As they
became more expert in their music, and in singing for their own
pleasure, they began to get ambitious, and gave performances
in public that packed the Town Halls and the churches. And

the chapels, too. They are at the heart of the history of British music. The princes of Europe built opera houses. By the unfortunate accident of history there has been since the beginning of the seventeenth century only one royal family in Britain—and there has been only one Royal Opera House. That in the eighteenth and nineteenth centuries was often in the hands of Italian impresarios, and staffed by Italian singers.

The princes of England, the merchant princes who made their money in the squalor of the Industrial Revolution, they built too—not opera houses, but chapels. The valleys of the industrial North and of Wales are full of these gaunt, bare, utilitarian and often unattractive buildings. In most villages, and in many small towns they were the only possible halls in which cultural activities could be staged. The Methodists, who had taught the people to sing hymns, and to read music, taught them as well to sing oratorio, and the choirs explored the repertory of sacred works. So, as the nineteenth century moved into the twentieth, while continental singers were based on their opera houses, English singers spent their working lives travelling hard from Town Hall and Mechanics' Institute to chapel and church, for these were the halls in which they earned their living, as hired soloists with amateur choirs.

I was once engaged for the annual 'Sing'—it was actually called that—of a village church choir in the North. There were three services in the day, which had a minimal interruption by prayer from the Vicar, and an enormous programme of anthems from the choir, organ solos, and a big group of oratorio solos from me at each service. Three concerts in the day—I was on my knees by the end. But the audience—I beg their pardon— the congregation were tireless, and their appetite for singing was insatiable. In the valleys they have great interest in singers and singing, in techniques and traditions, and, like Italian audiences at the opera, they are by no means reluctant to indulge their expertise and criticise singers. Once, in Wales, I was singing in the annual *Messiah*. At the interval we retired to the artists' room, and there I sat quietly drinking a cup of tea and minding my own business. A member of the committee came up to me, and asked me to sign his programme. His little girl, he assured me, would so much treasure my autograph. I got out my pen and began to write, and, as I did so, he bent over me and, in a confidential bellow that rang round the crowded room, he told me that he had heard me broadcast in *Grand Hotel* on the previous Sunday. 'Tut, tut, tut,' he added, 'Shocking it was!' But he was generous enough to allow some improvement in my performance—'Now I've heard you in the flesh, I'm satisfied!' It was consolation for me that at least he found my flesh satisfactory.

In Sheffield in 1939 the principal trumpet of the Northern Philharmonic Orchestra came up to me in the interval, a big man nearly as tall as I am, much heavier than I—and then I weighed eighteen stone—with a flowering walrus moustache. He told me, without preliminaries, that he had played t' *Messiah* more often than any other man living. I asked how many times he had done it. 'Bloody 'oondreds!' he said. 'I played troompet obbligato in "Troompet shall sound" for Santley.' This shook me. Sir Charles Santley, the finest baritone of his time, was born in 1834, and became a legend in British singing. Meeting someone who had played for him was like meeting someone who knew Moses. 'I was lad of thirteen,' he said. 'Fifty-one year ago. I'm in my fifty-second season.' I said mildly that if ever he had to give up playing the trumpet and went along to the Garden and showed his belly to Beecham, he'd find himself on the stage singing *Meistersinger*. 'I do a bit of singing already,' he said. 'I sang "Troompet shall sound" at smoking concert last Wednesday. *And* in between phrases I played troompet obbligato!' A mental picture of this enormous man singing a phrase, and then belting out the high notes on his trumpet, and then singing again—this was too much for me, but I managed to say tactfully that it must have been very difficult. 'Nay, there's nowt to it,' he said. 'Troompet part's difficult, but there's nowt in t' noomber' —and with a patronising flip of his hand he swept aside the long line of British basses from Santley to Owen Brannigan.

There is a story of the Larks of Rossendale which demonstrates the same pride and independence, and their musicianship, too. When the first printed copies of the *Messiah* were on their way to Rossendale, the Larks marched to meet the wagon that was bringing them. They turned, formed up around it, and escorted it in triumph into their valley, singing choruses of the *Messiah—by heart*. Their spirit lives today. The physical size of Northern choirs, and their delight and pride in their magnificent, virile tone, have led to a fierce competiveness in performances that has helped to make them some of the best choirs in the world. At the annual *Messiah* in a Yorkshire town, the orchestra were sorting themselves out on the platform when the doors opened, and in marched the choir to their places, serious and formidable, hundreds of them. It was obviously going to be a loud and strenuous evening, and the principal double bass nudged his mate. 'Hand me t' rosin, Fred,' he said grimly. 'I'll show 'em who's King of Glory.'

In Europe, they worked in opera houses. In England, we worked in town halls and chapels, and, in between seasons at Glyndebourne, it was with choirs like these I sang for the four years before the war.

Travelling, rehearsing, and singing on the same day—it was hard work, but exhilarating, to sing with choirs that took the *Messiah* with the same hard physical qualities that they brought to their cricket and to Rugby League football. And, like other English singers, I went on week after week until the war began, and all contracts were cancelled on the spot.

FIVE

War and the Garden

I RESENTED THE war. I didn't want to waste time fighting. I
wanted to sing. Every day it lasted was a day lost, and it cut
four years and Lord knows how many performances out of my
life, at a time when my voice would have been at its best.
Month after month I brooded about what I was missing, the
fun and the excitement. When the Queen's Hall was bombed, I
took it as a personal affront. One of my engagements which was
cancelled in September 1939 would have taken me for the first
time to sing on that famous platform. Now the Germans had
destroyed it, before I had had a chance to sing there. I wallowed
in self-pity for the part of my singing life that was slipping away.
And life in the army was no compensation at all for what I was
losing.

I had a Territorial commission for a couple of years before the
war, and I left for training with my A.A. unit the day after the
season at Glyndebourne had ended. The *Daily Express* celebra-
ted the occasion with a headline—OPERA STAR MISSES LONDON
DÉBUT—and a slick paragraph:

One of the artists was missing when the Glyndebourne Opera
Company came to London to sing at a reception at the May-
fair Hotel last night. Members had been looking forward to
introducing David Franklin, former schoolmaster and their

latest 'discovery'. But, instead of singing operatic arias, David was in camp. He is now a militiaman.

I wrote coldly to the editor and pointed out that he was wrong on two counts. It would not have been my first appearance in London, and I was by no means an impressed militiaman. I thought the great British public should be told the true facts on these two important matters, and I remained his truly. To my astonishment, he didn't seem to mind. At any rate, I can put the record straight now.

We went straight from that training period into the war. About the third week in August, starting, I thought rather unfairly, ten days before the Germans, we left our headquarters in South London, and I led a convoy of lorries through the Blackwall Tunnel late at night en route to the lump of the East coast that it was our task to defend. Our progress was somewhat delayed by meeting head-on in the narrow tunnel a convoy of vehicles of another exactly similar anti-aircraft unit, this one based in North London, and moving fast to its allotted positions in Kent. The dottiness of this arrangement was the first sample of the confusion and the bewilderment in which we all lived for the first weeks of the war. I had been working for a producer and a conductor of genius, who planned every detail with exquisite accuracy. The army wasn't nearly as efficient as Glyndebourne; and I found it extremely frustrating. That frustration, the anxiety of being at war (was I going to get killed?), my neurotic obsession with the singing that I was missing, the strain of irregular hours and of standing to at night in case of raids, the quality of army food and of improvised living conditions, all combined to land me, almost in a matter of weeks, in hospital, where I was brought to bed of a fine duodenal ulcer, the first of a series that I was to collect during the war. I was dieted, dosed, X-rayed, discharged from hospital, boarded, down-graded to Category 'C', and transferred from my unit to a desk job, and by the beginning of 1940 found myself a staff captain at the headquarters of Scottish Command.

Believe it or not, for nine months there I was responsible for a fleet of ships, which carried troops and sailors and airmen from the mainland of Scotland to the garrisons in the Orkneys, the Shetlands, the Western Islands and the Faroes—and back again. Soon after I took command of my desk, we acquired a new Major-General in charge of Administration, and the great man made a tour of his staff so that they might be presented to him. He came into my office one morning, ushered in by my Colonel, who said, 'This, sir, is Franklin, who runs your shipping for you.' 'I see,' said the Major-General, keenly. There was a pause while he fixed me with a penetrating soldierly eye. 'And what were you in civvy street, Franklin? Something in one of the big shippin' lines, eh?' 'Sir,' I said, simply, 'I am a professional singer.' 'Good God! What an extraordinary thing!' said the Major-General.

I moved from that desk to another, where I abandoned my ships, and instead shifted whole divisions about by road, with such success, it seemed, that I was promoted to Major, and the appointment of Deputy Assistant Quartermaster General—it sounded imposing, but was in fact a long way down the hierarchy—in Northern Ireland. I trundled British and American convoys round those narrow roads for nine months. On one very wild afternoon, I flew in an open Lysander to watch from the air the results of my planning on the ground, and was, I regret to report, sick all over the American 34th Division. Then I was transferred to South Eastern Army—our headquarters were on Reigate Hill—and worked at the planning of a minute section of the logistics for the invasion of Normandy. I was unhappy and impatient, working under great tension, and for three years I had had very little singing.

While I was in Scotland, I had broadcast several times, in programmes for the Forces by the Forces, and pretty awful they were. One week, I sang 'The Song of the Volga Boatmen', as a tribute to our great Russian allies. The following week, as a companion tribute to our great American allies, I offered, as the compère said, 'a rendition' of 'Ol' Man River'. In the third

week, as a tribute to Londoners in the middle of a blitz, I sang
'Old Father Thames'. One of my friends in the office cuttingly
suggested as my contribution to a possible fourth programme
'River, stay 'way from my door'. In Northern Ireland, the
Entertainments Officer involved me in a ghastly programme
called 'Tommy Entertains', or something like it—and personally I would have queried the choice of the word 'entertains'.
As we had in Northern Ireland the first American formation to
arrive in Europe, this was planned as a big hands-across-the-sea
lark, brothers in arms, and all that. We contributed a British
army band, and Major David Franklin, while the Americans
provided their divisional dance band (what a way to go to war!),
a military band and a crooner. One of the regular spots in the
series was a special song, specially written by a special soldier-
composer. Unfortunately, he had been delayed by his military
duties, and his manuscript had arrived in Belfast only twenty-
four hours before transmission. The Americans rightly, as it
turned out, mistrusted the musicianship of the crooner, and had
had relays of pianists working all night on him to teach him the
words and the music. They had had alas no success, for, when
he was asked to run through the number with the band in rehearsal before the broadcast, he stood in embarrassed but complete silence.

We then had a splendid scene, which I tremendously enjoyed.
The producer strode backwards and forwards over the stage—
we were doing the broadcast from a theatre—with a gaggle of
assistants twittering in his wake. 'We'll have to cut the number,
Gordie.' 'For God's sake, we can't cut the number—we need
the three minutes.' 'How about doing the number without the
vocal, Gordie?' 'It's a jingle-jangle. You must have the vocal.
What's a jingle-jangle without the vocal?' 'What indeed?' I
said to myself, and walked on to the stage, and asked them,
'What key's this thing in?' 'What the hell's it got to do with
you?' asked the distraught Gordie. 'If it's in my range,' I said
with quiet dignity, 'I'll sing for you.' 'You will? Great, David,
marvellous, wizard. We've just got time for a run-through,' he

said. 'You'll want the music.' I agreed that the music would be a help. 'Quick someone—get the music for David,' Gordie shouted, and a studio manager snatched the manuscript from the hands of the crooner, who had, it is true, little enough use for it, and brought it to me at a run. There were two sheets, one of which had words without music, and the other, music without words—and then just a bare vocal line, without any suggestion of the orchestral part, or even instrumental cues. They crowded round me, anxiously watching me as I glanced through the voice part. 'Right,' I said briskly, 'No trouble at all. I can sing this lot.' They slapped me on the back, said I was a real pro, thanked me for Saving the Show, and shouted, 'Studio quiet, please, for the run-through' at each other. I asked the master-sergeant leading the dance band if he would be good enough to indicate the approximate point at which he would like me to join in proceedings, and he said, 'Sure thing, Major.' 'Thank you,' I said, politely. 'You're welcome, Major,' he replied with equal courtesy, and off we went. He cued me in with a gesture that was an ingenious and tactful combination of downbeat and military salute, and, glancing rapidly from the words in my left hand to the music in my right, I sang my very first jingle-jangle. I can remember now only the opening couplet:

> He used to row her over the ferry,
> But he won't need to row her any more . . .

Time has mercifully eroded the rest of this work from my mind. The run-through was apparently successful. The producer came out of the cubicle making ecstatic signs of approval, and five minutes later, to the humiliated envy of the crooner, I was on the air rowing her over the ferry, making my début as a dance-band crooner, and, incidentally, an anonymous début, for I had asked that my secret should be kept. Twenty minutes into the programme Major David Franklin, of Glyndebourne Opera and H.Q., British Troops in Northern Ireland, was to make his contribution to allied understanding by singing 'In diesen heil'-gen Hallen' from Mozart's *Die Zauberflöte*, and I thought that

IIIa. Act 3, *Der Rosenkavalier*, at Covent Garden, 1947, with the chorus jeering at D.F. as the disgraced Baron Ochs.

IIIb. *Ariadne*, Glyndebourne, 1952. Fourth from the left, Murray Dickie, seventh, Mattiwilda Dobbs, eighth, Richard Lewis, ninth, Sena Jurinac, eleventh, D.F. and, fourteenth, Sesto Bruscantini.

IVb. Dignified old priest—D.F. as Sarastro (in *Die Zauberflöte*).

IVa. Disreputable old rake—D.F. as Baron Ochs von Lerchenau.

understanding might well be endangered if it became public knowledge that I had usurped the place of the regular crooner with the U.S. 34th Divisional Dance Band.

This was a tantalisingly small ration of singing for three years and more, and my impatience with the war, my longing to get back to work, and the pressures of the office, sent me off to hospital with another ulcer. I was hustled through what the army said was a cure, and sent back to the office, where I lasted for no more than a few weeks. An ambulance took me back to hospital with a third ulcer, and another medical board pronounced me finally unfit for service. I became a civilian again, free to start singing once more. But not immediately. I had the sense to realise that I must get myself fit again for the hard physical life of a singer, and got a job as the school bursar of St. Albans School. (Incidentally, out of the army, my duodenal symptoms gradually improved, and finally disappeared. At their worst, if I were offered a gin-and-something before a meal, I had to ring for an ambulance before I drank it. But working harder as a singer than ever I did in the army, I could eat—and drink —things that would have been poison during the war. This, I think, proves something or other of interest in the field of medicine.) I taught a few periods a week, too, to the fifth and sixth forms. I asked the Headmaster what I was supposed to teach them. 'Doesn't matter,' he said. 'Educate 'em.' I stayed eighteen pleasant months, and, when I was fit enough, went to London for lessons with Jani, and felt my voice clicking back into place. The old excitement, ambition, the pleasures of singing grew strongly again. I had friends on the Arts Council who were very helpful to the soldier returning from the desk, and offered me a number of concerts.

To their astonishment, I turned them down. Didn't I want the work? I needed it badly—I had a flourishing overdraft. But I could not then spare time for singing concerts, and earning fees. I had more important work to do when I left St. Albans. I had to spread the news around that Franklin was back in circulation. I had nearly five years' leeway to make up. I wanted to arrive with a bang, and I spent months organising the bang. I wrote beguiling letters to societies for whom I had sung before the war, and even more seductively to those for whom I had not. I wrote to every conductor I knew, and to a fair number of those I did not know. I asked the B.B.C. for an audition.

B.B.C. Music Bookings were reluctant. It was not necessary for me to audition, they assured me, for they knew my work well, and my reputation. They couldn't know my work, I said, because they hadn't heard me for five years, and a fat lot of good was my reputation, if I wasn't getting any broadcasts. I kept nagging, and in the end was included in the auditions for the next Prom season, to be held in the Albert Hall. This was not my first appearance in that vast arena, though that, as one of 2,000 London school-children in a Victory Concert in 1919, adding my pipe to our shrill performance of 'Land of Hope and Glory', was not an entirely adequate preparation for the ordeal twenty-seven years later of singing in Albert's Great and empty Hall. It would not have been a comfort to know that the night before his début there, Chaliapin was missing from his hotel and was eventually found on the platform, staring incredulously at the wide open spaces of the auditorium. It would have added to my own terror. So would the story of another great singer, which fortunately I did not then know, who, as soon as he saw the size of the Hall, quickly decided that he was ill, and cancelled his recital which he was due to sing next day. It was no good indulging my fear—I needed this audition, and I told myself sternly to go on and sing as loud as I could. I went on and sang as loud as I could, and was offered my first Prom. And with that Prom came a steady flow—not quite a stream, but certainly more than a trickle—of broadcasts.

My first appearance in opera after the war was in the Theater des Westens in Berlin. It was in 1945, soon after the end of the war with Germany. ENSA arranged a tour for British troops by Sadler's Wells. It was all done in a hurry, and some of the principals had already accepted concerts in England during the period of the tour. The air would be full of Sadler's Wells singers flying to England by R.A.F. Transport planes, and back again to Germany, and, while they were on the move, the Wells would be short of several principals. So ENSA engaged me to fill some of the gaps as a guest in the company for the middle three weeks of the nine-week tour. It was a strange experience. Being processed for Germany was very funny indeed. ENSA had offices in Drury Lane Theatre, and there I was inoculated against all sorts of diseases, and fitted up with passes that would take me into the British Military Zone, through the Russian Zone, and into Berlin. It took hours. There were several companies in the pipeline the day I went to Drury Lane. The *Having Fun!* company, en route to Madagascar, and the *Off The Ration* company, bound for Iceland, took the whole thing calmly. It was old stuff—they'd been doing it for years. One rather elderly soubrette, a blonde in *Having Fun!*, did make a scene when it came to her turn for a typhus injection, and protested that she had been done for typhus before. 'And what I say is this', she argued emphatically, 'if it was good enough for Malta, it's good enough for Madagascar.' I thought she had a point. When at last it came to my turn at the head of the queue for travel documents, the bored girl clerk didn't even raise her head. 'Name?' she asked. 'David Franklin.' 'Company?' 'Sadler's Wells.' 'Opera or ballet?' she asked. 'My good woman,' I said, from my six feet seven inches and eighteen stone, 'do I *look* like a ballet boy?'

My three weeks 'stint was depressing. The singing was fine. The theatre in Detmold, and the tiny baroque gem of an opera house in Bad Oeynhausen, were untouched by the war. But the theatre in Berlin had part of the roof taken off by a shell, and, covered by tarpaulins, was still wet and cold. The city was at its worst. There was the stench of destruction everywhere. The underground had hundreds of bodies still swirling about in flood water, and it was sealed off, for fear of epidemics. There were tanks and planes lying burned out in the Tiergarten, and graves along roadside verges, with Russian and German steel helmets hanging askew on rough wooden crosses. The wardrobe in my bedroom still had a spray of machine-gun bullet-holes in a graceful curve across the door. It was better not to look at Berlin, but to take refuge in the familiarity of the routine of rehearsal and performance. I remembered seeing, in the middle of the 1938 season at Glyndebourne, newspaper bills announcing 'NEW CZECH CRISIS', and feeling that Hitler and his conquests were strangely unreal. The reality of life was in the fantasies that we created in the theatre—nothing else mattered. And, years later, it was easier to believe once again that it was only the theatre that mattered. Berlin, outside the theatre, was an unreal dream.

But the war could still intrude upon us, and it was fun to watch Sadler's Wells at war. At lunch, one day, served to the company canteen-fashion, the manager banged on the top table for silence, stood up, and addressed us very soberly. 'I have had a communication from the General Officer Commanding British Troops in Berlin,' he began, 'and I have to insist that you obey the orders that he has given. There are parties of Russian troops—ten or twelve at a time—touring the city in lorries. They are kidnapping women on their own, and taking them off into their own part of the city.' Complete silence. 'No women members of the company may go out at any time on their own. By day, there must be at least two women together, and by night, no woman may go out unless she is escorted by at least one male member of the company, or one male member of the British Forces.' Eyes widened—this was war. (I did, I confess, wonder how much a Sadler's Wells tenor, or indeed baritone, could do to protect the honour of a soprano, or indeed, a contralto. But this was an unworthy thought, and I tried to put it aside.) The manager sat down, and the company were uneasy at the thought of the dangers around them. Then one of the mezzos let out her eldritch laugh. 'Russians, did you say, darling? In lorries? Ten or twelve of them? I see. And they take you off to their sector? Well, I must say'—and she did say—'the only thing to do would be to sit back and enjoy it!'

Safely back in England, I went on a tour of music clubs in

Lancashire, and had a phone call one morning from Rosemary Hall, who worked in the Arts Council in Manchester, a good friend and a helpful one, to say that she had fixed an audition for me with Barbirolli. I found an accompanist, hastily rehearsed, presented myself, and sang. It went pretty well, for I sang next season in every Hallé Choir concert. I think this was the first time that any singer had achieved this. This was an important occasion for me, for it not only brought me the extraordinary experience of working for Barbirolli, who brought great tension and excitement to everything he did, it not only lifted me one step nearer the top of my professional tree, but the Hallé shop window showed me off to a good many other choral societies in the North. I was getting myself well established.

There followed another important development. I auditioned in 1946 for the new company that was being formed to work at Covent Garden. I was told at once that they would want me, and was dizzy with excitement. But I was still called twice more for auditions, each time being told again that I was in. At last, a contract came. I signed it happily, and began a very busy period of my life, and an absorbing one. I was to work my way for the next few years steadily through the bass repertory—Rocco, Sarastro, Bartolo, Pimen, King Mark, Hunding, Fafner, Pogner, Sparafucile, Ochs. I went on singing a lot, too, outside the Garden. Like every other singer, I had to. We had contracts that were as permanent as anything can be in the theatre, for forty, sometimes forty-odd, weeks in the year. Whether your contract was renewed at the end of the season depended not only upon your standards of performance, but upon the goodwill of the management. If a German singer falls out with the upstairs office, there are scores of other theatres where he can look for work. But leave the Garden, for whatever reason, and there was only one other permanent and resident company to go to—the Wells. There was, true, one other company in London at that time, the New London Opera Company at the Cambridge Theatre. They began by playing *Bohème* every night for six months—it must be a unique arrangement in operatic history—

while they learned and rehearsed other operas. They worked up a repertory of five or six operas, with imported Italians, a British ensemble and a British chorus, and an orchestra of London players. They began to feel that they were permanent—there was even wild talk that they were going to buy the Garden, turn us out, and work there themselves. Then suddenly after two years, and after members of the company had taken leases of flats, and were buying cars and refrigerators on H.P., a notice went up at the Stage Door that the run would finish in two weeks' time. The boss was broke, and his singers were out of work.

This was a grim reminder—not that I needed it—that in the midst of life we are in death. It made me more determined than ever to keep at least part of my concert work going, as an insurance. In spite of the endless difficulties of fitting outside work into the schedule of performances at the Garden, the strain of overnight journeys, and warnings from singers like Widdop, it still had to be done. I begged, nagged, craftily persuaded, to get my N.A.s. The N.A. is a feature of English operatic life. It is a date on which you are officially accepted as Not Available for rehearsal or performance, and so are free to sing outside the theatre. The trouble was that the major choral societies made their arrangements for concerts and contracted their singers sometimes eighteen months ahead—I once was engaged over two years in advance—and, in the early days of the new company, the management did not always know what it would be doing three months ahead. So you had to be persuasive to get your N.A., and, once you'd got it, you had to be strong-minded enough to stick to it, even though the management changed its mind and decided that it wanted to use you that night after all. It could work the other way. You could be refused your N.A. because you were cast to sing on the night you wanted to be off, and you would have to refuse a good and showy concert or a broadcast—and when the throwaways came out, you could find that the office had swopped their schedule round, that you weren't singing, and you would

have to watch the man who got the job after you had said
'Sorry, I can't' make the success that you could have had
yourself. Maddening.

Opera, broadcasts, oratorio, concerts—I sang and sang. I
enjoyed every sort of singing. The theatre smelt of history, and
I was excited to think that I was working on the stage where
every great singer of the past had sung, that I was wearing
costumes that they had worn—some of them, in *Meistersinger*
for instance, had been used for thirty years—that I was using
their dressing-rooms. Great dancers, too. If I had a ten o'clock
rehearsal, and got in a few minutes early, I went across the
stage to leave my coat in my dressing-room. (The stage was the
safer route for me. There was a staircase on the prompt side,
but it had a very low ceiling, and I got tired of banging my
head against it.) Every morning, Massine was finishing a private
workout on the empty stage, using a flat for exercises on the
bar, sweat pouring off him. As Johnny, my dresser, explained,
'Fifty-two he is, and a grandfarver, and still 'opping around
wiv the best of 'em.' Massine said that the first day he didn't
have his hour of exercises would be the day that he would have
to give up dancing. Back in 1947 and 1948 he never missed.
We shared the theatre with the Ballet, and our first production,
The Fairy Queen, was a joint effort by the two companies. It is
an odd mish-mash, of Shakespeare's story of *Midsummer Night's
Dream*, the dialogue arranged by other hands, snippets of
music—my first part was 'Sleep', in a masque, and I was on
and off the stage in forty-five seconds flat—and ballet. It was
useful in getting the company working together, and for building a stage staff, and keeping the theatre open at night while,
by day, we were learning other operas as fast as we could.

It was inevitable that, apart from *The Fairy Queen*, we should
have little to do with the ballet. We were not at all the same
type. Johnny told me one evening: 'You ought to of been 'ere
this morning, guv. Ballet dress re'earsal. Laugh? You'd 'ave
bloody died. There's two geezers that share your room 'ere.
One 'ad this new fevvered 'at, and 'e asked the uvver wot 'e

fort of it. 'E said it was marvellous—made 'im look just like a woman!' Johnny did his grotesque imitation of a refined accent. ' "Reely? Oh, my dear, you couldn't of said anyfink that would of pleased me more!" ' And he went on, 'Straight up, boss, that's just wot 'e said.' As I said, we were not at all the same type. There was a small section of the Ballet, seconded so to speak to us for ballet sequences in opera productions—*Aïda* Act II, *Carmen* Acts II and IV, Act I of *Rigoletto*, and the Apprentices' Dances in *Meistersinger*. But they never liked dancing in opera, and thought it was *infra dig* to have to take second place to the singers. John Cranko said to *The Observer* in an interview in 1968, about his Ballet at Stuttgart:

> We're still slaves to the opera. Opera producers keep our dancers sitting on stage waiting to do hoppity-skip. So the kids often miss dancing in a ballet. . . . The last nut to crack is to free the ballet from the opera.

But I found it fascinating to watch the athleticism and the absorbed fanaticism of the dancers at close quarters—and sometimes comic. In the tavern scene in Act II of *Carmen*, after the dancers had done hoppity-skip, a nice little girl from the ballet had to fling herself into my lap, arms round my neck, while I passionately buried my hot lips in her neck (that particular piece of hoppity-skip was very inflammatory). I aimed my burning kiss at the down-stage side of her, and one night, as I bit her, she said primly into my up-stage ear, 'Good evening, Mr Franklin.'

'Good evening, Poppy,' I said, into her ear.

'Mummy asked me to give you a message,' she said. 'She heard you last night at the Albert Hall.'

(I'd had an N.A. to sing *Gerontius* for Barbirolli.)

'Mummy said," Poppy went on, 'that she thought you sang most beautifully, and she was very moved.'

'Please thank your mother,' I said, coming up for air, and then diving back again into her neck, 'and tell her that I am delighted she liked the performance.'

Of all the situations in which I could imagine being congratulated on my performance of 'Proficiscere, anima Christiana', I thought this the most improbable.

But then a lot of highly improbable things happened in those first years of the new Covent Garden Company. It was a big operation to start from scratch. Many of the singers had never been on a stage. One, cast in a seductive part, began every move with a thrust of her hips in the direction in which she had to go, and then, as it were, followed them across the stage. 'That woman moves,' said John Gardner, 'in a series of pelvic surges.' John was a répétiteur, a fine musician, and a pianist with ingenious if unconventional technique—but he had never worked in a theatre before. Only two of the répétiteurs had ever coached a singer. The rest had as much to learn as the singers. The producers were a job-lot, too. They varied from a Swiss who put on *Die Walküre* in traditional style, and then announced that any of us could sing our parts in any theatre in Europe—it was always the same—to a man who had produced plays in the West End, but knew little about opera, even the opera that he was producing. I had been brought up by Ebert, who had every group, every movement, every gesture, planned months before he met the cast, and planned against the music. It was strange to work now for a man who played it off the cuff, and pushed eighty-odd singers round the stage into various patterns to see what they looked like. At one point, Dennis Noble swaggered on to the rostrum at the back at his first entrance, and launched himself into his aria. 'Stop!' said the producer, and turned to the répétiteur. 'How many verses are there of this thing?'

Peter Brook was different. Whatever else could be said of him, he was different. Told what to do in the greatest detail by Ebert, I had, by doing what he told me, learned something of the craft of acting. Brook had his own method. Tom Williams said one day after a trying rehearsal, 'That so-and-so doesn't know what he wants—he only knows what he doesn't want.' In a sense, this was true. He had a very clear picture of what he wanted in the end, and this he could project to the audience. His production of *Figaro* made the story clearer, and the characters more real, than any other I had seen. But he could not direct you immediately to what he wanted, as Ebert did. Ebert has a magnificent speaking voice, and just speaking our singing roles, he could bring out the tone, the emphasis, the colour that he wanted from us. Brook hasn't voice enough to work this way. Ebert had been a very great actor. Brook is a terrible actor. He cannot move, or sit, or stand, or use gestures, or do anything that is part of the actor's technical stock-in-trade. Ebert told you exactly what to do with hands and feet—even what to do with an eyebrow. Brook had to rely on words, and sometimes the right words would not come. At the end of *The Olympians*, the gods had to disappear in the distance along a heavily perspectived road into the cyclorama. But we didn't disappear. Being not gods but only mortal, we remained the same size, and instead of getting smaller we seemed to get bigger, not only walking but overflowing the narrowing road. Peter called to us from the stalls 'Act *perspective*, dears!' Robert Helpmann protested—'Every muscle of my back is *rippling* with perspective,' he said.

In Brook's production of *Bohème* we had a lot of trouble with the horseplay in the first and last acts. There was a fair amount of experience knocking around on the stage. Rudolf Schock was from Hamburg, Silveri had done Marcello—and, oddly enough, Colline—all over Italy, I'd done Colline for the Wells, Grahame Clifford, the Bénoit, had been for years with D'Oyly Carte. The only Bohemian who had little experience was the young Geraint Evans, and Geraint caught on quickly. Brook encouraged us to experiment with the difficult sequences. 'No,' he'd say, 'that's not what I want.' So we went into a sort of rugger scrum, devising another mixture of what we could jointly suggest, from Hamburg and Italy, and the Wells, and the Savoy operas—and we'd call out to Brook in the stalls, 'Try this one.' And we'd play the scene again and again. And again. Finally, it was what he wanted, and then it was good. But finding out what he wanted was *very* hard work.

Brook is imaginative, in spite of the difficulty he had in communicating with the cast, and logical. He decided that my great height was an enormous advantage, and he must exploit it. So, when I played Pimen in *Boris Godonov*, he actually built it up. To give lifts to a man already six feet seven sounds dotty—but it worked magnificently. I had five inch platform boots. They were hellish to walk in. Until I got used to them I tottered on to the stage like a tart, and I was always in danger of turning my foot over and damaging an ankle. I had a domed wig, too, and boots and wig took my height up to over seven feet. In my first scene I sat in my monkish cell, patiently writing my history of all the Russias. As the curtain lifted, I stopped writing, raised my head, and sat quite still (it was Richard Burton who said 'Stillness is important') as I sang Pimen's solo scene. At the end, I got up and slowly walked off-stage. Brook had the table made especially low, and this made my seven feet look even more. After minutes of sitting still, this slow movement to towering height hit the house like a bomb.

The partnership between Brook, of great talent in the theatre and no experience in opera, and Karl Rankl, a very experienced routine conductor, was a strange one. In the dressing-rooms, we heard rumours of rows, and on the stage, though they tried to hide them, there were obvious signs of tension. Rankl had been through the standard apprenticeship, from répétiteur up, and had a wide knowledge of the repertory. But he never felt that he was secure—there had been a lot of criticism over the appointment of a foreign Director of Music of the first state-subsidised British opera company—and he had little idea how to handle people, or English people, and particularly English orchestra players. He was an Austrian, but had Prussian ideas of discipline. He publicly ticked me off for calling Brook 'Peter'— I must address him as 'Mr. Brook', Rankl said. He did not understand the casual Christian-names-at-first-meeting tradition of English opera companies, and never realised that calling him 'Peter' did not affect my respect for him as a producer or my discipline in obeying his direction. For Rankl, the stage was as sacred as a cathedral. One morning one of the Welshmen in the company strolled on from the Stage Door, in hat and coat. Rankl ran after him, swore at him, and snatched his hat off. The Welshman was furious—I thought for a moment that he was going to clobber Rankl—and Rankl was furious, too. And neither of them understood why the other was so angry.

This lack of communication was typical of the man. He was always very tense in the pit. The obituary notice in *The Times*, after his death in 1968, described his conducting as 'hysterical'. It was, alas for our new young company, just the right word. On the first night of *Bohème* he was so worked up that he ran into the pit, on to his rostrum, and into his first beat while the audience were trying to applaud him, and while some of the players still had their instruments in their laps. At rehearsals, an endless stream of petulance poured out and, in the first few months, all of us—singers, orchestra, production staff, music staff—became heartily tired of his complaints. On 1 April 1947 he was offered an opportunity to forget the unease of his relationship with the orchestra, to make friends, and start again. Alas again, he rejected it. We were to rehearse Act III of *Rosenkavalier* with the orchestra, and promptly at ten, Rankl climbed on the box, said a curt 'Good morning, gentlemen' and announced that he would begin with the Pantomime, and that he would beat two. He raised his hands, looked round expectantly, and plunged into his downbeat. With completely dead-pan faces, the orchestra played the prelude to *Carmen*. Rankl was astonished, and his beat faltered to a stop—and, with immaculate discipline, the orchestra faltered with him. Rankl snatched the music from Joe Shadwick's stand—Joe led the orchestra. 'But this is *Rosenkavalier* that you have,' said Rankl, 'why do you play *Carmen*—why?' Joe explained to him that on All Fools' Day we play jokes on our friends. If only Rankl had had the wit—or the humanity—to realise it, the

important word was 'friends'. The orchestra had offered him
the olive-branch. But Rankl told Shadwick not to be silly.
'Rehearse properly,' he said angrily, and they began the
Pantomime. Fifteen minutes later, when he had stopped them
to clear up some problem in the score, he turned to Shadwick
and said anxiously, 'When I come into the pit tonight to
conduct *Magic Flute* what will you play?' 'For God's sake,' said
Joe, 'we shall play the *Flute*, of course. This was just a joke.'
'A *joke*?' said Rankl—he couldn't believe it. I thought then
that, handling the orchestra as badly as that, he couldn't last.
He did stay another five years or so, but it was an uneasy reign.

But, while he was there, we worked hard. We were always
learning new operas, always rehearsing. Some of the performances we put up were not very good, and the critics often
said so, though not all of them seemed to realise, or at any rate
wrote that they realised, that the management was as new to
the business as the singers, and that they had to learn their
jobs—planning, casting, of conductors and producers as well
as singers—while we were learning ours. They also had to
learn how to avoid emergencies. Too often, in those early
years, we ran on doggedly into a crisis, and the office set about
handling it, when it was already too late. For more than two
years, I sang Zuniga, a small part, in every performance of
Carmen, without a cover. I asked the opera manager to get
someone to learn it. It was understandable, I said, that if a
Carmen or a José were ill, and no replacements were available,
another opera must be put on instead. But to have to cancel a
performance because Zuniga had a cold would be too silly.
But nothing was done. One morning, I woke up with a tempera-
ture of 102. I rang the theatre, not without a certain grim
pleasure, and said that I couldn't play Zuniga that night, and
put the phone down. There was an instant panic. The office
rang back, swore that a cover would start work on the part
next day, and begged me to Keep the Curtain Up. Weakly,
I suppose, I agreed. I wrapped myself in a heavy coat, was
driven to the theatre, began to make-up, tentatively tried out

my voice, and found that everything above a G, all the way up to my top F, had disappeared. Peter Gellhorn, who was conducting, agreed to give me a free hand, to re-write Zuniga as I went along, to squeeze what he had to sing into what was left of my voice. The opera manager came to my room, chatted me up for my hardihood in saving the show, and turned to go. I called him back, and asked him about the form of the announcement to be made in front of the tabs. (Normally, it is better not to tell the audience that you are ill. They'll spend the evening telling each other what a shocking show you are giving. If they aren't told, they'll most likely not notice a thing. But this was a special occasion—there was so little left of my voice that they were bound to notice.)

'I'm not going to have any of that nonsense about asking for the audience's indulgence. Indulgence be damned!' I said. 'The management ought to go down on their knees and thank me for having the guts to appear like this. I'm not going on unless the audience are told that I'm singing against my doctor's orders.'

'Well, old man,' he said, 'there won't be any announcement tonight, as a matter of fact. The tenor's ill too, and it's been decided that we cannot announce to the audience that two of the cast are singing against doctors' advice.'

'Why not?' I asked.

'Well, it would make us look as if we are in difficulties,' he said.

'And aren't you?' I asked. 'Pass me my hat and coat from the peg.' I began to wipe off my make-up.

'Where are you going?' he asked.

'Home,' I replied.

I got my announcement.

Looking back on those early years now, it seems as if they were filled with one crisis after another. I had a heavy cold one night, when we were to play *Rosenkavalier*, and said I could not sing. The management put on something else, and the audience queued at the box office for their money back, and they had to hand over £300. Six months later, when we were again doing *Rosenkavalier*, I had another cold. The management weren't too keen on handing back another £300, and, as there was no cover for Ochs, they persuaded me to go on. Somehow I got through it, but next morning I couldn't even speak, and I didn't sing for the next month. 'Saving the Show, is an over-rated form of courage.

There were other kinds of crisis. One morning in 1948 I was going up to the staff canteen in the amphitheatre. The recognised route was through the flies, and I looked casually down on to the stage, and there, sixty feet below, was a meeting of the stage staff, gathered round a man on a box.

'Morning, Charley,' I said to the fly foreman. 'What's going on?'

'Union meeting, Mr. F.'

'*Union* meeting?' I said.

'You know we're going back into the Wagnerian line of business, Mr. F.?' he asked. 'That meeting is about rocks. Rocks is props, you know.'

I did know. Just in case you are not familiar with the philosophical basis behind this principle, I should explain that sets—a castle, an Egyptian temple, the town of Nürnberg—are the responsibility of stage carpenters. Lighting—stage lights, lamps on the set, flaming torches carried in procession—are always handled by the electricians. Props—chairs and beds, swords and daggers, marriage contracts, fans, little grassy knolls—are handled by property-men. So are rocks. But not Wagnerian rocks. As Charley said, 'Act II of *Walküre* is nothing but rocks. And not little hand-rocks that you can pick up and walk about with easy. They're bloody great rocks about fourteen feet cubed.' And props had made their stand on the firm line of demarcation that rocks is props, but not Wagnerian rocks. 'That's a union arbitrator,' said Charley, pointing to the man on the box. 'Arbitrating, that's what 'e's doing.' I afterwards heard the solution that was arranged. The refusal of both sides, stage carpenters and props, to handle Wagnerian rocks was accepted. On nights when we did *The Ring* a special casual-labour Wagnerian rock staff was recruited.

It would be wrong to give the impression that emergencies were only to be found at the Garden. They are the breath of life in every opera house. There was the Strange Case of the Missing Scenery in Dresden in 1845. It was the first performance of *Tannhaüser*, and 150 tons of scenery had been ordered from Paris for the occasion. I did a bit of research into the logistics of the operation. Not all the journey could be done by rail, and a hundred miles or so had to be covered by horse-drawn wagons. The scenery was not available for the dress rehearsal, nor for the first performance, and the stage director was told to do the best he could. So, when the procession marched in Act II into the Halls of Song, they found themselves, to their astonishment, marching into Act II of Weber's *Oberon*. There were emergencies even at the most meticulous of houses, Glyndebourne. We were a day off the public dress rehearsal of *Die Zauberflöte*, and running a private dress rehearsal. The lift came up with the Queen of the Night, who sang her first act aria. When it went down again, Bing was there with her return ticket home. It came up again with another Queen. We didn't see her again, either. In Act II, in the afternoon, a third Queen appeared—and she went down on the lift, and home. A fourth Queen appeared, in a tweed costume. There wasn't time to find out who she was, even. At the first night, a fifth Queen sang the part.

At the Garden, too, singers quietly disappeared, though, as time went on and the management knew more about what to look for, they made a number of triumphant decisions. I was lucky enough to be on hand when one such triumph was revealed. It was at the North Western Polytechnic in Kentish Town, an unlikely site for a revelation, God knows. In the second and third years of the company, after a good deal of criticism of some of the singers, guests began to arrive from abroad to crown our performances with a Mimi, a Musetta, a Boris, or a Violetta. (This sort of infiltration is not possible

va. End of a career. Conversation piece at Covent Garden, during a rehearsal of *The Olympians* in 1950. Kenneth Schon, talking to J. B. Priestley, and Moira Fraser. Behind them, Peter Brook talking to Robert Helpmann. Extreme right, not talking to anyone, D.F.

vb. *The Olympians*, Act 1—the Gods. Left to right, Kenneth Schon (Jupiter), Margharita Grandi (Diana), D.F. (Mars), Robert Helpmann (Mercury), Thorstein Hannessen (Bacchus), and Moira Fraser (Venus).

vɪa. A new career. D.F. checking a script before a broadcast of *Weekly Echo*.

vɪb. And another. Working off the cuff, without a script, Frank Muir, looking curious, and D.F., looking emphatic, in *My Music*.

except in opera. West End actors may have to contend with Americans or Australians, but they never have to work with a Danish Hamlet, a Norwegian Nora, or even an Argentinian Charley's Aunt.) We were always rehearsing *Bohème* with visiting singers. They got a day's stage work—if they were lucky. Not on the stage, which was always too busy. Hence rehearsal rooms in places like the North Western Polytechnic. A call with the orchestra was much too expensive. A day on the stage, in which we walked through the moves with them, one piano rehearsal with the conductor, and they were ready for their Covent Garden début.

We thought these rehearsals were boring. We knew the production backwards, and disliked having to make a framework for a foreigner who was going to steal the limelight which we would very much have liked for ourselves. We were called one day to rehearse with a new Mimi. She was Spanish, we heard, and had done a good audition. We met her, good-looking we thought, a little plump perhaps—though not for a soprano— quiet and retiring. For the first two acts, as singers say, we 'marked' it, we sang in half-voice, dropping down an octave from the top notes, or singing them in falsetto. This was just routine—no point in pushing the voice. We had no idea what she was like—she was 'marking' too. We broke for coffee, or for what passes for coffee in Kentish Town, and they began the Act III quartet. Geraint Evans, who was singing Schaunard, and I sat and read the paper. Rudolf was Rudi Schock, Musetta was Ljuba Welitsch, and Marcello was Paolo Silveri. With the new girl, they were cruising gently along, workmen doing a chore. Suddenly, something happened. The new soprano let out her full voice. It was like cream, smooth and exciting, remarkable in quality and size, effortless in production, with easy, balanced flexibility, and a long range crowned by thrilling top notes. Geraint and I dropped our papers, and sat gaping at this phenomenon. Schock, Welitsch and Silveri were astonished, and, I thought, a little alarmed. This girl was someone to reckon with. Schock took off his coat, Silveri loosened his collar, Welitsch cleared her throat, and all four of them cut loose in one of the most exciting performances of the quartet—even with a battered old upright piano—that I have ever heard. The new girl's name, by the way, was Victoria de los Angeles, and one of the things which I most enjoyed in my singing days was being in the cast of her English début.

We had a good many Americans, several as residents, most as guests for a short series of performances. They were part of the first wave of singers from the U.S.A. who moved into Europe after the war. Nowadays, pick where you like, there are Americans in the cast. Some of ours were excellent. The best Gilda I ever heard was a negress, from the South, who found a career at home difficult, and worked both at Glyndebourne and at the Garden. She had a fine voice, and had been beautifully schooled, and managed both the tessitura and the coloratura of Gilda with exquisite poise. But she had something more. Most coloraturas are mature, experienced women who somehow, in the skill with which they perform Gilda's music, give it a sophistication which contradicts the basic assumption that she is an innocent in the flush of first love. The experts give the impression that she is a girl who has knocked about a bit. This coloured girl added to her technical expertise and the beauty of her singing the unsureness that came from the position of her race in America, and this, though it was fortuitous, gave an air of shyness that made her performance quite irresistible.

But the sense of character that others showed was not always so complete. I played Ochs with an American Marschallin. I made an entrance and a leg in the first act, bent over my lady's hand, and kissed it, and, as I did so, caught the unmistakable fragrance of chewing-gum. (Dear God, Maria Thérèsa chewing gum!) At the end of the act, as we walked off together, I asked her if I was right. 'Yeah,' she said, 'keeps my throat from getting dry.' Fascinated by the obvious physical problems, 'What do you do with it,' I asked, 'when you are actually singing?' 'I park it,' she said. 'I got a hollow tooth.'

I think one of the reasons why we had a fair number of Americans working with us was that in those days we sang operas in English, and there was a common, if mistaken, belief that Americans sing in English. (There were difficulties of communication off-stage, too. We asked an American baritone to dine with us and, when I was helping him on with his coat before I drove him to the Tube, I tactfully asked him if he would care to spend a penny. 'On what?' he asked, bewildered.) Certain sounds seem to suggest that they sing in un-English—the 'a' in words like *wrapped*, or *flat*, or *hang*, for instance. There was an American Sophie who sang in ecstasy night after night, 'O rupture!' I mentioned this to Jess Walters, an American baritone, who sang several seasons with us. He hotly denied it. I told him that he did it himself in *Olympians*, at the end of Act I, when as Zeus come back to earth, he had to give a terrible warning to the mortals. He drew himself up to full height, lifted godlike hands, and sang, 'Beware the lightning flush!'—as if, I said, he were pointing out the dangers lurking in a new and speedy system of plumbing. 'I do not,' he said, offended and incredulous. 'Want to bet?' I asked him. At the next performance, true enough, 'Beware the lightning flush!' he sang—and immediately turned to me and in an astonished and perfectly audible voice said, 'By God, I do!'

There were other racial peculiarities in the pronunciation of English. I waited expectantly every night in *Meistersinger* for an Austrian Sachs to sing encouragingly to Walther as he walked to the singing rostrum, 'Zir Walther of Stolzing, zink the zonk. Ye masters, zee if 'e goes wronk.' And what a Balkan soprano can do to Aïda or Musetta has to be heard at close quarters to be believed. This was one of the reasons why the policy changed, and why now performances at the Garden are usually in a language which the audience do not understand. I think it is a pity that the difficulties that continental singers find in getting tongues and lips round English words, and their reluctance to re-learn roles in another language, should have resulted in English audiences being cut off from an understanding of the piece they have paid to hear. Busch and Ebert drilled me at Glyndebourne in German, and later I found my first performance of Mark in German not impossible. In fact, Rankl said enthusiastically that I sounded just like a German bass in the part. I thanked him, and took the opportunity to add that it was no more difficult for a German to work in English than it was for me to sing in German—but he didn't see the point.

And the point is that singing is an act of communication which depends on words, and cannot even begin to work unless the singers are using a language which they share with the audience. It is true that some translations are bad, and some foreigners find English impossible. But the solution is to get better translations and singers who *can* sing English. It is not the right solution to switch to a language of which the audience understands nothing. It never has been. Joseph Addison wrote in March 1711, in *The Spectator*:

It happened also very frequently, where the Sense was rightly translated, that there was a necessary Transposition of Words, which were drawn out of the Phrase of one Tongue that was very natural in the other. I remember an Italian Verse that ran thus Word for Word,

And turned my Rage into Pity;

which the English for Rhime sake translated,

And into Pity turned my Rage.

By this means the soft Notes that were adapted to 'Pity' in the Italian, fell upon the Word 'Rage' in the English, and the angry Sounds that were turned to 'Rage' in the Original, were made to express 'Pity' in the Translation. It oftentimes happened likewise, that the finest Notes in the Air fell upon the most insignificant Words in the Sentence. I have known the Word 'And' pursued through the whole Gamut, have been entertained with many a melodious 'The', and have heard the most beautiful Graces, Quavers, and Divisions bestowed upon 'Then', 'For' and 'From'; to the eternal Honour of our English Particles.

And Addison went on to explain the solution of these difficulties that the management adopted:

> The next step to our Refinement was the introducing of Italian Actors into our Opera; who sung their Parts in their own Language at the same time that our Countrymen performed theirs in our native Tongue. The King or Hero of the Play generally spoke in Italian, and his Slaves answered him in English; the Lover frequently made his Court, and gained the Heart of his Princess, in a Language which she did not understand. One would have thought it very difficult to have carried on Dialogues after this manner, without an Interpreter between the Persons that convers'd together; but this was the State of the English Stage for about three Years.
>
> At length the Audience grew tired of understanding Half the Opera, and therefore to ease themselves intirely of the Fatigue of Thinking, have so ordered it at present that the whole Opera is performed in an unknown Tongue.

And later in the same paper:

> I cannot forbear thinking how naturally an Historian who writes two or three hundred Years Hence, and does not know the Taste of his wise Forefathers, will make the following Reflection, 'In the Beginning of the Eighteenth Century the Italian Tongue was so well understood in England that Operas were acted on the publick Stage in that Language'.

He was right. Two hundred and fifty years after he wrote that paper, Operas are acted on the publick Stage at the Garden (at Glyndebourne, too) in that Language—and in German, French, and Russian. The resident English have had to relearn their roles, and the whole Opera is performed in an unknown Tongue.

Though in my day we were groping towards an acceptable standard of performance, at least we groped in English, and the audience could grope with us. We had one other advantage over the British singers who have followed us into the Garden. Foreigners, allowed to sing in their own languages, fly in, rattle off stock performances that they have been giving for years in theatres all over the world, and fly out to rattle them off somewhere else. There are a handful of British singers who have had the talent and the luck to join this international jet set, but they are not part of the resident British company who once again have been left to do the bits and pieces—roles known in the trade as 'a cough and a spit'—that they have always had to do at the Garden. They are back where they were in the days between the wars, when Beecham ran a short summer season, the leads were sung by continentals, and the British had only the crumbs that fell from their lips. (Robert Easton once told me that the only rehearsal he had in *Das Rheingold* was to be told to keep one pace to the left and one behind the Fafner, a German bass, and so followed him all over the stage like a half-back shadowing a centre-forward. How could the British establish themselves as principals under such handicaps? How could they even learn the beginnings of their trade?) There is, I suppose, one difference. Beecham's seasons lasted six, seven, maybe eight weeks. Contracts at the Garden are now for the year—but it is even more frustrating to do coughs and spits for forty-two weeks in the year than it was for a couple of months, and to spend a working life as a sort of living back-projection to frame the stars. We were luckier—and this was the advantage we had over the present generation of British singers. We sang the big principal parts. We had the excitement, and the fun—and we also learned how difficult leading parts could be.

SIX

Baron Ochs von Lerchenau

OCHS WAS the biggest part that I had tackled.

Before the war at Glyndebourne I had sung the Commendatore in *Don Giovanni*, Sarastro in *Die Zauberflöte*, Banco in
Macbeth, and one or two little bits and pieces. The Commendatore is not easy to sing, but the only problems are technical, of
voice production. If there is a top to your voice, and you have a
good D, and an E flat, and an E natural, if you can stand still,
and belt out the last scene without losing any of the edge from
your tone, you have all that is needed. The characterisation is
drawn in bold and economical outline—no subtleties, and only
one change of colour, in the first scene, when he is mortally
wounded. And then, in a heart-rending trio, which Mozart
dared to write for a baritone and two basses—almost a unique
combination, I think—the Commendatore dies after some
touching calls for help, as he feels life leaving him. But this,
too, is written simply, and the problem here as well is only
vocal, to sing fairly high in the voice, and still *piano*. In any
case, the trio is very short. By operatic standards, the Commendatore is an unconscionable time dying, and though as a
young man I found this trio a test for my infant technique, the
test did not last long.

The main demand of the part, for sustained resonance at
the top of the voice, can be made much more difficult, if the
producer is the sort who fancies himself as an innovator. Put

135

the Commendatore, as usual, in the middle of the stage, give him something solid to stand on, let him sing, and the music will make a tremendous impact. Ebert did more than put me in the middle of the stage—he had me high on a rostrum, which lifted me clear of Don Giovanni and Leporello, and clear of the orchestra, too, so that I was directly in line with most of the audience sitting in the raked auditorium, my voice could attack them directly, and I had a chance to dominate the scene. But in 1967 I saw a production at Glyndebourne in which the statue, come to life, did not stalk into the Don's palace. Instead, the palace went to the statue. There was some sleight-of-hand with the set, which was made up of square towers, painted differently on each side so that, by being twitched round, a new scene could be suggested in a matter of seconds. The producer could not resist the temptation to play with his set in the last scene. We heard the menacing stone footsteps of the Commendatore, coming to supper as he had promised, but at the exciting and terrible moment of his entry there was a blackout, the towers were twitched round, the lights came up again, and, dammit, we weren't even in the palace. The dining-table, the wine, Don Giovanni and Leporello were still there, but they were now surrounded by the cemetery, and slap in front of the statue. This air-lift made nonsense of the story and of the music, for the terror and pity in the scene come from the statue's coming to life, and moving stonily into his murderer's palace. This one had not even come alive. He was still there, motionless on his plinth. And, instead of singing freely on the open stage, the unfortunate Commendatore had to sing behind the set standing on a step-ladder. Rintzler, who sang the part, has a glorious voice, with a rich, dark tone and remarkable resonance. But in this scene he had no chance to dominate, as he should have done. Muffled in the eccentric position in which the producer had placed him, he could scarcely be heard.

In Edinburgh, when Glyndebourne took *Don Giovanni* to the Festival in 1949, I ran into the same sort of difficulty, luckily of much less importance, and because of the wayward fancy, not of the producer, but of the conductor. He was Rafael Kubelik, and he insisted that in the cemetery scene it is impossible for the statue, standing on his plinth, to get a good ensemble with the three trombones who accompany his two sentences (and he has only two in the whole scene) unless they are all four physically together. I tried to argue that a singer is used to singing on the stage with the orchestra in the pit, that they don't have to climb up and stand close around him for each aria. I said that three trombones were no different from any other part of the orchestra, and that the cemetery scene is no different from any other scene in any other opera. I said—and possibly this was a tactical mistake—that I had done thirty-odd performances at Glyndebourne for Busch, with me on the stage and the trombones down in the pit, and we had no trouble getting together. But Kubelik would not listen.

He was the boss. A stand-in from the chorus was dressed in an exact copy of my statue-costume and make-up, and stood on my plinth. One morning, when we had finished a three-hour orchestral rehearsal, they kept me and the trombones in the theatre, and we tried to find the right place to sing my two ghostly sentences. I did point out that it would be odd for the statue to be seen on the stage, and for his voice to come from somewhere else, but I was over-ruled. So I was sent with my three trombones first to the O.P. side, and stood in the wings, and sang. 'Not good,' they said from the house. Kubelik and Ebert and Strasser were listening from half-way back in the stalls, to judge the unearthly acoustic that they were looking for. 'Now try the prompt side,' they ordered. We did. 'No good,' they said again. In quick succession, with one of the music staff who conducted us, I and my ambulant trombones tried behind the cyclorama ('Hopeless'), in front of the cyclorama ('Also hopeless'), up in the paint-frame ('Franklin, why don't you sing?' 'I *have* been singing!' 'We can't hear you. Sing louder.' 'I can't. If I do, I'll rupture myself.' 'Then it's no good—come back to the stage'), in the orchestra pit ('Too open'), in the passage leading from the pit to the band-room with the door half-closed ('Too closed'), with the door open ('No. The acoustic is dead').

By now it was half-past one, and I wanted my lunch. I climbed out into the pit, popped my head over the rail, and, as they sat talking about what could be done in this crisis, I said heavily that the only place we hadn't tried was the gents' lavatory in the passage. I thought I was being funny, that it would bring them to their senses and make them realise that the whole thing was too damn silly, and call it off, so that I could go and eat. But to my astonishment they took me seriously. 'That is a very interesting suggestion,' they said—and there was another flurry of whispers. 'Try singing, with you in the corridor, and the trombones in the lavatory with the door open,' they commanded. We did. That was better, we heard, but now they wanted to try the effect of *all of us* in the loo. This was a great success—apparently, the white tiles gave the exact other-world sound they wanted, and so this was the final disposition of our forces. Every night that we played *Don Giovanni*, I performed professionally in a lavatory, for the first and so far the only time in my life. The conductor of me and my group, one of the répétiteurs, exercising his first independent command in the Glyndebourne company, was John Pritchard. Incidentally, and this gave me great pleasure, in the middle of my first sentence in the scene—'Di rider finirai pria dell' aurora'—one night when the performance was being broadcast, the automatic flushing system flushed all over the Third Programme. With typical Glyndebourne attention to detail, a note was made in the stage manager's prompt-book that in future the tap in the loo must be turned off every night at the end of the interval before Act II.

Providing you are not mucked about by the conductor or the producer, and are allowed to stand on the open stage, and just sing, the Commendatore has few problems. Banco, too, was uncomplicated. It was athletic singing, and this was fun. He has some gorgeous tunes, and a splendid aria before his

death scene. The characterisation is all on one level, a dark
and sustained melancholy that is not difficult to design and
project. Of the parts that I had sung before I began to study
Ochs, Sarastro was the most important, and the most difficult,
though, compared with the Baron, Sarastro was simple.
The part is not big, and easy to learn. The two arias—'O Isis
und Osiris' and 'In diesen heil'gen Hallen'—are very familiar,
for every bass has sung them over and over again in concerts.
(I once read, in a programme of a concert in a Lancashire
town, that I was due to sing 'Oh! Isis and Oh! Siris', a title
which gave, I thought, a subtly plaintive touch to the serenity
of the priest.) I already knew the arias, and I had only the few
pages of the Act I Finale, the Act II trio, a couple of sentences
of recitative, and the spoken dialogue, to learn.

It was quickly done. The melodic lines are firm, and clear.
There are no problems in the structure—Mozart's harmonic
schemes are economic and familiar—and the orchestral texture
is simple. There are, especially for a young bass, and I was a
baby of 29 when I first sang the part, some difficulties of
technique. The top D in the very first entry was for me not
at all easy. The second syllable of 'Erheitre' is awkward, and
awkwardly placed on a D, just at the break in a bass's voice.

He can sing open up to a C, and possibly a C sharp, too, providing it is on a comfortable vowel, and in the middle of a legato phrase where he can keep his support flowing steadily. An E flat, and an E, and an F—if he has one—a bass *must* sing covered. But the D is a no-man's-land. Singing it open is dangerous, and it may come out 'white'. Covering it, he may well pull the vowel back, so that the tone is darkened, and the vowel distorted. In this phrase, for instance, the 'ei' of 'Erheitre' is difficult to place comfortably in the head. Open, it sounds insecure, unsupported. Covered, it will lose brilliance, and may be darkened into an 'aw'. 'Er—haw—tre dich.' Not a nice sound.

But the rest of the passage flows easily in the voice and, musically, it is clear, simple and easy to understand and to memorise. Sarastro even has strings playing his line in unison with him. This makes it easier for him to learn his music, but it also makes it essential that he should sing *legato*, for otherwise, if he makes separate attacks for each note, the strings will expose him, and underline his lack of control. Singing with the smoothness of a string-player's line is not easy for a bass, but it is a valuable exercise in technique.

The characterisation of Sarastro is straightforward. What changes of mood there are to be found are, again, simple, and almost stylised. Sometimes, he is the stern High Priest.

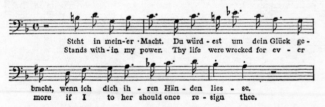

Sometimes, the gentle father-figure.

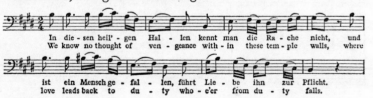

He has only one ensemble—the trio in Act II. Sometimes, his authority must dominate. Elsewhere, he must be able to modify his tone, so that he can accompany the other voices when they lead.

With these few changes of mood, of presentation, of colour, and with a good tone, a flexible line, and the ability to sustain dignity in delivery and in his stage presence, Sarastro should not be a difficult role for any competent bass.

Baron Ochs of Lerchenau is quite another matter. It was not only the biggest part I had tackled—it is incomparably difficult. It stretches the singer to the limit of his capacities— voice, intellect, physical stamina and musicianship. And perhaps it is in musicianship that he is most cruelly tested. The vocal line is extraordinarily demanding. The intervals are awkward, unfamiliar. The orchestral part, even when you see it in a simplified piano reduction, can look quite terrifying. The rhythms are subtle, shifting, complicated. The counter-

point is fast-moving and elusive. Beginning to learn the part, trying to fit your awkward intervals into a complex orchestral structure—at first it's a nightmare. You have to understand the harmonies, to see where the counterpoint is leading, before you can weave your own line into the whole texture.

The range is enormous. Ochs has a low C at the end of Act I, and stretches up more than two-and-a-half octaves to a top G sharp. Sarastro's range by comparison is short. He has several top Ds, and touches on E flat twice, but, though the part is well known as one of the great *basso profundo* roles, it goes no lower than a low F. (One of the women's magazines, gossiping about the social scene at Glyndebourne in 1937, unwisely strayed into the field of music criticism, and girlishly cooed, 'Our own David Franklin, as Sarastro, has a wonderful, organ-like low D.' I showed this notice to Busch, who said firmly, 'If Sarastro sings a low D, you vill hear about it first *from me!*') Ochs plunges a whole fourth lower than the *basso profundo* Sarastro, and must climb up, too, above the stave into un-known baritone country. For, besides the G sharp, there are two F sharps, and sixteen top Fs scattered through the part. Banco has one top E, a deliberate parade of physical power at the climax of his aria. Ochs is constantly singing Es, not as climaxes, but as part of the normal conversational lie of the voice. There are so many top Fs that coming down to an E, which in other major roles is a mountain peak of effort, seems oddly enough like a relaxation.

It is not only the extremes of the range that Ochs must have that hold a problem. The *tessitura*—the general level of the part—is phenomenally high. Look at this passage, written for a bass!

It looks like baritone music—but then no baritone could attempt the low Es, the Ds, and the one low C.

Very few singers have the two-and-a-half octaves plus that Strauss wrote for Ochs. The range is inhuman. So every singer edits the notes to suit his own capability. It is accepted practice. If he had a voice a shade lighter than a full *basso profundo*, if he is a step nearer to a bass-baritone, he will dodge the low C and content himself with the octave above. Another man will find the depths of the part comfortable, but will shave off some of the top notes. I was one of those that found the C fun to sing, but I didn't like the look of the top G sharp, and I didn't think much of the F sharps, either, and I used the lower alternatives that Strauss thoughtfully provided in this passage:

But, where he had not been thoughtful enough for my taste, with Rankl's agreement and often at his suggestion, I sang my own private alternatives.

I did sing the Fs. I enjoyed them. There is a great sensual pleasure in singing Baron Ochs. But it is a pleasure in which one must not over-indulge. The truth is that the part is over-written, not only in the calls it makes upon the singer for short periods of intense physical effort in particular bars, or for pages at a time, but in the stamina he needs to sustain the whole part. Sarastro has seventeen pages of music to sing, most of it serene and gentle, and all of it carefully placed well inside the limits of the voice. There is room to spare at each end. Ochs has 203 exhausting pages, that keep him for the most part at full stretch, with nothing left in reserve. When I first began work on the part, Rankl told me that I must learn to 'pace' myself, like a long-distance runner, through those 203 pages, and find the places where, because the writing was in the middle of the voice, or because the orchestra was for a while more lightly scored, I could take it easy, relax, rest the muscles of my support, get my breath back, and get ready for the next burst of energy. Ochs is the bass's Grand National, and he has to work out how to keep up a steady gallop all the way round, and still have enough strength in reserve for scores of giant fences that Strauss has built into the part.

I once heard Percy Heming talking to Edie Coates at the Garden about this same question of 'pacing' your way through a long part, when she was preparing Carmen. 'The audience know the opera by heart,' said Percy, 'and they'll be waiting for the big moments when you can let fly. If you can't let fly, thumbs down for Edie. You must save yourself, to make sure of the climaxes. The audience will be a bit unsettled, a bit anxious, if they hear you holding yourself back, saving yourself. But they'll be content to wait, once they know you've got it. So you *must* show them what you've got as soon as you get on. You've got a nice showy, legato phrase, as soon as you come on to that rostrum at the back, at your first entry. Take it out and let 'em have a good look at it straight away.' ('What do you think this is?' asked Edie. 'The Windmill?') 'Then, when they've seen it,' said Percy, 'you can tuck it away again, and go easy. You can patter your way for twenty or thirty pages, and they won't mind, because they know that, when the big stuff comes, *you've got it ready.*' This was the tactic that I had to learn for Ochs.

In operas written up to the middle of the nineteenth century, the pages of recitative which separate and lead up to the formal set-piece arias and ensembles make welcome rest-periods for singers. Against the light, skeletal accompaniment of harpsichord or piano, sometimes with an added cello, they can sing in a light, conversational tone that rests and refreshes the voice. In spite of one critic who mentioned 'reams of exhausting recitative', there are no recitatives in *Rosenkavalier*. The narrative sections that carry the story-line are set as vigorously as the set-pieces, with a tremendous, driving accompaniment from the orchestra.

That last top F has to be held for eight-and-a-half bars. It is the end of a passage in Act I, in which Ochs boasts of his sexual powers, of his obsession with women, and his considerable successes with women. There are fourteen-and-a-half pages of it, and, at Strauss's tempo, it can take over four minutes. It is like running a four-minute mile. *The Observer* wrote of it at our first performance that it is 'an appalling hurdle' but conceded that Mr. Franklin took it 'in a manner which on the whole did him credit'. It was reassuring to learn that at least parts of it did me credit. But this fiendish section is only about a fifth of Ochs' commitment in the first act, in which he has seventy pages' vigorous singing. And he still has two acts, and 133 pages, to go. Obviously, when you begin to learn the part, it must be trimmed, not only by shortening the range, by taking out some of the top or some of the bottom notes, but by cuts, sometimes pages at a time. That scabrous narration is always ruthlessly cut down. And cuts through the whole opera—and, come to that, in every opera in the repertory—are established and traditional. It is interesting to listen to a recording—better, to several different recordings—with a score, and discover what particular combination of cuts individual conductors use. This is not vandalism, but a necessary safety precaution. Singing Ochs uncut, with every bar and every note kept in, the strongest voice could be pulled to pieces, even before the singer reaches the stage for his first performance.

For learning the part is itself an exhausting process. There are two ways of doing it. If you can read what some people call 'the dots', you take them with a rehearsal pianist—a répétiteur —a page or a few pages at a time. If 'the dots' are a hidden mystery to you, the répétiteur must play you your part slowly and methodically, a couple of bars at a time (203 pages of it) over and over again, until you have memorised the sound and the rhythms and the words. But whether you can read, or whether you have to have the notes banged out for you, you must sing them, over and over and over again. It is a long and painful ordeal. It took me three months to learn the part. (Rankl told me that this was the fastest time he had heard of. One very famous Ochs took six months, and Rankl himself as a répétiteur spent a whole year on the job, working with another bass.) It was like keeping office hours in a torture chamber. Regularly, at ten each morning, I met my répétiteur at the Garden in one of the dressing-rooms which had an upright piano installed.

Most of the work I did with Reginald Goodall. Reggie won't mind my saying that, though he is a distinguished and under-rated, neglected conductor—he has never been given the opportunities that his great talent deserves—he is not the best pianist in the world. He is a wonderful teacher and, as répétiteur, taught me to find my way through the bewildering intricacies of the score of *Rosenkavalier*, and helped me to understand the style and the character of the music. I knew at the time, and told him so, how much I got from his knowledge and experience and patience, and twenty-one years later I am still grateful to him for what he taught me. But his piano-playing was never more than an ingenious approximation to the notes printed in the score.

There are difficulties in playing an opera on the piano. In the vocal score, at the beginning of Act III, there is this note by Carl Besl, who arranged the orchestral score for piano—'In an arrangement for two hands it was not possible to do more than indicate the main features of this Fugato which is in six and more parts.' This is a good working description of Reggie's pianistic technique. For two hours each morning, and another two hours after lunch, he resourcefully 'indicated the main features of the orchestral score', and I felt my way a little nearer each day to knowledge and understanding of the music. Four hours' singing a day, five days a week, with occasional performances in the evening—I was playing Zuniga in *Carmen*—and concerts and broadcasts, too, was quite enough singing for me, thank you.

When you are sight-reading new music, you use as little voice as you can, but every now and then you have to let yourself go. It becomes an irresistible urge. I can think of three reasons why this happens, even in the dullest routine rehearsal. Singing half-voice—perhaps for singers 'half-throttle' would be a more significant term—can get very tiring because, deliberately holding the tone back, instead of allowing the machine to pour out in full flood, the throat gets tense and hard. So, secondly, letting fly, in full voice, for a while, breathing fully, using all the support, getting the instrument to work efficiently, is actually, in spite of the extra effort, a refreshment for the voice. Thirdly, when you 'mark' the part, and sing the top notes *falsetto*, you misuse your technique. Singing out helps you to place the tone, work the voice into a technical pattern of performance. Singers always talk about 'singing a part into the voice'. It is like running in a new engine, and Ochs took a lot of running in. There is a fourth reason—singers are vain. They love to show their splendid voices to an audience, even an audience of one patient répétiteur, and after an hour of 'marking' they feel a need to compensate for clumsy stumblings through a new passage, and, on familiar ground, to 'take it out and let him have a good look at it'.

So, singing flat out all the time (and I have known singers who have done that, who could never bear to save their voices) or 'marking', or switching from one to the other, whichever way you do it, learning a long part is a physical marathon. Reggie and I went on and on. You do what you can to vary your tactics, to get variety into what is a monotonous task. Reading new sections is the most tiring work of all. So, every day, we would begin by pushing on and breaking the back of, say, ten new pages. Then, after an hour on them, we would switch back to a previous section where the notes and the rhythms were already accurate, and becoming so familiar that I was half-way to memorising them and I could sing in full voice for a while. We'd run through that several times, with me trying to sing without the score, and taking a quick look at it, if I found myself groping for an entry. And, to finish the session, we would go back to the new section with which we had started, and try to get it running a little more smoothly.

I learned to count my bars all through the opera. You always get important leads from the conductor, but I knew that I must be self-supporting. If there were an emergency in the orchestra, or the conductor forgot to fling me a lead, if he were busy with another singer, or with the chorus, I must be ready to find my own leads. I remember going home by bus (there were no cars to be bought in those first years after the war), and singing Ochs to myself in a whisper, feeling the words come to my lips and my tongue. At first, I had the score open on my lap, and I got along without it as far as I could, turning over the pages automatically without looking at them, as I thought my way through a scene. This was enormously helpful later in performances, because on the stage I actually *saw* the pages in front of me, floating over the heads of the audience, and I read my music from them, and saw each page turn as I came to its end.

For the first weeks I stumbled often, fumbling for notes and words. The words needed as much coaxing into place as the notes. We were using a new translation, written not by a singer, but by a writer, Alan Pryce-Jones. The *Daily Telegraph* was to give its opinion later, in its notice of the first performance, that 'whatever the language, one never hears the words in a Strauss opera'. I found that depressing, but *The Times* was not to agree, for it referred to 'Mr. Franklin's excellent articulation', and I assumed this meant the words could be heard. *The Spectator* announced that 'Strauss himself wrote most of Ochs's music so that the words should be largely unintelligible'. *The Scotsman* took an opposing view and thought I had 'exemplary diction'. Whatever the critics thought—and it is both illuminating and delightful to see how readily they disagreed—we ourselves thought the words were important, and we did everything we could to make them tell.

Sometimes it meant re-writing them. When Ochs takes formal leave of the Marschallin at the end of Act I, he sings this phrase:

Eu - er Gna - den ... ha - ben heut
I am speech - less ... stunned by your
Why your High - ness, ... 'tis too much,

durch un - - ver-sieg-te Huld ... mich tiefst be - schämt.
in - com - - par - a - ble kind ... com - plais - anc - y.
your kind - - ness and your charm ... have left me dumb.

What Pryce-Jones wrote is the line beginning, 'I am speech-less'. There were several things wrong with it. After a fast gallop through the act, with climax after climax at the top of the voice, a phrase stretching over two octaves down to the low C needed careful preparation, and lots of breathing spaces. In the German, there was a breath to be taken after 'Gnaden', after 'heut', another after 'Huld' and a fourth (thank God for monosyllables!) after 'tiefst', just before the approach to the final C. But, if I were to make sense of Pryce-Jones, I could not take breath in the gap the German gives after 'heut', because this would break the sense of his words. 'I am speechless, stunned by your—BREATH—incomparable kind complaisancy.' It would not be tolerable. In fact, if I were to take the *sense* of the words as of first importance, there would be only one breathing-space, after 'I am speechless'. I could not breathe after 'your', I ought not to breathe after 'kind' and fracture the sense of the words again, and, dammit, it was impossible to breathe in the middle of 'complaisancy'. But this would mean singing the whole phrase with only one breath, and, breathless and tired after a heavy act, I should find it impossible.

And there was another point. 'Complaisancy'. The *O.E.D.*

adds '(rare)'. It is a nice literary word, but useless for a singer. The 'ee' sound of the last syllable was hopeless for the low C. I needed a full, dark, round vowel on which I could get my throat open. And, if I managed to get the word to the audience they would not hear the unfamiliar 'complaisancy' but think the word was 'complacency', and therefore wrongly assume not that I was fulsomely thanking the Marschallin for her gracious agreement with, and acceptance of, my plans for marriage, but, instead, accusing her of being incomparably *self-satisfied*.

The sentence that in the end I cooked up for the phrase is the bottom version, that begins 'Why, your Highness . . .' It is true that this is scarcely a literal translation of the German, which near enough would read—'Your Grace, you have today by your inexhaustible favour, put me deeply to shame.' But at least I was as near to the original as Pryce-Jones, and, better, mine was singable. There were lots of lovely monosyllables in the Franklin version, it had the same punctuation gaps as the German, and I had the breaths where I should need them.

We made a number of other changes, this one for instance because the word-rhythms did not match the music:

Again, the top line is what Pryce-Jones wrote. (1) It ignored the first of the notes that Strauss had written. (2) It put a stress at the beginning of a bar on the word 'her', where it sat awkwardly, and (3) it sent me on to the stress of the first beat of the next bar, with the last syllable of 'Majesty', an impossible distortion of the word. And, since that note was a top E, it was moreover almost unsingable. My revision, the lower one, put the accents on '*no*ble' and 'Imp*e*rial', where they belong, and gave me 'crown' to sing on the top E, a much easier, more grateful vowel at that pitch. The dotted quaver, semi-quaver, and quaver at the beginning of the phrase did put a false accent on the 'be-' of 'before', but I made a tiny alteration in the music-rhythm, and sang three semi-quavers after the third beat of the bar, and then words and music rode together, their accents fitting easily.

In another passage, we thought it necessary to make changes in the words, to help the audience understand them. Pryce-Jones had written the sort of line that, in a book, a reader could re-read, and slowly work out what was intended; but our audience would hear the line *once*, and must get an immediate understanding. Here there was no question of not fitting the music, or distorting rhythms. It was only a matter of picking the right word, in the right place.

PRYCE-JONES	FRANKLIN
(a)	*(a)*
Be not out of countenance, Rofrano, that your father once sowed his wild	Be then not ashamed, my dear Rofrano, that your father once sowed his wild
(b)	*(b)*
oats. He follows in the act	oats. He's not alone in that,
(c)	*(c)*
a noble company, the late lamented Marquis;	he stands with the élite, the late lamented Marquis;
(d)	*(d)*
I won't deny I'm of it too.	I won't deny I've done it, too.

I made four changes. *(a)* 'Out of countenance' was, we thought, too literary. 'Be then not ashamed' is much more direct, and easier to understand. *(b)* 'He follows in the act'—would an audience at once realise that 'the act' was that of fathering bastards? I linked it more strongly to the sowing of wild oats, with, 'He's not alone in that'. *(c)* Could the whole phrase 'He follows in the act a noble company' possibly mean to the audience that the Marquis was but one of a number of the aristocracy of Vienna that had begotten bastards? Again, I thought it could not, and my complete phrase, 'He's not alone in that, he stands with the élite', had much more chance of making the point. *(d)* 'I won't deny I'm of it, too'. Of what? If you have time to read back and pick up the allusion, you will realise that what was intended was that Ochs, too, is a member of the group of noble bastard-begetters. But it was unlikely, or rather impossible, that the audience could *immediately* associate 'it' with 'the noble company' a couple of lines before. So, I finished with, 'I won't deny I've done it, too,' again words that were familiar, and short, and direct.

There were many other revisions. For instance 'Tis a confounded imposture' became, 'Sirrah, you play the comedian', because this gave a more convenient vowel for a top note, and, incidentally, because it was nearer to the German original. 'What histories befall a man of quality' was altered to, 'What accidents befall a man of quality', because 'histories' is more literary and less direct than 'accidents', which is familiar in colloquial use in this context. 'But first I'll drain my glass' became, 'But first I'll drain this glass', because 'this' gave me a stronger consonant—the 'th' sound—with which to attack a *piano* top F. And in the waltz song at the end of Act II, I changed, 'And better, for a raffish air to boot' to, 'And better, for a cheerful air as well', because (1) 'cheerful' on the top note was better in the voice than 'raffish'; (2) because the first syllable of the word lasted five beats, and a drawnout 'ra ... ff—' with the consonant coming at the end would give the audience little clue to what the word was eventually to turn into, while 'cheer . . .' would immediately establish itself; and (3) in any case 'raffish' is an unfamiliar, and 'cheerful' a very familiar, word; and (4) 'to boot' is archaic, and 'as well' part of the colloquial vocabulary.

Gradually and patiently we smoothed out the difficulties, and gradually I sang Ochs into the voice, and my memory. I can remember the feeling of triumph when for the first time on the bus home I could sing silently through a complete act, with my score unopened on my lap. The part became more fluent and more certain until, after twelve weeks, I could sing through the whole opera, or any part of it, at the drop of a hat, from memory. (I became so certain of it that, when we came to performances, I could turn to Rankl, when he came up to the stage for the final call with the principals at the end, and cheerfully apologise to him for the mistakes I had made that night—and tell him exactly what they were, and where.)

Then we started the second stage of rehearsals, ensemble calls round the piano in Rankl's room, with a répétiteur playing, and Rankl conducting, coaching, directing. For me, it was more a rehearsal for fitting dialogue passages together, because Ochs has little ensemble work; and, when he does sing with the others, he either dominates them or babbles away regardless, completely separate from the rest. Of real ensembles, like the magical trio in the third act for the Marschallin, Sophie and Octavian, Ochs has nothing. There are therefore no problems for him of balancing with the other voices. He never accompanies, never gives way to another singer.

His only problem of balance is with the orchestra. The full roll-call of instruments is 113, and, when they go hell-for-leather, as they normally do when Ochs is singing, his problem is to make himself heard. Not really his problem, I suppose—or my problem, back in 1947—but that of the conductor. The trouble with Rankl, then the musical director, was that he was so anxious to get a good performance, and to establish himself against opposition, that he could never relax when he was on the box, and managed to communicate to his singers his own considerable, uneasy tension. He couldn't delegate responsibility to the orchestra and let them play, nor could he give the singers room to sing. The more uncertain and nervous he felt, the more rigidly he tried to control the performance, and his four-in-a-bar became four downbeats in the bar. With every beat a strong one, the orchestra played louder and louder and, for example in the strenuous 6/8 narration in Act I, I couldn't even begin to follow Strauss's direction that it should be sung in an easy 'conversational' tone. 'Conversational'? I was fighting for my life, to prevent myself drowning in orchestral sound. And, because Rankl was so rigid and unyielding in his phrases, it was difficult to find room to breathe, let alone attempt any subtleties of phrasing.

Day after day we sang with the orchestra in the crush-bar at the Garden and, at about the same time, worked at stage rehearsals, which were seldom actually on the stage, because the stage was always busy. When there was a performance, either of opera or ballet, at night, every afternoon was taken up in setting for the show. There were ballet dress rehearsals, technical rehearsals, lighting rehearsals in the mornings, and it was only in the last week or two that we got on to the stage, and actually worked in the *Rosenkavalier* set. Until then, we rehearsed in the 'top room' of the pub opposite the stage door, or in the bareness of the Holborn Hall, or sometimes in the crush-bar. The set was marked out with chairs, and gaps were left to suggest a door, a window, or a marble staircase. It was often difficult to remember which chairs were really chairs, on which you could sit, and which were walls.

There is one factor in the production of an opera which I think audiences and people in the straight theatre, and certainly some critics, do not realise. Ochs is Ochs, not because of the way he moves, or the words that he sings, though these each have an importance in the creation of character, but fundamentally because of his music. *The Stage* was to write, after some criticism which it offered of my performance:

> Still, let us be generous: Mr. Franklin was probably trying to sing the part as Strauss wrote it.

This is 'generous'? To suggest that the deficiencies in my Ochs came from my singing what Strauss had written? To imply that I might have been more successful *if I had not sung what Strauss had written*? *Punch* did not waste time with words like 'probably', and was forthright:

> Baron Ochs is a disgusting character in spite of the enchanting waltz tune associated with him.

This was nonsense, and revealed a complete ignorance of the way that a singer finds a characterisation. If he sings his 'enchanting waltz tune' as it is written, he cannot be a disgusting character. It is *his* tune. Its elegance is his elegance, its warmth is his warmth, its appeal his appeal.

There is here a tremendous difference between the way that

an opera singer builds a part, and the work of the straight actor. The actor works from the beginning with the rest of the cast. They start by reading the play, probing for the writer's intentions, guided and directed by the producer, feeling for changes of pace and of colour. The singer has his changes of colour already laid down in the composer's explicit directions, his changes of pace dictated by the composer's metronome marks. The actor, after several readings, moves on to the stage and begins rehearsals with his script in his hand, working the part into his memory together with the moves, the gestures, and the groupings that the producer asks him for.

There are two practical obstacles to the singer's working in the same way as the straight actor. It took me three months to memorise Ochs, another bass six, and a third a year. No one could memorise such a part *in the middle of stage rehearsals*—and anyhow it would be impossible to rehearse on the stage with scores. The vocal score of *Rosenkavalier* is $9\frac{1}{4}$ inches wide, $12\frac{1}{4}$ inches long, $1\frac{1}{4}$ inches thick. It weighs three pounds. When it is opened, so that you can read the music, it is $18\frac{1}{2}$ inches wide, $12\frac{1}{4}$ inches long, it still weighs three pounds, and you need two hands to hold it. How then do you manage a sword in the duel scene, or your bit of slap-and-tickle with Sophie in Act II, and Mariandel in Act III? With both hands full of an enormous score, how can you even drink a glass of wine, for instance?

All of this means that a singer must come to his first stage rehearsal with the music memorised and the score discarded. It is in fact a contractual obligation in opera houses like Glyndebourne, with an *ad hoc* company collected for a short festival season. And it follows that, once the music is memorised, and the composer's directions followed, *the characterisation is already set*. The producer in the straight theatre can mould, develop, alter. The producer in opera can only take the character that the composer has designed, and that the singer has worked into his voice and his mind, and help him to develop it, high-light it by putting him into the stage set, and into the framework of the other singers of the ensemble. The producer

can strengthen a performance, but he cannot alter it.
Joan Cross, who produced *Rosenkavalier*, recognised this,
from the wide experience that she had herself had as a singer.
'You can never direct, but only develop,' she maintains. 'You
cannot make an artist do anything foreign to his personality.
You cannot make an artist do anything that is not there in the
music. You have to take the singers as they are, in physique
and personality, and work with what they've got.' And the
singers a producer has to work with are cast primarily on
voice. You want an Isolde? There are possibly at any given
moment a dozen women in the world who can sing the part.
The only one available is fat? Then you must reconcile yourself
to a heavyweight Isolde.

For Ochs the essential requirements are more than two-and-
a-half octaves, what *The Stage* called 'the utmost musicianship',
and stamina. Probably, there are, again at any given moment,
six men in the whole wide world who can manage it, vocally
and musically. And you can think yourself lucky to have one
in the resident company of your opera house, whatever his
shape and size. I was young—thirty-nine at the time, and that
is young for a bass—six feet seven, and about eighteen stone.
And this was half the trouble.

The critics remembered, or were to write that they remembered, Richard Mayr, a great and well-loved singer, and a
favourite Ochs for years. In a hotel in Salzburg, there is a
Richard Mayr Room. It is a basement room, with stained-glass
portraits, lit from the other side, of Mayr in all his favourite
parts—Ochs, Sarastro, Rocco, the lot. He was idolised in
Vienna, and some of the adulation rubbed off on to the
audience at Covent Garden and the critics. He was short and
tubby. Joan Cross told me—I never saw him—he was 'cuddly'.
None of these are adjectives that could be applied to me, and
the critics seemed to punish me for it. The *New Statesman*:

One simply cannot believe in a lanky, bony Ochs.

I wonder why? 'Lanky, bony'? The portrait facing page 113,

at least to my eye, scarcely suggests that I was bony, but then I must declare an interest. *The Observer* was to write:

> The best plan is to shut one's eyes, remember how Richard Mayr acted this part, and keep both ears on Franklin's voice.

You can judge a performance *with your eyes shut*? *The Spectator* said:

> That he was tall and thin inevitably tells against him to those who remember Mayr, and he is certainly too young-looking.

'Inevitably' is a significant word. It seems that some of the critics made up their minds beforehand that my job was to try to look like Mayr, and to play the part as he did. I did not look like him, and I did not play it like him. Mayr was a good Ochs. Ergo, I must have been a bad one. It was a simple piece of logic.

The *Birmingham Post*, almost alone, realised what I was up to. It wrote that I 'showed an original conception'. *The Observer* conceded, 'At least, he sings the part, as distinct from shouting his way through it', and *The Stage*, in the backhander it dealt me—'Still, let us be generous: Mr. Franklin was probably trying to sing the part as Strauss wrote it'—had stumbled on to the truth of the matter. *The Stage* critic wrote also for the *Evening News*, and in that setting went a bit further. He even dropped the word 'probably' and nailed his colours to the mast. 'David Franklin sang this cruelly difficult music vigorously and accurately (I think I even heard the low C).' (He did.) Singing and not shouting, and singing accurately—these were something of a novelty in the part. Joan has told me that Mayr sang sometimes out of tune, and often inaccurately, but got away with it in the theatre because of his immense charm. And it can be confirmed from the records of *Rosenkavalier* that Mayr made with Schumann and Lehmann that not every note that he sang was firmly in place. In any case, I wouldn't have been fool enough to try to copy Mayr. I was approaching a part in the only way that I knew, the way I had been taught at Glyndebourne, *through the music.*

From the music I was sure that Strauss saw Ochs not as a low comedian, but as a man of breeding. We both felt, Joan and I, that there was evidence, too, in the text. He is a cousin of the Marschallin, Maria Thérèsa, and if he is that close to the centre of the Court, even though he lives on an impoverished estate in the country, he must have been brought up within its code of manners. He is so near to Her Highness that he has an entrée to her levée. Her servants try to keep him out in Act I only because Octavian has been with her all night, and it would be indiscreet, with her husband away at the wars, for Octavian to be seen in her bedchamber.

But the more important evidence of his nobility lies in the music. There is first the waltz-tune. I have already written, a few pages back, that anyone who has this tune 'associated with him' cannot be disgusting, and I don't in the least mind repeating myself here. The melody of the waltz is elegant, warm and appealing. If you sing it *legato*—and I did sing it *legato*—its elegance and warmth and appeal must soak into the character you are building. Secondly, there is the orchestra theme (p. 150) that accompanies Ochs's formal leave-taking of Her Highness. It is first heard at his equally formal first entry, and Joan used its flourishes of demi-semi-quavers for me to make my series of 'legs', and for ornately deferential gestures of the hand, matching the ostentation of the phrase, before Her Highness. (It appears again to mark Ochs's formal presentation at Court of his esquire, Leopold.) As a third example, there is a second entry-theme, crammed with pomp and circumstance, 'nobleman's music', for his first visit to Faninal's mansion in Act II. Each of these three motives, elegant or ceremonial, *insists* that Ochs must have known how to behave as a man of breeding should.

The essential weakness of Ochs, in which lie the seeds of his final disgrace, is what Joan called his tactlessness. He has immense pride in being one of the Court circle, and an overwhelming conceit that makes him assume that the Court will good-naturedly and broadmindedly accept his adventures, that he finds amusing (for others as well as himself), fashionable (everybody's doing it), and natural. So, at his first entry, over the formal music, he makes his ritual bows. But he sees Octavian disguised as a girl, and passed off by the Marschallin as her maid, and he cannot resist, even in the middle of making a leg, the chance of making an immediate pass at her. He believes that any servant girl is fair game for a nobleman, and should feel honoured at being 'passed at'. The footmen have to whisper a reminder to him that Her Highness is waiting to receive him. 'Disgusting'? The Marschallin laughs when she sees Ochs at work on the 'maid'—it *is* rather amusing to see a womaniser chasing your own disguised lover—and Ochs immediately takes this to mean that Her Highness is a woman of the world and likes a little bit of fun. He launches himself into his boastful account of his sexual techniques, certain that she will appreciate and enjoy it. 'Disgusting'? When, a few minutes later, over his formal entry-music again, he presents his Leopold, he cannot resist hinting, man of the world to woman of the world, at the wrong-side-of-the-blanket reason for the astonishing resemblance that Leopold bears to him. 'Disgusting'?

When he is received by Faninal, over the second of his formal entry-themes, he airily patronises his host, who is very *nouveau riche*, and Ochs delights in the superior social status which enables him to play the condescending aristocrat. 'Disgusting'? This same music is used again in Act III, after Ochs has been disgraced before the Marschallin. He bows, over the theme as the stage directions indicate, 'with the grace of a man of the world', and, again man to man, he laughs gently at the trick that has been played upon him. Very good fun it has been— most diverting. He assures Her Highness that he finds the whole episode delicious and entertaining, and that he is quite ready to be magnanimous and forget the whole thing. This, he believes, is how men of the world carry off a delicate situation. 'Disgusting'? Tactless, stupid, insensitive, we thought, but not disgusting.

He is absolutely astonished when the Marschallin icily dismisses him from the Court, and forbids the marriage that he has arranged with Faninal's daughter. I believe that there is in the music of this scene a hint of compassion for Ochs. If he were just a coarse vulgarian, there could be no pity, no regret. Aristotle, in his *Poetics*, discussing the elements of tragedy, insists that its essence is the story of a man brought to adversity:

> Not the spectacle of a virtuous man brought from prosperity to adversity, for this moves neither pity nor fear: it merely shocks us. . . . Nor again should the downfall of the utter villain be exhibited. A plot of this kind would, doubtless, satisfy the moral sense, but it would inspire neither pity nor fear: for pity is aroused by unmerited misfortune, fear by the misfortune of a man like ourselves. . . . There remains, then, the character between these two extremes—that of a man who is not eminently good and just, yet whose misfortune is brought about not by vice or depravity, but by some error or frailty. He must be highly renowned and prosperous—a personage like Oedipus, Thyestes, or other illustrious men of such families.

If pressed, I would readily concede that this passage does not wholly apply to *Rosenkavalier* and to Ochs. Aristotle is concerned with tragedy, and *Rosenkavalier* is a comedy of manners. Ochs is out-ranked by Oedipus, and by Thyestes. But his family is noble, and his rank makes his fall more terrible. No one would have pity for a mere vulgarian in disgrace—how can a vulgarian be *disgraced*? Ochs *must* be a man of breeding, a nobleman at home in the Court, for the Marschallin's dismissal of him to be as devastating and terrible as it is for him.

There is one other point, in which Aristotle can help to explain Ochs. The misfortune that brings the tragic hero crashing to ruin must be brought about 'not by vice or depravity, but by some error or frailty'. This is the nub of it. The majority of the critics held Ochs guilty of 'vice and depravity', and so thought him coarse and disgusting. Joan and I believed that there was only an 'error or frailty' in his character, and that this was his stupid, conceited tactlessness. If we were right, what seems to be some evidence of 'vice and depravity' must be met. There are three counts against Ochs— (1) his disgraceful boasting to the Marschallin about the women he has enjoyed, (2) his attempt to seduce Mariandel/Octavian, and (3) the coarseness of his behaviour towards his intended bride, the innocent Sophie.

May it please your Lordship. Against the first charge, m'lud, I contend that it has already been established in evidence that my client, Baron Ochs, was misled by what he took to be Her Highness's amusement at his attentions to, he believed, her maid. I need not add, m'lud, but I do, that it was a deliberate and fraudulent attempt to deceive my client, for Her Highness's—shall we say?—'friend' to take part in this disgraceful, transvestite impersonation. My client fell into the trap set for him, thought that he was being encouraged by Her Highness to be frank, and so unfortunately, as he now realises, began to describe to Her Highness certain personal experiences that he had been led to believe she would find entertaining.

On the second count, I ask m'learned friend if he has never heard of the *droit de seigneur*? Is my client to be blamed because, like others of the nobility, he considered that his birth and rank entitled him to full enjoyment of that right?

To the third charge, the answer we make is, first, that there was no coarseness in his treatment of Fräulein Faninal, and, alternatively, if there were coarseness, it was an error, not of depravity, but of judgment. It is not disputed that at Court, in the presence of Her Highness, the Baron's general behaviour has always shown full awareness of the respect, the formality, that are rightly paid to Her Highness. But, with respect, m'lud, to be a guest of Faninal is quite different from being a guest of Her Highness. Faninal is an upstart, a man ignorant of the manners of high society, and the Baron believed that a relaxation of the rigidity of polite behaviour would indicate his willingness to overlook the great differences in their social position and, despite them, to be friendly towards a commoner

who is unfortunately not a gentleman. Indeed, so far from
resenting the Baron's bearing, Herr Faninal—I beg your lordship's pardon—I should have said 'Herr *von* Faninal', but his
purchase of his ennoblement has been so recently negotiated
that it is easy to forget it. So far from resenting the Baron's
bearing, Herr von Faninal said, before witnessses, referring to
the simultaneous presence in his house of the Baron, and
Octavian, Court Rofrano, who was acting as the Baron's rose-
cavalier, 'Wär nur die Mauer da von Glas, dass alle bürger-
lichen Neidhammeln von Wien sie en famille beisammen so
sitzen sehn'. If I may assist the court by offering a translation?
Your lordship is most kind. Herr von Faninal said, 'If only
the walls there were of glass, so that the unenvious citizens of
Vienna could see them together here, sitting en famille!' Far
from taking offence, Herr von Faninal was delighted at the
unaffected simplicity of my client's behaviour, and wished that
all Vienna could witness it. It was not until Octavian, Court
Rofrano, was suddenly aggressive that the situation became
tense.

The prosecution now contend that the Baron inspected
Fräulein Faninal as if she were a horse. Our answer is that the
Baron is a farmer, and an expert in the breeding of horses, that
he regards the breeding of his future children as a matter of
great importance in his family, and that it was therefore
natural that he should take careful stock of the physical
characteristics of the lady he had selected to mother those
children. It could possibly be argued that my client's good
nature, his willingness to suspend the rules of society in the
company of those who did not understand them, had led him
to behave with unusual frankness and unexpected freedom,
but, even so, the most that can be alleged against him is not
coarseness, not depravity, not vulgarity, but only, perhaps, a
lack of tact.

These were the arguments on which we based our approach
to the part of Ochs. The next step was to plan how he should
be projected to the audience. This again was a long process. As

in every opera, Joan began by blocking out the moves. In some operas, the arias give the producer's powers of invention a rest. Sarastro is brought on to the stage, firmly planted on his rostrum in his spotlights, and there he stays for six minutes, with the company of priests respectfully and statically grouped around him. Rocco, Colline, Ramphis, Banco, Hunding, Pogner, and Pimen, all have periods of several minutes' singing at a time with a minimum of movement, when all they have to do is stand and deliver. But *Rosenkavalier* needs a continual bubble of movement, and it is a trial of a producer's imagination and ingenuity, to contrive actions that are natural-looking, fit in an attractive stage picture, and both tell a story and define the characters.

The pattern that Joan planned for me was simple, designed to fit the colour and the mood of the music. Over the formal phrases, in the presence of the Marschallin, I was to move elegantly, with easy gestures, and the confidence of a man used to the Court. When the music changed, and babbled and hinted and chuckled knowingly, I was to brag confidentially to Her Highness, with a knowing leer, a significant nod—but I must never touch her, save when I kissed her hand in the etiquette of greeting or leave-taking. I might think her a woman of the world, but I must know, and keep, my place. She was above me, and physically out of my reach. With Mariandel/Octavian, I could move beyond the sly glance, the wink, and the dig in the ribs, to a fondling, exploring hand that, in Act III, could go so far as to try to undo her/his restricting corsets, and to the eager pinching of an attractive bottom. Sophie I was to examine and handle greedily and eagerly, like a horse-breeder who knows he has a bargain for the title which he has to sell. Faninal got in turn a patronising clap on the back, a casual approval of his house and his wines, and a careless indifference. All servants, mine, the Marschallin's, and Faninal's, I was to treat with contempt and insolence.

These things we planned and practised and developed in the routine of rehearsals. We ran scenes over and over again, with piano accompaniment, until the action became more fluent, and the points we had to make more telling. Orchestral rehearsals, dress parades, dress rehearsals followed, first with piano and then with orchestra. The first rehearsals on the stage with the orchestra bring another difficulty for the singers, and an odd one. They have become accustomed to the piano accompaniment that they have been working to for months—indeed, they have memorised it. What the orchestra plays often seems quite different from what they expect. For one thing, the piano reduction has to leave out a good deal of a thick orchestral score, and, for another, if the solo instrument on which they have been depending for their cue into a particular entry is positioned under the stage-apron, they cannot even hear it. They must memorise a completely different sound. Then came the first complete dress rehearsal, AS PERFORMANCE, as the call-sheet announced, with full scenery, lighting, costume, and make-up.

The make-up that I planned for Ochs was fun to do. You will see from the portraits reproduced facing p. 113 that there was a considerable difference in the appearance of Ochs and Sarastro. I hoped that I had made Sarastro remote, austere, ascetic. I hoped, too, that I had made Ochs look like—Ochs. But there seems to be, in those portraits, a difference in the actual physical shapes of the two faces. Ochs's face is round, with a curling lip, bulbous nose, and puffy, sagging cheeks. Sarastro has a long, thin, pointed face, sunken cheeks, and thin lips. Sarastro's ornate crown, which I privately thought looked like a jelly-mould, and his beard at the other end gave additional length to the face. Ochs had a high wig, but pushing it back on the head framed the dome-like forehead, lost some of the height, and so helped to emphasise an almost circular outline. So the one appeared thin, and the other chubby. Ochs's thick eyebrows brought out his sensual quality, and curling Sarastro's high over his eyes made them bigger and more striking, gave him dignity, and the cold glance of authority. The two noses were easy, and I did not use a false one. Sarastro's was heavily shaded on each side for its full length, and so seemed thin. The shading of Ochs's nose was carried outwards half-way down, and the ridge and the tip were high-lit with a lighter colour, so that it appeared to blossom into a bulb. The lines in Ochs's cheeks brought out their roundness, and carrying the lines down past the jaw added for good measure a couple of double-chins. I made Sarastro's cheeks sink in by emphasising and extending the shadows under the cheek-bones. I took Ochs's lips out as far as I dared, and curled the corners downwards and thickened the lower lip. I used the opposite tactic with Sarastro's mouth. The lips I made thin, and short, and absolutely straight. So, from one face, I made—I hope I had made—two contrasting faces.

Throughout rehearsals, Joan insisted that we must get away from Mayr. My Ochs must be a countryman, with sensual appetites, but not disgusting. And not old. This, she held, was essential. *The Spectator*, for example, disagreed.

He is certainly far too young-looking.

But why should he be old? He brazenly boasts to the Marschallin that he delights in the freedom that man has to enjoy sex all the year round, not being limited, as animals are, to certain seasons of the year. He relishes each summer when an army of girls comes from Bohemia to work on the harvest, and it is pleasant to persuade two or three of the girls to stay with him in his farm-house, and work for him in the fields, and 'work' for him at his home at night, whatever task he sets them, until November. (Two or three girls all through the summer, until November, and he is *old*?) German girls are for his taste just as attractive, but they have a different flavour, sharp and dry, like wines from the North. 'Would I could be like Jupiter happy in endless disguises,' he shouts with enthusiasm, 'I should never be idle.' There are many ways, he says, to capture what, if he had known the phrase, he might have called The Monstrous Regiment of Women. (Only a regiment? Ochs had had a brigade.) This one must be wheedled, that one is a shrew, another will giggle and quickly lose her head—there is a special enjoyment in this type—and there is another that has a touch of the devil that gives a zest to her final capitulation. Even an ugly woman, poor and in rags, can provide an extra excitement, with her astonishment to find a fine nobleman can realise that, beneath her tattered dress, there is a body from which he can take pleasure. Some must be overcome by strategems, others attacked like lightning, so that, before they know that he has begun, they find themselves sprawling defenceless. And always—Ochs was an epicure of sex—he likes to have masses of hay in which he can lie in comfort. This is his credo, as exhaustive in its survey as Leporello's 'Catalogue' aria, and as exhausting. Can such an Ochs really be *an old man*? A *seigneur* who takes often-repeated pleasure from his *droit* must surely be a man in his sexual prime.

This sexy narration, the 'four-minute mile', was a problem. It is marked, successively, 'Throughout in the tone of easy conversation', 'Always very quickly and distinctly', and 'All in a low voice, very confidentially'. I have already pointed out, at p. 142, the high *tessitura* of the voice, and at p. 145 the vigour of the orchestral scoring, which make easy, confidential, conversation well-nigh impossible. There is a further difficulty. The metronome marking is $\downarrow \cdot = 144$, which means that Ochs is expected to sing 432 quavers to the minute, over seven to the second. When, as often, separate syllables of the words are set to separate quavers, it is therefore required of Ochs that he should be able to sing, uncomfortably high in the voice, against a heavy orchestra, seven distinct syllables in a second. Ochs has a problem indeed. If he can get the words clearly to the audience, good—more than good, it is a miracle. If the words become just an incoherent gabble, at least he may be able to present to the audience the picture of a man oozing with conceit, confident that the Marschallin is fascinated by his charm—and a shattering bore. This was most important to the characterisation, because, by making Ochs a bore, I could plant his vanity, his self-satisfaction.

But this was a tricky wire to walk. Make Ochs too much of a bore, overdo his obsession with women, overplay his grossness, and I should turn high comedy into farce. It was difficult enough already. Ochs's cowardice in the duel scene in Act II, the mechanical japes which frighten him in Act III, his clumsy attempts to seduce Mariandel/Octavian, these were very near to slapstick, the slapstick would destroy character, and turn Ochs into a buffoon. I saw this happen, after I had left the cast of *Rosenkavalier*, and after I had left the Garden. Joan's original production was still being used, but, each year as it reappeared, a resident producer would take charge, and rehearse it again in the pattern that Joan had made. That is what should have happened—in theory. In practice, after the first performance, and the producer has moved on to another opera, another house, another country, gradually performances get careless. Singers forget, leave out, or alter what they were at first directed to do, and the show becomes untidy and loose. Three years after its first performance, Joan's *Rosenkavalier* had not exactly worked itself loose—it had fallen apart.

There is a small part in Act II, for the Doctor, who has nothing to sing, but is called in to mime attendance on Ochs, and bandage his arm, after Octavian has pinked him in their duel. The fact is that singers who have nothing to sing get frustrated and, with a tiny part to mime, they try endlessly to build it up with a bit more business here, and new props there, just to get a little piece of recognition. This particular Doctor had persuaded the producer that it would get a bonus laugh if, instead of bringing with him an instrument-case, he were to carry on a carpenter's carpet-bag, complete with hammer and, God help us, a saw. The only hope of keeping Act II at the level of high comedy is that everyone should act with restraint and with discipline. The Doctor's tasteless, grotesque miming with saw and hammer, treating a man with a flesh-wound, tore the fragile texture of the act in pieces, turned a noble comedy into a squalid farce, and Baron Ochs von Lerchenau into a clown.

Singers are dependent upon one another in performance. I first learned this at Glyndebourne, when I was rehearsing Sarastro. The second aria—'In diesen heil'gen Hallen'—is more often than not sung as a kind of concert-piece in costume. The singer gets himself into his lights, takes a deep breath, and works at producing a good *basso profundo* tone. But there is more to it than just vocalisation. The aria is the key to the whole opera, in which Sarastro defines the teachings of the Temple of Wisdom, and, so that I could be seen to be the teacher, Ebert gave me, as a pupil, Auliki Rautawaara, the Pamina, a good singer and a most beautiful woman. She stood, as Ebert directed, in front of me, with her back to the audience, and put her hands in mine. I ignored the audience, looked at Pamina, and sang only to her. It was an expert production device and I found it invaluable; and later, when I sang Sarastro at the Garden, I asked the producer if I could avoid the concert-piece image of the aria there, too, and had another beautiful pupil to sing to, Elisabeth Schwarzkopf. It was in this scene that I first realised how much a singer can do to make a success of another's aria.

It was in the last act of *Rosenkavalier* that I was to realise how much a singer can do, too, to destroy the work of another. Ochs takes Mariandel/Octavian to a private room in an inn. He warms her up for the seduction which he plans with dinner and wine, and sends the waiters away, and insists that he himself will serve the meal. Joan told me to give the girl one spoonful of whatever it was we had to eat—generally, the catering department sent down to the stage a helping of cold potato salad—to give myself the second spoonful, turn back to her plate as if I was thinking of giving her more, hesitate, make up my mind, turn the dish upside down, and crudely scrape with a spoon all the food from the dish *over my own plate*, thus rather craftily planting with one stroke both my table-manners and my greedy appetite. One night, as I leant across the table to put the dish down, my Mariandel/Octavian quickly switched plates, so that I had the smaller portion and she the enormous one. We had a short discussion of the matter after the show.

ME: And why the hell did you switch the plates tonight?

SHE: I thought it might be rather fun. It got a laugh, didn't it, darling?

(She had been on the stage long enough—*just* long enough—to think it is part of the business to call everyone 'darling'.)

ME: But, dammit, it was the wrong sort of laugh. *I'm* the funny one. You're supposed to be my straight man.

SHE: Well, darling, I like to put something new into every performance.

ME: I, on the contrary, like to keep every show exactly as the producer rehearsed it.

SHE: Well, they always say it takes all sorts. . . .

ME: But don't you see, you silly woman, that for two whole acts you have been building the character of a nobleman, and that, in that one piece of clowning, playing to the gallery for a laugh, you destroy your whole night's work? No nobleman would ever, even in disguise, insult his host by pinching his plate. If you want to turn Octavian into a buffoon, go ahead. See if I care. Only don't you dare to interfere with any of my work again.

She didn't. I suppose that taking my work as seriously as I did was to take it for granted that it was worth taking seriously. After the first performance of *Rosenkavalier*, I had my doubts. I was very badly roughed up by some of the critics, though they did not by any means seem unanimous.

David Franklin's Ochs lacked grossness as his voice lacked resonance. (*Daily Herald*)

Love—fifteen.

David Franklin has the voice for Ochs . . . (*Daily Telegraph*)

Fifteen all.

One could not help admiring Mr. David Franklin's resource, his excellent articulation, and his euphonious agreeable singing. (*The Times*)

Thirty—fifteen.

Mr. Franklin's singing was first rate. (*Birmingham Post*)

Forty—fifteen.

A defect, and it is a serious one, is that the Baron (David Franklin) has not the physical or vocal weight for the part. (*Manchester Guardian*)

Forty—thirty.

The defect is the Baron Ochs, for which part David Franklin seemed not to have the right weight of voice or manner. (*Time and Tide*)

Deuce.

BARON OCHS WAS MISSING. The Covent Garden company achieved the astonishing feat last night of performing Strauss's *Rosenkavalier* without Baron Ochs. (*Evening News*)

Advantage—the critics.

I do not say that the Baron Ochs of David Franklin is the authentic Ochs in spirit and detail. But I should have no hesitation in saying that it is completely successful of its kind, and must, I think, be vastly impressive to anyone who has never heard the opera before. In Mr. Franklin's case exemplary diction and a magnificent vocal equipment make him most effective as an admittedly Anglicised but nevertheless persuasive version of the disreputable, tragi-comic figure of Baron Ochs. (*The Scotsman*)

Deuce.

The only real disappointment was Mr. David Franklin. Tall and thin, he gave the character a touch of ecclesiastical authority instead of showing us, as he should have done, a grand-operatic Falstaff, and his voice had little of the right quality. (*Truth*)

Advantage—the critics.

The acting is deplorable, except for the footmen when they are standing to attention. (*Daily Mail*)

Game!

Only it was not a game to me. No one enjoys being whipped in public, and I felt bruised and hurt. There were private consolations. Harold Rosenthal, the critic and a good friend, told me with relish about one of his colleagues who in the first interval said he was astonished that, though the opera had been translated from German into English, the tenor's aria in Act I had, extraordinarily enough, been rendered into Italian. Harold gently explained that the aria was in Italian in the original—the tenor was supposed to be an Italian, entertaining the Marschallin with an aria in his native tongue. So it was left in Italian in the English version. 'Interesting,' said the critic. I found it comforting to think that the basis for at least one critical judgment was, if not ignorance, at any rate only imperfect knowledge.

When I was dressing for the second performance, unhappy after my caning, and wondering what sort of reception I should get from an audience who had read the notices, Percy Heming breezed into my room, and tried to cheer me up. 'Don't forget, dear boy,' he said, 'that any of the critics would give his right arm to be sitting where you are now, preparing to go on the stage of the Royal Opera House.' It was a charming thing to say, and I warmed myself with it. But I knew it was not true. Some of the critics had begun careers as performers, and either had not made the grade or finished the course. But it was silly to try to persuade myself that they were all longing to sing opera—though I did get some simple pleasure from imagining what X, or even Y, could have made of Baron Ochs.

There were other and public consolations. Ten months after that first performance, the *Evening News*, which had then announced dramatically that Ochs had been missing, said of the first performance of the following season that I was the corner-stone of what was the best production in the Garden's repertory. I had not altered my ideas or my approach. My performance had become smoother, and I had probably found more confidence. But I played it exactly the same way as I had always done. In 1947, I had been 'missing'. In 1948, I was the corner-stone. Ah well.

In 1947 *Theatre World* had made a concession.

It is far from easy to be dogmatic about the playing of this difficult part.

Two of the critics found it easy enough:

David Franklin's Baron Ochs never comes within hailing distance of von Hofmannstal's conception. (*Observer*)

As David Franklin, he has a natural gift for humour of a certain broad kind, but simply to be yourself on the stage is not good enough, especially when the species of humour natural to you is not the sort the composer and librettist had in mind. (*Sunday Times*)

The odd thing was that, after such great confidence that they knew what Strauss and von Hofmannstal wanted and I did not, a few days after the first performance I had a delightful letter from Frau von Hofmannstal, who told me not to let myself be upset by the critics, because, although my Ochs was new, though it needed time to settle down, my approach to the part was *just what Strauss and her husband intended.*

And, in June 1959, the music critic of *The Times*, writing about the first fifty years of the opera, said this:

It is worth recalling that when Mr. David Franklin sang the part at Covent Garden some ten years ago, von Hofmannstal's widow commended his performance because of its razor-edge balance between breeding and decadence.

That made pleasant reading. But by the time I read it, I was no longer a member of the company. Eight years before, I had left the Garden.

SEVEN

Franklin Dav

SUDDENLY, IN 1950, singing wasn't easy any more. There was a sense of strain in my voice, and I had to use much more effort than ever before. The top lost its ease and its fullness, and it became dry and hard.

It was extraordinary, and I was astonished to find that my collars had become very tight. I sang *The Creation* one night in Derby, and I felt myself so strangled by my dress-collar that in the interval I borrowed a penknife, and slit the stud-holes to give myself an extra quarter of an inch, so that I could breathe. I had no idea what was happening to me. I thought it would be simple enough to cope with the problem by buying bigger collars. For years I had used a $17\frac{1}{2}$, which is big by ordinary standards. But I had taken it for granted that it was natural enough for a man of my size. I asked Austin Reed's to make me a dozen collars, two inches deep—I needed that depth because of my height—and size 20. The salesman shook his head, and said apologetically, 'Sorry, sir. I'm afraid we can't touch it. That's an engineering job!' After persuasion, I did get my big collars, but was surprised, and worried, to find that they did not help. I still felt constricted, and obviously the constriction, whatever it was, was inside my throat, and not an outside pressure. It was time to go to see my doctor.

He sent me to a consultant physician, who said I had an

174

enlarged thyroid. (My father had told me, when I was in my teens, that there was a family tendency to thyroid trouble. I thanked him for warning me, and then forgot it. It could not happen to me.) The physician sent me to another consultant, a surgeon. He was, I discovered, a chest man, and I asked him why I had been sent to him? Surely the thyroid is in the neck? He explained that mine had developed a sort of pendant, like a carrot, which had grown downwards behind my chest, and was lying snugly alongside my windpipe which, as the thyroid grew, it was steadily closing. No wonder singing was difficult. My thyroid was beginning to strangle me.

It was decided, and I had to accept, that there must be an operation. Otherwise sooner or later I should die rather unpleasantly, garrotted by my own thyroid. It was planned to do the job at the end of the season at the Garden, in the summer break of 1950. Once this thing was out of my throat, I should be able to breathe normally. 'And sing normally?' I asked. There was an ominous silence for a moment.

It was not going to be as simple as that, I was told. (The thyroid is connected, they say, to the recurrent laryngeal nerve, which controls the operation of the vocal cords.) It was possible, the surgeon said, that my voice might be affected. Everything possible would be done, naturally, but he must be honest with me, he said, and warn me that damage to my voice was—well, possible. I must prepare myself for it, just in case. . . .

By God, that's not easy, I thought. I couldn't have been more shocked, more appalled, if he had told me that I had only six months to live, and, in effect, that was just what he had told me. Singing and my family—there wasn't room for anything else in my life. A few months before, I had been interviewed by a writer who was preparing a book on singers of the day, and after he had got all the biographical details he needed he asked me what my hobbies were. This stopped me dead. Hobbies? It would be silly to have offered my family as a hobby, but I couldn't think of anything else. I thought I ought to produce something for the man, and asked if reading in bed at night counted? It didn't. But there was nothing else—I rehearsed and I sang. Finish.

I had been infatuated with singing from the moment I started at Glyndebourne. I enjoyed the sensuous pleasure of feeling a phrase slide through the throat, of feeling good resonance in the head. I enjoyed clipping crisp consonants on to the flow of the vowel sounds, I enjoyed the intellectual challenge of learning difficult music. I enjoyed the fun of performances, the unvaried routine of a production, which made me meet the same singer every night on the stairs as I went up to the stage, and she was coming down from it, or brought me alongside the same electrician re-aligning the same spotlight at exactly the same moment. I took pleasure from these things, because I enjoyed being a member of a team moving through an intricate and disciplined pattern. I enjoyed singing with an orchestra, feeling the voice ride over the rich sound they made. I enjoyed the casual friendliness amongst singers—and the intense rivalry that lay just beneath the surface. I enjoyed the beauty of the Royal Opera House, and working on its historic stage. I enjoyed the professional status that the Garden had given me. I enjoyed my contract, too. Even if I hadn't been paid for it, I should still have gone on singing, but to get paid for doing what I loved made me one of the lucky ones, and I knew it. We lived, not extravagantly, but comfortably enough, on my opera pay, and on the concerts and broadcasts that I did as well. And, not least, I loved music. Any sort of music fascinated me. Great music moved me, always deeply, sometimes uncontrollably. One night I was singing Mark and in the last act of *Tristan*, when I had finished the last sentences I had to sing, I stood listening to Flagstad in the 'Liebestod'—and it was just as well, I thought, that the producer had me with my back to the house, for the tears were running down my face. I removed my make-up, changed, got a cab to Euston, took a sleeper to Manchester, a cab to my hotel, a bath and breakfast, another cab to Belle Vue, and at ten o'clock Barbirolli began rehearsing the Hallé in the prelude to *The Dream of Gerontius*—and by five past ten I was in tears again. A thoroughly weepy weekend, but this was what music did to me. I was hooked on it.

I must prepare to lose all this? I wasn't very good at it. I tried. But all I could do was to try to persuade myself that it wouldn't happen. 'You'll be all right,' I told myself desperately. There would be a successful operation. 'He's the best surgeon there is for this sort of job,' I reassured myself. Nothing to worry about—my recurrent laryngeal nerve would be unharmed. (Damn the recurrent laryngeal nerve! A week before I hadn't even known that I had the thing, and now everything I wanted to do with my life was hanging on a tiny, delicate thread.) I found me difficult to persuade. I was scared, and every week I was more scared. Those months were awful, and worse was to come.

The terror of losing my voice tightened the singing muscles, and as this additional tension was added to the considerable physical pressure on my throat, performances became more and more difficult. That summer we were preparing *Götterdämmerung* and I had been cast as Hagen. I had already sung Hunding, Fafner, Pogner, and King Mark, and Hagen would be another specimen in my collection of Wagner's bass parts. For me, it was to be the great prize, a wonderful role, with sinister, vigorous music, and I had always wanted to sing it. But I was never to perform the part. A couple of months before the first performance, my thyroid took a stronger hold on my windpipe, and gave it an even more vicious squeeze, and my voice suddenly disappeared in the middle of a rehearsal. I went in panic to the surgeon. His fingers probed into my throat, and I wished he wouldn't, because it hurt. He could see—dammit, I could see it myself every morning when I was shaving—that my larynx had now been pushed three-quarters of an inch out of alignment, and the pressure on it was enormous. He operated next morning.

It was done in the Brompton Hospital, because of the chance of thoracic complication. I was told next morning that it had gone smoothly, but if this was a smooth job, I wanted to have nothing to do with a difficult one. I felt horrible. An eight-inch wound in the neck is extremely painful and I do not recommend it. (If you are desperate, the gas oven, sleeping pills, even the river, are all more acceptable. Take it from me—cutting your throat is out.) In the morning, the surgeon, bright and clean and aggressively antiseptic, arrived with his team. 'Better up than in,' he said. 'Seven inches long it was, and it weighed over a pound.' The idea that anyone should have *weighed* the chunk that he had cut from my throat I thought quite revolting. 'How on earth you ever sang a note with that pressing on your larynx, I just don't know,' he went on. 'It's a remarkable specimen, and we've pickled it. We shall use it in our post-graduate teaching here.' 'It's all very well for you, flashing my ex-thyroid all over the place,' I said, weakly, 'but I must remind you that I am under contract to the Royal Opera House, and I must ask that, whenever you display my thyroid to a medical class, it must be announced that Mr. Franklin's thyroid appears by kind per-mission of the General Administrator of the Covent Garden Opera Trust'—and I sank back painfully on to my pillows. Even without rehearsal, I thought, I had played the scene rather well.

I was there for three weeks, though all the other patients on my floor were there for at least as many months. I think I was the only one who was lucky enough to go home with both lungs still in position. The physiotherapist was disappointed in me—not that I kept both lungs, but that I made much less use of them than she expected. I first met her the night before the operation, when she came into my room and announced that she was going to teach me to breathe with my diaphragm. 'Oh, good!' I said, 'I shall enjoy that.' She explained that this was so that I should be able to breathe out of the bottom of my lungs the last dregs of what she called 'the nasty anaesthetic', after what she also called my 'op'. She told me to lie back and relax, said that she would put her hand on my 'tummy', and, though I should probably find it difficult, I must try to breathe with my tummy against the weight of her hand. 'Like this?' I said, and took a quick breath, and shot her hand a couple of inches upwards. Her eyes popped, and she asked if I could do it again. I obligingly repeated the performance, and she asked what my job was. I said that I was a singer and that I had been trained to breathe for years, not with my chest, but with—and I gave her a coy simper—my 'tummy'. She conceded my competence in this field of physiotherapy, and left me in peace.

But after the operation—this was where she had her disappointment—she began talking enthusiastically about testing my vital capacity. There was a slight and embarrassing misunderstanding here because I thought she was referring to my virility, and I said lecherously that I should enjoy whatever tests she had in mind. But, it seems, 'vital capacity' means only the amount of air that can be drawn into the lungs. Every Brompton patient was tested. Big as I am, and still with two lungs while most of her patients had only one, poor devils, and being moreover a singer with a big development of the diaphragm, she was sure that I should set a new record for the hospital. In fact, I did nothing of the sort. I came second to a little man who had only one lung to work with. I inhaled until I was dizzy, and blew into the balloon-thing until I had spots in front of my eyes, but I never got anywhere near the little man's figure, whatever that was. I thought there was an interesting point of technique here. The singer breathes with his diaphragm in order to get the deepest possible support for his tone. He does not breathe high in the chest, because this tightens the muscles of the throat, and anything that affects them will damage his tone. I could take a breath big enough for a long phrase, and in a split second, but I had been drilled in low breathing. I did it with the diaphragm, and the top half of my lungs was unused. So, in this particular athletic competition, I was a bad second.

After my convalescence, I had another battle, which I won. This was fun. The operation, which had been organised in the private wing of the hospital, so that I retained my doctor's choice of a surgeon, cost several hundred pounds, and I included it amongst my expenses in my tax return. I thought it was worth trying. My accountant was gloomy, said he would do what he could, but had to report complete failure. So I asked his blessing, and went to see the Inspector of Taxes myself. We went three brisk rounds. I began by arguing that it was incontestable that this was an expense necessarily incurred in pursuit of my profession. If I had been a bank manager, I could have gone on without treatment for much longer; but, as a singer, I needed to be able to breathe much more than a bank manager, and the operation was therefore professionally inevitable. The Inspector conceded that, if I could not breathe, I could not sing and, if I could not sing, I could not earn fees and, if I could not earn fees, I should have nothing on which I could pay taxes. But, he said, it would be as logical to claim as a professional expense what I spent on food and clothing. Without them, I should die, and so he wouldn't be able to get any tax from me. Why, he suggested gaily, didn't I claim for food and for clothes?

I was delighted, for I had been lying in wait for this one. 'But I do claim for food and clothes,' I said, 'and you allow my claim year after year. Not for all my food—not for my breakfast and the Sunday joint. Not for all my clothes, my pyjamas or the tweeds in which I play golf. I put in a claim— and you allow it—for food I eat professionally, when I have to lush up someone who may be useful, and for professional clothes I wear at concerts, even for make-up that I wear on the stage.' I thought I saw him twitch, and I pressed it home. 'I'm not claiming for all my medical expenses,' I said, reasonably. 'Not for every bottle of aspirin, or for the sticking-plaster I use when I cut myself shaving. I'm claiming only for those medical expenses that I say were necessary for the exercise of my profession.' He admitted I might have a debating point, but said there was no precedent for accepting medical expenses for tax relief. I'd got an ambush ready for this one as well.

'Suppose,' I said, 'a singer had a special lightweight set of teeth, because National Health gnashers would have thickened his diction. Would the cost of them be a professional expense?' He definitely twitched this time. 'I do happen to know a singer,'

I said, 'who did have a special dental plate made, and was allowed to set it off as an expense.' 'Damn!' he said, 'I told X not to say anything about it!' 'Oh?' I said, 'X has had it, too, has he? He wasn't the one. The one I know is a mezzo, and very nice teeth they are. That makes two of them.' I asked how he could make a distinction between special teeth for singing, and a special operation for singing, and at last he gave in. He would accept the surgeon's fee, and my hospital expenses, as professional expenses. 'Thank you,' I said, 'And now, what about the hotel bills for my convalescence?' He went sour, and said that I should not press my luck. So I didn't—but at least, to the surprise of my accountant, a thyroidectomy was established as a professional expense.

But this concession from the Inspector—I liked to think of it as a cleverly planned tactical victory—and the fact that I was no longer in danger of self-strangulation, were the only two benefits that I could count from the operation. In spite of the skill and the care with which it had been done, the removal of the lump from the throat did damage the recurrent laryngeal nerve, and as soon as I started singing again I knew that the top notes were gone. For months I had frightened myself with the nightmare of losing my voice—now I was to live through it. Bliss's *Olympians* was scheduled at the start of the new season, and I was cast as Mars, a vigorous, bull-headed part. Rehearsals began three months after the operation, and the first performance was a month after that. I acted my head off, used every trick of the trade I knew to try to cover up, but it was no good. I sang badly, and everyone knew it. They said that it was a mistake, that I should never have been asked to sing so soon. Steuart Wilson, who was Deputy General Administrator, told me that they should have sent me to sit in the sun for six months, and given me time to recover. I was desperately worried, and this was a godsend. Yes, I told myself pathetically, I was pushed into performances before I was ready, when anyone could have seen that what I wanted was more time. I was of course lying to myself. I had not been pushed into singing Mars. I was eager to do the part, because I was anxious to convince the management—and me—that I was as good as ever. I didn't really need time to recover. There would never be time enough for that. My top notes had gone.

My friends in the company, the chorus, the orchestra, audiences, the critics—they all knew it. So did I. The difference was that I would not admit it. I couldn't—I was much too frightened to face it. You may well think that I was making far too much of a common misfortune. Others have had operations, and have learned to live with them, even with thyroidectomies that have harmed their voices, and why couldn't I? The answer is that there is a special relationship between the singer and his voice. No one enjoys finding out that his friends think his voice unattractive, but the bank manager or the dustman can in time learn to accept it. For the singer this is impossible. His living depends upon the quality of his voice— and not only his living. His ambitions, his pleasures, his satisfactions, and his pride, all grow out of its beauty, warmth, power, size and flexibility. Every voice is an essential part of the personality. But for the singer it is more than personality—it is his life. And mine had suddenly come to a full stop.

I was desperately anxious to prove that I was not finished, and so took on performances that, comfortable enough a few months before, were now outside my reduced capacity. I had humiliation after humiliation, as my voice gave way. It worked in fits and starts. Some nights, it wasn't too bad, but I could never tell when, reaching for a top note, I should find nothing there, and there would be a terrifying gap in the phrase. The top Es and the Fs had gone, and with them my nerve had gone, too.

I had always slept for a couple of hours in the afternoons before a performance, until it was time to leave for the theatre. I still went up to bed, but I didn't do much sleeping. I worried, sometimes I shook with fright, and I can remember afternoons when I cried, real tears. This was the greatest humiliation of all, to see myself, an enormous man forty-two years old, lying in bed and crying like a child, because in a few hours I had to go on the stage and sing. Up till then, I had taken great pride in the size, the resonance and the stamina of my voice. I enjoyed it, when the loudspeakers called me down to the stage. I loved the excitement of listening to the overture from behind the curtain, waiting for it to go up and start me off to compete with a big orchestra and a big audience. I was nervous on first nights, or when someone special was in front, but it was a pleasant feeling. I wanted to get at them, and I couldn't wait. That was all over. I didn't want to get at them now. I wanted to crawl into a corner and hide, and I couldn't. I still had to go on and sing with my voice in shreds.

I wrapped myself round with self-pity. I suppose it was the easiest form of escapism, and I romantically dramatised the mess I was in. I cast myself as the hero, struggling to rescue himself, and alone. It wasn't true, of course. My friends were very concerned, and offered advice and sympathy, but I didn't want it. It would have meant my having to accept openly the basis of their concern, that I was finished as an opera singer, and I wasn't yet prepared for that. Instead, I ran away from it. When people tried to talk to me about my voice, I curtly insisted that it was going to be all right, and shut up. I talked about it to only three men—Steuart Wilson, Norman Allin and Percy Heming. Each of them tried to help. I had some lessons from Steuart and Norman, and months of work with Percy. Their trying to help me implied a belief that my voice could be repaired, and I could talk about it with them, but with no one else.

The management never mentioned it or my performances, or said one word of encouragement, and this made me wallow even more in my fantasy of the Lone Hero. I told myself they didn't care. I know of course that it wasn't true. David Webster has since told me that they were very worried, not only because I had been a valuable member of the company, but because of the problem of my future. The Garden, in any case, was not then a comfortable place for singers. The company had growing pains. The critics lashed out at our performances, and Equity and the I.S.M. at the engagement of foreign singers in leading roles. Inside the company, the home team were suspicious of the management's intentions, and extremely jealous of the imported singers. In addition, there was a battle for power going on in high places. Rumours of the fight leaked down to us from time to time, and we found them very unsettling. So it was easy for me to persuade myself that the management were much too occupied with their own affairs to spare time to help a poor devil of a singer who had had his throat cut. (I must have sounded like someone out of *East Lynne*.) Of course they were busy, but if I had let myself think about it—and I couldn't let myself think—I would have realised that it wasn't that they didn't care. It was tact, or embarrassment, or compassion, that kept them away from me. How do you talk about the future to a man who has no future?

So I went on torturing myself with their indifference, brooded on what I decided was their callous neglect, and began to get very angry about it. As it turned out, getting angry was a good thing, for it made me start thinking, after Christmas, of resigning from the company, and becoming a free-lance. I'd show them, I told myself bravely. Exactly what I was going to show them was not at all clear. But I would show them . . . something or other. My friends tried to persuade me to hang on. After all, I had fair-sized cheques coming in each week, and it would be silly to throw up this security. Wait, they said, until you get better. I said that the Garden had made me so frightened that I should never get better as long as I stayed there. (I was wrong, for it wasn't the Garden that had broken my nerve. Me and my recurrent laryngeal nerve—we'd managed that all on our own.) I must get out into the cold, cold world, and there, I said, my courage and my voice would come back. I was still lost in my fantasy of the Lone Hero.

That year must have been hell for my family. Our two daughters were too young to realise what I was going through, but old enough to realise Daddy was awful to live with, moody, depressed, ready to blow up at the drop of a hat. One night, when the anger I felt at the way I imagined I had been treated had reached a crisis, I walked for hours round Hampstead Heath and in the small hours crawled home exhausted, sat on my wife's bed, and told her that at last I had made up my mind. I must leave the Garden. It meant throwing away the security of my contract. I couldn't even guess whether they would renew it. (Secretly, I thought they would, if only out of charity. But who wanted charity? I was a singer, and I had been a proud singer.) Did she mind? Mary said the only security worth having was peace of mind. Even with our weekly cheques, I'd been impossible to live with, and she was glad it was over. We said nothing to the girls next morning, and, when I went out after breakfast, Susan, the younger one, asked what had happened to Daddy? He seemed happier, different somehow.

Daddy *was* different. He was going to Show Them. But what? This was a problem, and there were a couple of difficult years ahead until I worked out the right answers. At first, I believed—I had kidded myself—that it was only a question of regaining my confidence, and then my voice and I would be in full flow once more. I would re-establish myself in concerts and broadcasts. It took more bitter humiliations to make me finally accept that my time as one of the leading singers in the country was up. I really was finished. I still gave a performance of sorts. I had enough experience on the stage and on the concert platform to use my height to *look* competent and strong. People had said that my diction was good, and in recitals I used the way I handled words to cover up the gaps in my voice. But I couldn't do that in oratorio. 'The Trumpet shall Sound' isn't a patter-song—either you can sing it, or you can't, and I couldn't. At last I had admitted it—but this capitulation was private. I was still too sensitive and too hurt to tell anyone else that I knew I could no longer sing as I had done in the old days. I pretended that I was going to be as good as new, in time. All I wanted was more time. Behind that protective screen, I was desperately unhappy, but at least I had stopped panicking, and I had begun to think. This was a beginning.

I could not make a living with my private fantasy of the Lone Hero, and so he disappeared. But what should I do? Schoolmastering? I could, I supposed, teach Latin and English and History, but I hated the idea. I had left the staff-room to find fame and fortune, and I would crawl back, beaten, only if we were starving. In any case, I had lost fifteen years' increments, and I should get far too little pay for my age and the needs of my family. The classroom would be a poor substitute for the stage, and *somehow* I wanted to go on working as a performer.

What sort of a performer? Opera was out—though one or two last opportunities came along. The day after I left the Garden, I began rehearsals of Peachum in the English Opera Group production of Britten's vivid and astringent *Beggar's Opera*. We played a season at Aldeburgh, another at the Cheltenham Festival, and three weeks at the Lyric, Hammersmith. I was always sentimental about theatre history, and I enjoyed working on the stage where Frederic Austin's famous production had run for years after the first war. Aldeburgh, too, was a delight. It is a gem of a town, and its associations with *Peter Grimes*, the tiny hall and its improvised dressing-rooms, the beach and the sound of the sea just outside—these were all a relief from the vastness, the gloom, the vegetable smells of the Garden, and the unhappiness that I had had there. I played several seasons more at Glyndebourne, as the Haushofmeister in *Ariadne auf Naxos* and as the Bassa Selim in *Entführung*. These were speaking parts, and my last appearances in opera.

I was to be offered another contract. The manager of the D'Oyly Carte Company rang me and offered me a job as principal bass. The man they had was ill (and was to die within six months, poor chap) and they wanted someone to start working into the parts he played. There were one or two obvious advantages. The strain on the voice would not be heavy. Gilbert and Sullivan needed good diction, and mine was supposed to be pretty good. I had a fair amount of stage experience, and I was used to discipline, and this would be useful in the highly stylised productions that the company put on. I'd have to put up with being on the road for forty weeks in the year, and tours in America, and my home life would just about disappear. But they offered me the same salary that I had had at the Garden, and I was told that it could be a job for life. The only thing against it was that I didn't want it for a week, let alone life. I have never enjoyed G. & S., and churning out the same twee Victorian jokes about parliamentary trains and elliptical billiard balls would have driven me insane. That evening at supper I told my schoolgirl daughters that I had been offered the job. Two knives and forks clattered down on to their plates. 'Oh, no!' said Susan, in dismay. I said it meant security. 'Let's face it,' said Janet, 'you're difficult enough to live with now, but if you are going to do Gilbert and Sullivan for the rest of your life, you'll not be difficult. You'll be impossible.' 'Take it easy,' I said, 'I turned it down.' 'Thank God for that,' said Janet, and 'It was a jolly rotten trick to frighten us,' said Susan. I thought it interesting that the kids, young as they were, had got the right idea. What mattered was not so much how regularly my money should come in, but that I should be content with the way I earned it. If Daddy was happy, the family was happy, too. If Daddy was frustrated, the family went through hell.

Oratorio was out, too, as well as opera. Song recitals? Lieder programmes? Well, maybe. I could select things that were within my powers. To avoid stretching the voice unduly, I could juggle with key-sequences, and have songs transposed. But there was a limit to what I could do. You cannot avoid every climax. You cannot build a complete programme with no excitement in it. Besides, there are always younger, fresher, and *cheaper* voices on the way up, breathing down your neck. The youngsters—they hadn't had their voices wrecked by an operation—could out-sing me. What I wanted was something distinctive to attract the music-club market, something which other singers could not perform, something in which their fresh voices would not have so great an advantage. I needed something in which there would be no competition.

I began to think about lecture-recitals. Most lecture-recitals by singers are no more than a collection of songs, with chatty introductions to each song. These I should find even more difficult than straight recitals, because mixing singing with speaking is not easy, and talking and singing for an hour and three-quarters would be dangerous for my damaged stamina. My speaking voice was unaffected, for it is naturally deep, and the loss of my top notes had left it unaltered. The singing was the difficulty. I must find a shape to the programme in which I could sing, and do all the singing, at the beginning when I was fresh, and do the talking afterwards. This meant that I couldn't just string together chatty introductions to the songs, and give them to the audience *after I had sung the songs*.

I must find a theme, and one that would come naturally after I had sung. Not the songs themselves, or the composers—how about the preparations I made for a performance? Possible, I thought. I believed I could hold an audience with an account of the work a singer does in his studio. Better, his workshop. And there was my title—'The Singer in His Workshop'. Not bad, I thought. It gave a quick picture of what it was about, and it was unusual and, I hoped, attractive. (It isn't unusual these days—everyone has a 'Workshop' programme now, but I think I was the first to use it as a title.) Talking about the singer's deliberate and calculated projection, I should in fact be talking about the psychology of performance—but I mustn't frighten audiences off by telling them that. I must write it as an attractive and amusing look behind the scenes at the singer's working life.

There was a problem. I had the beginnings of a shape, though it was incomplete—a miniature recital of carefully selected songs, lasting say half an hour, and then, I reckoned, about an hour's talking. But I needed a good finisher. It would be an anti-climax, to begin with music, and finish with an hour's talk. I must have more music at the end, to round the programme off. But I knew that, after talking for an hour, it would be impossible to sing again. What about recording something? Maybe, but what? A performance of a song? That wasn't on, for playing a recorded performance from a tape would only underline what I was trying to conceal, that physically I could not sing again at the end of a long evening. Record a *rehearsal*? This had possibilities. Record a rehearsal of one of the songs that I had sung at the beginning? 'That's more like it,' I thought. I've sung, I've talked about the way a singer prepares his work for public performance, and then I play a recording of a rehearsal of one of the songs they've already heard, in which I could bring out the principles that I should have explained in the talking bit. Exactly what principles I should bring out I could decide later. But I should have to stop the tape from time to time in order to bring this-and-that, whatever they were, to the audience's attention. Clumsy, I thought. It wouldn't do. Then came the Bright Idea that was to pay the rent for a long time. I'd leave the tape running, and when I made the recording I would leave gaps in the singing into which I could slip whatever I wanted to say. I would start the tape as if it were a straightforward recording of a rehearsal, and when HE, the chap on the tape, did something wrong, I would make a critical comment on HIM and HIS singing. Then HE—I was fair bubbling with ideas now— could protest in an injured voice at my unfair criticisms. What I'd got was a cross-talk act between me in person and me on the tape. It would need very careful timing. (I discovered that the timing was in fact easy. It needed careful writing, and, once it was written properly, the timing couldn't go wrong.) I should in effect be giving my recorded voice a singing lesson, it would be the good finisher I needed, and it turned out to be very funny. I'd got what I wanted, something novel for the market, and something in which I should be free from competition.

189

It worked. I planned 'The Singer in His Workshop' carefully to fit, and to cover, the new physical limitations of my voice, but it became a success in its own right. In the first few performances I had a number of spontaneous reactions from the audience. Driving home afterwards, I remembered each reaction, and worked out how I had got it, from my timing, or a change of pace, or from a different tone I had used. Then, at the next performance, I reproduced the timing, or change of pace, or whatever, to see if I could dig out the same response from the new audience. And, as I went on, doing the programme again and again, there came more reactions, more laughs, more moments of silence—and they always seemed spontaneous. I did the 'Workshop' all over the country. I did a shortened version on television. In the next fifteen years, I gave something like 300 performances. I was back in business, and we were solvent again. I followed it with other scripts— 'Per Ardua ad Opera, or, How to Enjoy Opera Even Though You Are Musical', and 'Glyndebourne and Mozart'. These, luckily, were of a wide enough appeal to attract not only music clubs but ordinary lecture societies, and though it was a surprise to find myself hired to talk to a Philosophical, Scientific and Literary Society, it was good for business, and I found myself one of the busiest lecturers in the country, following round on the circuit TV personalities talking on 'Me and Television', archaeologists on whatever they'd just dug up, ladies who talked about 'Six Weeks in Norway on a Bicycle', and people who were by no means professional lecturers, but had just climbed something, or swum something, or fallen off something, and cashed in for a couple of years by talking, often quite inaudibly, about what it was that they'd climbed or swum or fallen off.

I produced operas in Wales, and in London and Birmingham with student casts. I taught singing, too, in London and in Birmingham, and my practice grew almost alarmingly. But, after the early nineteen-sixties, I found myself so busy with other work that I was forced to whittle my teaching down, and finally had to give it up altogether. It was hard work, but I did get pleasure and satisfaction from being able to help young people to do what I had enormously enjoyed doing myself. I was asked to adjudicate at music festivals. Thousands of singers, pianists, string players, choirs, all over the country, compete each year in hundreds of music festivals. The work itself is killing. I once found, when I arrived to begin work, that I was scheduled to hear 133 performances in the day. When I protested to the secretary that it was impossible to listen sensibly to as many, judge them accurately, and find time to make helpful and useful comments on each competitor at the end of the class, she said glumly that there had been a mistake in the compilation of the programme, and there was another class of 39 which had unfortunately been omitted, and this would bring my total for the day up to 172, and she didn't know what I would think about her. She very soon knew. I was never asked to that festival again.

Occasionally—very occasionally—someone manages to produce a breath-taking and moving performance that lights up the whole day. I remember a contralto at a festival in the North, who sang an aria from the *St. Matthew Passion* which reduced me to tears. Even an hour later, when I delivered an adjudication of the whole class, my voice trembled when I talked of the exquisite quality of her singing. I happened to catch sight of her, sitting in the third row from the front, as I spoke. There I was, on the platform, moved to such an extent that I could scarcely speak, and there she was—sucking an orange.

Once I was asked to go to speak at a Rotary lunch in the middle of a festival week. I wasn't very keen on the idea, but the festival secretary asked me to go as a public relations thing to help the festival. They always managed to persuade one of the adjudicators to go each year, and they persuaded me. When I got to the hotel, I was offered a glass of sherry by the chairman who said, 'Can't think how you fellers stand it. The same song fifty-four times—it would drive me up the wall.' 'You've got it all wrong,' I said, 'it's not the same song fifty-four times. It's fifty-four different *people*, and if you like people there's always something to hold you interested.' I found even the bad performances interesting. For one thing, one could perhaps offer advice that might help them to sing better. There was, too, the fascination of discovering the motives that made people, ordinary people, clerks and miners and teachers and housewives and typists, willingly undertake the ordeal of standing up in public and singing. They sang, some of them, for love of music. They sang, some of them, because they had been bullied into entering by their ambitious families. They sang, many of them, because of their own ambition. They sang, and there were a lot of these, because of their own vanity. But whatever their motives, they gave me a lot of pleasure, and a good deal of fun. Once, again in the North, I was adjudicating the Rose Bowl, which everywhere is the solo championship and the climax of the festival. Six young singers, the winners of the individual classes, were brought to sit on the platform while I commented on and assessed each of their performances. The contralto had a huge, dark voice, not perfectly under control, for the vowels were swallowed and distorted. 'You must sing,' I said, 'with a forward production, with bright clear *open* vowels.' I turned to the audience of proud mums and dads and anxious teachers. 'A good question to ask any young singer before she goes off for the day's singing is this,' I said. 'Have you opened your vowels this morning?' I suppose it was a bit of a risk. There was a shocked pause for perhaps three seconds, while the audience checked back on what I had actually said, and realising that it really was not 'bowels' but 'vowels', burst into the biggest and most satisfying belly-laugh that I had heard. And I think it made a point.

The competitive nature of festivals is sometimes held to be open to question. The motto of the British Federation of Music Festivals insists that competitors are not rivals, but friends pacing each other on the road to perfection—or something like that. Personally, I didn't believe a word of it. The competitor who came on the platform with a look in his eye which made it clear that he had every intention of singing the others off the stage and right down the street—he was the man who came nearest to the cut-throat atmosphere of professional singing, and he was the man for my money. I believed in offering hard professional advice to singers—it did at least pay them the compliment of taking them seriously.

I sometimes became a little impatient with other adjudicators. After years of working in festivals, some of them had reduced judgment to a prefabricated formula. I heard one say in an adjudication, 'I come now to choir number 13. Their intonation was a little less than buoyant.' He meant that they sang flat. 'The intonation of choir number 14, on the other hand, was a little more than buoyant.' This lot had sung sharp. Another man was well known for his little book, in which he had for years made notes of telling phrases. He could be seen turning through its pages, until he found a good one—'A voice of dewy freshness,' he would announce. Using meaningless jingles like this saved him from having to make judgments. Good teachers are hard to find, and in areas where there were no good teachers one could hear a whole class of singers performing quite appallingly. But they wanted to sing, and what they urgently needed was practical help. I thought it was unhelpful—and the audience realised it was dishonest—for the adjudicator to say breathlessly, 'What a lovely, lovely hour of beautiful music we have had from these young people, haven't we?' We hadn't, and everyone knew it.

I believed in speaking my mind. I hoped I should not hurt the singers' feelings, but I would not compromise my own honesty as a singer. I would not pretend that a performance was good, if I knew it was terrible. But they were singers, even if they weren't good singers, and I had been a singer, and I felt at home with them. I had always had fun with singers, and I didn't see why I should not share my pleasure with them, If a joked popped into my mind, I offered it to the audience. too. And some adjudicators became impatient with me. One, a man older than I was, took me aside after that crack about keeping your vowels open, and after a preliminary announcement that he was speaking as an older man, recommended me to try to control my wit. At least, that was his general theme. What he actually said was, 'For God's sake, stop trying to be funny.' But I enjoyed trying to be funny and, years later, much to my surprise, found myself working as a professional comic.

This came from the longest chain-reaction of my life, which started, oddly enough, in a very serious broadcast on the Third Programme. Nothing could have been further from comedy. It was the first 'spoken word' broadcast I had ever done, and it opened up an entirely new field for me as a performer. It came very soon after I had left the Garden, and it was a good time to start something new. I was asked to take part in a symposium on the work of the composer. Sir Arthur Bliss represented composers, and a pianist, a string player, a wind player, a conductor, and I all talked about what we needed, and what we thought we had a right to expect, from composers. I've forgotten who the others were, because we never met. We each recorded separately, and the producer edited the tapes into the form of a discussion. I had seven minutes. It took me a long time to write and re-write my seven minutes, and talking into a microphone, instead of singing at it, seemed very strange. When I had finished, the producer was friendly, but professionally non-committal. The studio manager, however, said as I left, 'Never done this sort of thing before? You'll do a lot of it in future, take it from me.' I was quite happy to take it from him—every performer glows with pleasure at any praise that he gets—but thought that he was overdoing it. I believed that my seven minutes had got everything that I knew about singing, and I didn't think that I had anything more to say. And for some months, I didn't have anything more to say. I went on with my lecture-recitals, and my teaching, and working at festivals. I sang one or two more broadcasts, not very well— small song recitals, *Grand Hotel*, and *Those Were the Days*—and

I thought my broadcasting was finished. I had no idea that the studio manager was right.

Soon I was asked to write a series on opera for B.B.C. schools programmes. Opera had never been tackled before, on the grounds that it was impossible to hold children's interest in something which they could never have seen in an opera house. I had to start right at the beginning, and teach them what an opera was made of, how it was made, how it was rehearsed, and how it was performed. It was an experiment, which seemed to turn out successfully, because every year for some years I did a whole term's series, eleven programmes each time, dealing with individual operas, which I arranged for broadcasting from gramophone records in twenty-minute chunks. This was fascinating, and I learned a lot about radio technique.

Writing for schools had its problems. In my version of *La Bohème* the two lovers became just good friends. There was another crisis in *Carmen*. I had written a vivid piece of narration to introduce the 'Cigarette Chorus':

> The mid-day bell at the cigarette factory rings, the girls troop out into the square, where they join their lovers. They stand in pairs, their arms round each other, watching the grey smoke from their cigarettes drifting slowly upwards in the hot air of Seville, as they sing this Cigarette Chorus . . .

The producer said I must re-write that bit. As a matter of policy, cigarette smoking could not be referred to approvingly in any schools script. I said that it could easily be changed:

> The mid-day bell at the cigarette factory rings, the girls troop out into the square, where they join their lovers. They stand in pairs, their arms round each other, *coughing like mad* as they watch the grey smoke from their cigarettes drifting slowly upwards in the hot air of Seville . . .

This, I am afraid, was thought too flippant, though I've forgotten how in the end I got round it. These programmes were fun to do, and seemed, extraordinarily enough, to make a deep impression on a captive audience. We heard of one school where the teacher said that his children listened dreamily to 'O Isis and Osiris', every time we used it in the series. We had a report from another school, a tough secondary-modern in the Black Country, where a class protested at having to listen to a series on opera, and needed the threat of physical force to keep them in their places while I began the first programme. But eleven weeks later, they arranged on their own initiative an expedition to Birmingham to hear the Carl Rosa company in *Rigoletto*—and, what was more, added sixpence apiece to the cost of the expedition to take their form-master with them and pay for his seat.

I had another idea—or, rather, I pinched it from another series. In the B.B.C. Midland Region, they had a regular programme called 'Stories from the Ballet' in which a narrator told the story of some of the stock repertory ballets, to introduce some of the best-known music. My idea was a series called 'Stories from the Opera' which, like the companion ballet programmes, I arranged for a programme-slot of sixty minutes. But the difference was that I linked the episodes with narrations which I wrote for myself, as one of the characters in the opera. I told the story of *La Bohème* as Colline. I was the Doctor in *Traviata*, Zuniga in *Carmen*, Rocco in *Fidelio*. Sometimes I wrote scripts for others—for Marjorie Westbury to tell the story of *Hansel and Gretel* as the small boy (one of her specialities), and for the American baritone Jess Walters, as Sharpless in *Butterfly*. The programme established itself, was sometimes used not only in the Midlands, but in the Basic Home Service network, and it ran off and on for about five years.

I became a disc-jockey, of a rather highbrow kind. The Home Service had in those days a Sunday lunch-time programme of operatic records, linked in various patterns. One day I met the Head of Gramophone Department in the Club bar. She asked me if I had any ideas for the series. I said I had been toying with an idea called 'First Nights And Second Thoughts'. 'Lovely!' she said. 'Have you got your diary with you? Good.

Can you do eight Sundays, starting on June 5th . . .?' and
went on to give me rehearsal times, the length of each programme, and transmission times—and then said, with a sweet
smile, 'Now—what's it all about?' It actually was not a bad
idea, about operas that failed miserably at their first appearance, but afterwards established themselves in the repertory.
The interesting thing was that the series was accepted on the
spot on the title alone. I introduced a series of 'Music To
Remember' and in one programme my flippancy got me again
into a little trouble. I had to introduce the overture to
Rossini's *William Tell*. I was fascinated by the story that, after
its first production in Paris, it was proposed to put it on in
Italy; but there were official anxieties. It was felt that the
spectacle of a brave, democratic Swiss defying his Austrian
overlords could well stir up trouble amongst the patriotic
Italians, who might be provoked into similar resistance against
the Hapsburgs, who were still the masters of Italy. So the
setting and the title of the opera were changed, and it was presented as *William Wallace of Scotland*, the story of the struggle of
a brave, democratic Scot against those familiar oppressors, the
English. I thought this was a delightful story, and I wanted to
underline it, when the moment came for me to set the orchestra
playing, by announcing the Overture to Rossini's *William
Wallace*. But this was frowned upon. Pity, I thought.

I spread my tiny wings in another direction. I was asked by
Phyllis Tate and her husband Alan Frank, who publishes her
work—he is the music editor of the Oxford University Press—to
write the libretto for an opera that she had had in mind for
some time. This dropped right out of the blue, and it astonished
me. I had met Phyllis and Alan some years before, in my palmy
days as a singer, when I had sung in a broadcast of a work of
hers that I found extraordinarily difficult. But this was much
too slight a knowledge on which to take the risk of asking
me to work with her. I asked them bluntly, 'Why me?' and
Alan told me that they had 'asked around', as they say, and in
several quarters my name had been suggested as a singer who

could both read and write, and knew something of the techniques and the construction of opera. Phyllis had long been obsessed with the story of Jack the Ripper and this was to be our subject. It took me a year to plan the synopsis, argue about how many lines Phyllis needed for each act, and then write the words. I was not working at it full-time, by any means, but put in a day, or a morning, sometimes a couple of days together, in between my other work. For Phyllis it was two years' slogging, but the first performance, which was at the Royal Academy of Music, with a student cast, had a great success. One notice said that it was the best first British opera since *Grimes* and we sat back and waited for it to be taken up by one of the professional companies. It never was. We were disappointed because we felt that we had written a good, modern, interesting opera ready to take its place in the repertory. It was given a professional performance by an *ad hoc* company, which I was fortunate enough not to see, because I was told that it was quite awful. It had another student performance in Glasgow. The B.B.C. put it on in the Music Programme, when it was conducted by my old friend Charles Groves. And so far this is the sum total of the success that *The Lodger* has won. Later we were commissioned by the B.B.C. to write another opera for television. It was called *Dark Pilgrimage* but the subject was not one that we chose, and indeed not one that we enjoyed writing. The less said about it, the better.

Birdie's wings were getting stronger, and their span was wider. Four years after I had left the Garden, I had a bit of a ding-dong with the Post Office, which illustrated the growing variety of my work. We were moving to another house. There was a telephone already installed, and I filled up the official application to have it transferred to me. The form had a little window, in which I had to insert the details for my entry in the directory. NAME: 'FRANKLIN DAVID' I wrote, and added my address and the phone number. The form was promptly returned with a crisp official note telling me that the directory entry was 'inaccurate'. I rang the Sales Manager.

'Why inaccurate?' I asked.

'Christian names in full are NOT permitted by the regulations,' he said. 'There is great pressure on space in the London directories, and official instructions are that only initials are to be allowed in future. In the case of common initials, such as D, abbreviated christian names may be permitted at the discretion of the Telephone Manager.'

'Franklin D. is all I shall get?'

'Yes.'

'But that won't sufficiently identify me.'

'In the case of common initials, such as D, I have already said, abbreviated christian names *may* be permitted at the discretion of the Telephone Manager,' he said.

'Are you telling me that FRANKLIN DAV is the most that I can hope for?'

'That is correct, sir.'

'God damn it,' I said, 'I'm not that sort of a singer!'

'I'm sorry, sir,' he said. 'I don't understand.'

'In the circles I work in,' I said, 'I have never been known as Dave Franklin, and certainly *never* Dav Franklin.'

'I'm afraid that the abbreviation is all you are allowed, sir.'

'Wait a minute,' I said. 'Mine is a business telephone. So— correct me if I'm wrong—as a business subscriber I am allowed my surname, one initial or abbreviated christian name . . .'

'At the discretion of the Telephone Manager,' he cut in sharply.

'Naturally,' I said, and went on, 'plus one-word-of-professional-or-trade-description. That's right?'

'Quite correct, sir.'

'Good,' I said. 'Now we know where we are. I'll have my surname, I will abrogate my right to one initial or abbreviated Christian name . . .'

'*Abrogate*, sir?'

'Sorry,' I said. 'I will give up my right to an initial or a Christian name.'

'*No* initial or Christian name?' he said, astonished after the fuss that I had been making.

'*No* initial or Christian name,' I said firmly. 'Instead, I will have only my surname, plus one-word-of-professional-or-trade-description.'

'And what's that, sir?' he asked, bewildered.

'DAVID,' I said triumphantly.

'No, sir,' he said desperately. 'That's not professional-or-trade-description. That's a Christian name, and Christian names in full are not allowed. Words of professional-or-trade-description are like butcher, or physician-and-surgeon, or undertaker.'

'Look,' I said. 'To make a living, I sing, I lecture, I broadcast, I write, I produce operas in the theatre and on the radio, I adjudicate in music festivals. Give me one word of professional-or-trade-description that would cover all of those activities.'

'Very hard, is that, sir. Very hard indeed. I can't think of one, I'll be honest with you.'

'I can,' I said.

'And what would it be, sir?' he asked.

'DAVID,' I said fiercely.

He argued for a while longer but I had him on the run. FRANKLIN DAVID I have been ever since, but FRANKLIN DAV, as the G.P.O. wanted to call me, had recovered some of the ground that David Franklin had lost. And there was more still to come.

There has been in my life a strange five-year cycle. I am neither psychic nor whimsy. I do not believe that I have a Good Fairy and a Bad Fairy, fighting for possession of me to decide whether I get a pat on the head or a kick in the stomach. But the plain fact is that every five years, give or take a few months, something important happens. Sometimes it is splendid and exciting, and sometimes it has been horrible. To take the period since the Second World War, in 1946 I auditioned for Covent Garden, and was given a contract. Good. In 1951, after the loss of my voice, I left the Garden. Bad. In 1956 I was asked to do a series of programmes called *Fifty Years Ago Tonight*, from the

Midland Region of the B.B.C. Good. Peter Haysom Craddy was the producer, and it was his idea. It was a splendid one, and I wished that I had had it. It was that I should do the research to find music, all over the country, that had been performed fifty years ago to the night—no cheating—and that I should link the music with a background script about the artists who had performed it, the places where performances took place, and the people who lived near by. This was the first time that I had had an opportunity to talk about people and places, because until then all my radio work had been connected with music, either singing, or talking about music, and this was to prove a useful extension of my work.

I had another Bright Idea, one morning when I was shaving. I leapt at the telephone and with my half face still covered with lather talked for forty-five minutes to my lecture agent. The Idea was to adapt *Fifty Years Ago Tonight* for a lecture in any particular town. While I had been researching for the B.B.C. Midland series, my eye had often strayed from the music columns into the ordinary news. And fascinating things it found. What I wanted to do was to begin by talking about what had happened, in any town that hired me, fifty years ago to the day, sometimes in the very hall in which I was to speak, and then from these local beginnings to broaden into a picture of what was happening all over the country, in politics, in music, in the theatre, in ordinary social life—even in the shops. It went, though I say it myself, like a bomb and I spent hours in the British Museum digging into old newspaper files preparing for town after town after town. It became, I am modestly delighted to report, a very profitable exercise.

For the first few years after the Garden, I had had to make a deliberate and conscious effort to re-establish myself. Then a momentum seemed to develop and after that things started happening around me. In 1961, the next year of my five-year cycle, we moved from London to Worcestershire. I was convinced that London was strangling itself to death, and I didn't want to be there when it happened. Soon after we arrived in our new home, my wife asked 'Isn't it time?' I said, 'Five years after 1956 is 1961—yes, it is.' I wondered what would happen, whether it would be good or bad. It turned out nice again. Soon after we arrived in Worcestershire, the wind band of the Royal Shakespeare Memorial Theatre gave a performance of Handel's *Music for the Royal Fireworks*, and because I was now handy, the producer of the Midland morning magazine asked me to do him a piece about the very first performance of the music, in 1749. I dug out the *London Gazette* for that week, and there was splendid material there. The very first rocket that the Royal goons let off flew into the Royal Library, built of wood, in Green Park, and set it on fire. Half of them were detached to rescue it, some of them hacked it down with axes to save it from being burned down, and the others poured buckets of water over the flames, and these fire-fighting activities between them destroyed the Library. Meanwhile, the rest continued to let off fireworks. Their second rocket went straight to a young woman in the crowd and set her clothes on fire; the *Gazette* said she would inevitably have burned to death, had not a bystander, 'with admirable presence of mind, pulled off her clothes, but only down to the shift'—thus preserving not only her life but decency. Several people died during the night. A man perched on a tree in the Park shouted enthusiastic huzzas for the King, over-balanced, and broke his neck as he fell. Another drank the King's health so repeatedly that his head swam, and his mouth tasted horrible, and, bending over a lake to drink a refreshing draught, fell in and, poor chap, didn't come up again. Strangely, these disasters which I reported from the *Gazette* came out funnily, and the producer asked me to cover the actual performance at Stratford.

That I thought gorgeously comic. In the first performance, Handel had had 24 oboes, 24 bassoons, and 9 trumpets as the foundation of his band, and nothing could drown the sound they produced. But the band of the Royal Shakespeare Memorial Theatre was only nine strong. They embarked, looking, I said, very smart and seamanlike in their dinner-jackets, on a barge which was hauled out inch by inch on an extraordinary spider-web of ropes, into the middle of the river. They could scarcely be heard even when no fireworks were being let off, and every time the chaps doing the pyrotechnic bit wanted to let off another rocket, the band had to take five. There were hordes of strange vessels in the river. I was prepared to accept that I was wrong in thinking that in the dark I had seen a Red Indian war-canoe, but I swore that I had seen an army landing craft. The din in the audience on the river banks was indescribable. Transistor radios, the buzz—more than just a buzz—the steady roar of conversation, the noise of traffic over the bridge, shunting from the station, planes overhead—all these made a barrier through which I heard, very occasionally, the fizzing of a rocket, and faint wisps of sound from the band. I advised the organisers to hire an aircraft carrier (a River Trust was then working on making the Avon navigable) and the massed bands of the Brigade of Guards. There was no other way, I thought, to make the music audible.

When I recorded my piece, the studio crew laughed, and Michael Ford, the producer, asked me if I could be funny on things other than music. I said I could try. If I could keep it up, he said, he'd take anything I offered him. I began to offer him a lot. I started writing funnies for *Today*, and for what is techni-cally called the Midland opt-out from *Today*. I wrote about everything that caught my fancy: life in our village—and it is the sort of village that is full of quiet fun—a visit to a nudist colony, the files of the Patent Office in Birmingham, a very tatty escaped eagle, an ox-roasting, the 700th anniversary of the death of Simon de Montfort in the Battle of Evesham, and a scourge of beatniks that had camped in the Art Gallery in Birmingham. There was a wealth of comic material waiting to be found in all of them.

In the Patent Office, a specification for a humane mousetrap took my fancy. It was so designed that it did not kill the mouse, but hung a string round its neck, with a bell that tinkled when the mouse ran home. The devilish ingenuity of the idea was that other mice, hearing a bell ringing in their midst, would feel there was something spooky about their home, and would move next door in a body. It was thus not a device for extermination, but rather for the re-distribution of mouse population, and I thought that the invasion of another house by mice ringing bells might well lead to bad neighbour-relations. I liked, too, the invention of the Self-Raising Bowler Hat, designed for the assistance of gentlemen carrying parcels in both hands, and thus having no hand available to carry out the courtesy of raising their hats to ladies of their acquaintance whom they met on the street. The self-raising hat was delicately balanced on a structure which fitted on to the head, and the grave and formal inclination of the head would set the apparatus to work. The hat would raise itself—but would continue to go on rocking itself up and down all the way down the street. Rather un-English, I thought. The piece about the beatniks who had invaded the art gallery gave me the opportunity to announce an important discovery that I had made in sex-recognition. They looked all the same to me, with long hair on the shoulders, jeans and sandals, but I guessed—I couldn't be sure—that those with beards were men, and the clean-shaven ones were women.

I did a couple of broadcasts in *Today* about the Simon de Montfort festival. The battlefield on which he died is about half a mile from our home, and one of the armies in the battle marched to the fight over what is now our garden, and we took an interest in the planning of the celebrations. The committee gave their all to the project. An alderman said enthusiastically in the Council that Simon was going to do for Evesham what Shakespeare had done for Stratford-upon-Avon, which gave a curiously commercial air to the planning of a curious festival. Every organisation in the town was to contribute. The chess club was to organise a chess tournament, the rowing club and the swimming club a regatta and a gala, a play was written and was to be produced about Simon's last hours, the rambling club was asked to arrange a pleasant afternoon ramble over the approach routes of the four armies that converged on Evesham for the battle, and the music club were to plan a symphony concert of contemporary music by Worcestershire composers. I said in my broadcast that apparently no one had thought of working out the distances covered by the armies. I had, and they totted up to 126 miles, and I thought that 126 miles were a little more than a pleasant afternoon ramble. As to the concert, I pointed out, I thought helpfully, that the battle was in 1265, and the first symphony was written just about 500 years later, and that, if they wanted contemporary music, they had better brush up on their lutes and their rebecks. It got me into trouble in the town—but I had had my fun.

I was chatting with Michael Ford at lunch one day in the B.B.C. canteen in Birmingham, laughing about a commentator I had heard the night before. 'For goodness' sake,' said Michael, 'don't waste it on me. Write it down, and turn it into a broadcast.' I did—and it produced a sudden extension of my chain-reaction. With this script, it exploded.

> I wish they wouldn't go on so. Tell me once, or twice at the most, but if I haven't got the message by then, don't bother. Don't keep on. . . . (*Fast, crescendo*) 'It's a furlong to go and Monkey Nuts is running on well from Wallflower and Silent Noon. It's a great race, Monkey Nuts, Wallflower, and Silent Noon in that order, and (*fortissimo*) at the post the winner is Monkey Nuts, Wallflower is second (*voice gradually down to normal*) and Silent Noon third. And with that news, that the 3.30 was won by Monkey Nuts, with Wallflower second, and Silent Noon third, we return you now to the studio.

> And then the chap in the studio has to have his whack at it.

> Back in the studio we bring you up-to-date with our Results Service. The 3.30 was won by Monkey Nuts, with Wallflower second, and Silent Noon third. And there, coming up on your screen, you have your visual check.

> And although we can see it for ourselves on the telly, blow me, he reads it all over again: 'First, Monkey Nuts, second

Wallflower, and third Silent Noon.' Of course, he knows we're not very clever, and he feels he must help us with the hard words. But I wish he wouldn't.

I wish, too, that they wouldn't be so soppy when they introduce programmes. I heard one chap the other night, finishing with a charming, intimate message addressed to each of the 1,295,475 people listening then: 'Take . . . *very* good care of yourselves, won't you?' I can't answer for the other 1,295,474, but, speaking on behalf of me, I wish to state that I have been taking great care of me, since long before he asked me, because I've already given my promise to be careful to that nice Mr. Marples. This chap needn't think he can flannel me into leaving Mr. Marples, and joining his lot. Because I won't.

The other night, after the news, another programme started before I could switch it off. (*Wistfully*) 'Hullo,' said a voice. 'I know it's awfully late, but . . . *please*, can I drop in? Just for a little while? I *promise* not to make a noise.' Actually, I wish he could have dropped in on me at the time. In our house, the transistor gets taken to some very peculiar places.

So there it is then. That's what you have to say when you've finished your piece. They all say it, Mr. West, and Mr. Wolstenholme, and Mr. Baxter, and Mr. Swanton, and old Uncle Dimmock and all. I've never really understood *what* is there, then, but good enough for them is good enough for me. So there it is then.

(*very sexy voice*) Goodbye for now. Take . . . *very* good care of yourselves, won't you? (*even more sexy, in a whisper*) And, until we meet again, please, *please* remember just one thing. (*ordinary voice and briskly*) The 3.30 was won by Monkey Nuts, with Wallflower second, and Silent Noon third.

This little piece had an extraordinary success. It was used in the Midland morning opt-out, and in both editions of *Today*. By midday, it had been picked up by *Pick of the Week*, and repeated the following day, and months later, was used again in *Pick of the Year.* And it had an extraordinary effect on my future. Michael Bowen, a producer in the B.B.C. West Region, heard it, and rang Peggy Bacon, who was then producer of Children's Hour in Birmingham. He said that he'd heard a chap called Franklin, very funny with a script clutched in his hand, and asked her if she thought I could be amusing without a script. She thought for a moment, and then—bless her—said 'Yes'. And so, a few months later, I found myself on *Any Questions?*, and have been a regular ever since.

As it happened, I was also invited to be a member of the Midland team on the *Round Britain* Quiz, and both of these programmes I found a frightening prospect. Of the two, *Round Britain* is much more the more difficult, and I had the feeling that I was a sitting target for aged clergymen, sitting in remote rectories in Norfolk with an *Encyclopaedia Britannica*, rooting out recondite and obscure questions with which to torture me. As my wife said, when I was asked to do both programmes, you either know the answer to the Quiz questions, or you don't. She thought *Any Questions?* would be easier, because I could flannel my way out of a tight corner. I should be reluctant to think of my wise and urbane contributions as mere flannelling, but I confess that I did evolve a useful technique for dealing with M.P.s. Normally, if I saw a chance to make a quick bite and then leave the bones to the rest of the panel, I cocked a finger at Freddy Grisewood, he nodded, as he was re-reading the question, and then threw it to me. But if it was a political question, I carefully avoided his eye, sometimes taking the precaution of dropping a pencil on the floor, and waited until the two M.P.s —there's always one from each party—had had their say. I discovered very soon that in every question there is a key-word— abortion, the pill, devaluation, Vietnam—that sets politicians off on the prefabricated party line. I'd listen with blatant admiration to both of them, and then, when it was my turn, I'd say, openly, how much I admired their arguments, their fluency, their deep knowledge of the matter. Then I'd pause, and change the tone of my voice, and go on, 'But what you said has nothing to do with the question, has it?' And it never had. It was extra-ordinary how often I could use that ploy—and I did, ruthlessly.

Because of the funnies I had done for the early morning pro-grammes, and because of the work I had done on *Any Questions?*, in 1965 I became involved in work for Current Affairs. I was asked to do a weekly programme called *Weekly Echo*, in the Mid-lands, a commentary on the local weekly papers of the region. I was asked to write a pilot programme, to test the logistics of production. There were nearly a hundred papers to read; half arrived on Friday, and the rest on Saturday. The programme was to be recorded on Sunday morning, for transmission on Monday morning, and so the script had to be written on Satur-day. To give time for it to be duplicated, it must be finished by tea time, and the problem was to find out if there was time to read so many papers, and to write a fifteen-minute script, by that deadline. The planners asked me to do the pilot because they felt it was not appropriate to ask a journalist to comment on the news, and the work, of other journalists. I laughed at the idea, but said I'd do it, on condition that it was understood that I believed it was impossible. There wouldn't be time enough, and there wouldn't be enough material in the papers. I was wrong on both counts.

Weekly Echo has, at this moment, been running for nearly four years, and it is one of the greatest pleasures of my routine work. It is not a programme about papers—it is about people, the people of the Midlands, who do silly, criminal, human, touch-ing, infuriating things every day. The papers watch them at it, and I watch the papers. It is fascinating to see how often stories about a particular social question—water supplies, education, housing, coloured immigrants, the barring of the Press from Council committees, traffic, town planning—crop up simul-taneously and independently in papers all across the region, ready to be linked into a pattern of life in the Midlands. We thought at first that it was to be only a summary of the news, but it turned out to be delightfully funny every week. Mid-landers, bless them, have given me an unbroken series of comic pay-offs (a technical term for the end of a programme).

There was the rector who wrote with dignity in his parish magazine—the *Newark Advertiser* lifted it from the magazine, and I lifted it from the *Advertiser*—that there had been a theft from the Rectory. 'Whoever took the Rectory commode,' he added, 'should be warned. The seat has woodworm.' I finished the programme: 'Mind how you go. Good morning.' There was another parson who wrote in his parish newsletter, 'God has given us this great hope in immorality because it is the most natural thing in the world and the most reasonable. Without immorality, life is just a blind brief culver between two oblivions.' When this was brought to his attention, he said reproachfully, 'I don't think the typist and I speak the same language. I was writing about immortality!' A gushing woman columnist had a headline—'WHEN TO HAVE BABY'. Fascinated, I read on. 'Tax-wise, the best time to have a baby is a few minutes to midnight on 5 April.' The trouble was that she wrote this piece in January, which scarcely gave anyone time to make the necessary arrangements. A council in Suffolk gravely considered an offer by a firm who offered to supply piped, continuous music to their public lavatory, and in their sales letter argued that it would 'counteract the silence and emptiness usually present and give some life and cheer to the place'!

We spend a lot of time on the proceedings of local councils. I have been accused of making fun of them, and I primly replied that it was not necessary—they did it much better than I could. In a discussion on whether the Press should be admitted to committees, an alderman begged his council to reject the motion. 'If they printed everything we said verbatim,' he argued, 'the public would think we are a school of comedians.' I made no comment on this plea, but merely added that I had found that same week in another paper from a near-by town a report that Alderman X had said in a council debate, 'If I had an accent like Councillor Y, I'd go out and commit suicide.' Councillor Y replied hotly, 'The alderman sounds as if he was speaking with an apple in his mouth,' to which the alderman made instant and witty riposte—'At least, *I* have my teeth in!' We took reports from this paper and that, and by cross-cutting and laying one story against another, as one would in cutting a film, we found that we have a satirical programme, in which the people of the Midlands every week satirise themselves. And, like everything else in my work, it is enormous fun.

The next year of my five-year cycle was 1966 and, true to form, my chain-reaction exploded again. A Current Affairs man from London heard a couple of *Weekly Echo* tapes and liked them, so I was asked to do *Weekly World* from London. It is a commentary on the political weeklies, and to my astonishment —and, I am sure, to that of listeners who remember me as a singer—I found myself in the political pundit line of business. There is a panel of reviewers who each do a month on the programme, and I enjoy all of my stints as they come round. There was a second explosion at the same time. I've always allowed myself to indulge my taste in 'funnies' in all sorts of radio scripts, and Tony Shryane apparently enjoyed them. He is a remarkable radio producer and has a sensitive nose for successful programme ideas. He started *The Archers* and, up to now, has produced it continuously for seventeen years—and still is refreshingly sane. He started *My Word*, and has fourteen years of that behind him. In 1966, with Ted Mason, who has set the questions for *My Word* and has written hundreds of episodes for *The Archers*, he was planning a new programme to run alternately with *My Word*. This was to be called *My Music*, and they asked Frank Muir, Denis Norden, Ian Wallace, and me to take part, with Steve Race in the chair. This was how I became a professional comic, at the end of a long chain that had started fifteen years before with a highbrow symposium on the Third Programme.

My Music became an immediate success with listeners—and with us, too. I had worked with Ian, who knew Denis and Steve, and Frank and Denis had worked together for years, but otherwise we began recordings completely unknown to each other. And right from the start, we hit it off as if the series had been running for years. I found it the most enjoyable work I'd ever done in my life. Work? I could scarcely believe my luck in being paid for playing the fool, and having fun about music, in such entertaining company. Frank and Denis have long been the best comic writers in the business. The speed at which their minds work astonishes me. They can pick up an allusion behind a word and turn it brilliantly into an Instant Joke. They have been at it so long that it has become instinctive—almost compulsive—to play with words. A friend of Frank's told me that he dropped in casually one day and saw a new and splendid refectory table in their hall. He stroked it affectionately and said approvingly, 'Wood like that doesn't grow on trees.' Their facility runs riot in *My Music*. I was once asked to identify a children's choir from a snippet of a record that was played to us. I realised, cleverly I thought, that they were singing in German. 'Austrian, are they?' I asked. 'No,' said Steve. 'Boys?' I asked. 'No,' said Steve again, 'little boys and little girls.' 'No idea,' I said, and gave up. 'No marks,' said Steve. 'Pity. Actually it's the Obenkirchen children's choir.' I tried to justify my tactics, and explained that I had asked if they were Austrian and boys because I was after the Vienna Boys' Choir. 'That may well be,' said Frank brutally, 'but let's leave your private life out of this.'

Denis has a fantastic knowledge of who wrote what in the theatre musicals, but about serious music he once said that he envied me what he called my 'air of outraged omniscience'—a gorgeous phrase. In an early programme, he was called upon to identify an aria from *Rigoletto*. With Ian's help—we cheat and prompt each other without scruple—he discovered it was 'La donna è mobile'. Steve gave him his two marks, and then, off the cuff, asked Denis if he would care to translate the Italian. 'Yes,' said Denis at once, 'The bird's got a motor-bike.' That was the hit of that week's edition; but one of Frank's very best cracks was cut out of the transmission tape for policy reasons. I was set to name an overture of Beethoven's, of which a few seconds were played from a record. I have a blind spot about Beethoven. He wrote so cruelly for voices—*Fidelio* is appallingly difficult—that I suspect my mind has set up a defence-mechanism, and has rejected Beethoven. I knew it *was* Beethoven, but I had no idea what it was. Steve was kind and said he'd help me. 'It's founded on a play of Shakespeare's—there's a clue for you,' he said. I afterwards discovered it had nothing to do with Shakespeare, and anyhow his clue meant nothing to me. I said so. 'Bad luck,' said Steve. 'No marks. The play was *Coriolanus*, but Beethoven's title was the Overture *Coriolan*.' And, in an interested voice, Frank said, 'Whatever happened to the anus?'

Ian and I confessed to each other when we began that we had both been worried about our chance of being able to live with Frank and Denis in this sort of impromptu knockabout. Fortunately, we survived. We all developed, quite spontaneously, without planning or pre-arrangement, a series of programme devices. Frank nags at me, and scores off me almost at will. I treat him with heavy and dignified reproach. We both tease Ian. Frank has a go often at Denis, but I don't. Denis's reaction is so fast, and his wit so devastating that I don't take any risks with him. We all turn on Steve from time to time. One night, Frank complained that Steve, knowing what the questions were to be, had time to prepare his impromptus beforehand, and loftily explained to him that 'the chairman is not supposed to be funnier than the members of the team'. And these regular techniques have made *My Music* develop from a quiz game on music into, not perhaps a situation comedy, but a comedy of character, in which the five of us airily toss question and answer from one to the other, and the fun bubbles out week after week.

It was a remarkable development for me. And there was a third explosion in 1966. I'd read *Warwickshire and Worcestershire Life* at the barber's, and in the waiting-room at my doctor's surgery. The editor astonished me by writing to ask me to write regularly for him. I misunderstood, and said that I wasn't the man to write about Angela ffrench-Smythe's latest dinner-party, glossy magazines weren't my line, and I wouldn't anyway have time to do the leg-work. But he said that his board had issued a policy instruction that each glossy in their chain must now have a controversial page—and I'd been cast to write it, if I wanted. I wanted. Ever since, each month I have written about anything in the two counties that has taken my eye—local politics, gypsies, advertising, village life, town developments—and have at will made fun or serious criticism of it. So now I was comic, political commentator and journalist. I could scarcely believe it myself.

It was in 1966, too, that there came a fourth development. At the B.B.C. in Birmingham, I had worked on *Weekly Echo* with Helen Fry, a Current Affairs producer, who, in that year, was transferred back to London, to work in a section of the B.B.C. that specialised in productions using material from the thousands of records held in the B.B.C. Archives. I had lunch with her one day in 1967 in the B.B.C. Club in London, and met her boss, Harry Rogers. She had deliberately arranged this meeting, because she wanted me to work for her and for the section, and, by the time we finished lunch, I was committed to several scripts for their *World of Sound* series, and, more important, to a big feature programme about Glyndebourne. This, as it happened, was to lead to another wide extension of my work, to a series of programmes which profoundly disturbed me as I wrote the scripts, but, in the end, helped me to lay old and painful ghosts.

Helen had an idea for a perfect title—*Glyndebourne Revisited*.

EIGHT

Glyndebourne Revisited

THE IDEA for the programme which Harry Rogers suggested
was that I should wander round Glyndebourne, chatting about
people and things that I might remember as I wandered, listening to voices from past seasons in the B.B.C. Archives, and to
music from Glyndebourne recordings. There was a mass of
material, and I had first of all to find some way of organising it.
I planned a route—the front hall, down the passage to the
Small Dining Room, into the Organ Room, through the doorway beside the organ into the theatre and on to the stage, down
the stairs to my old dressing-room, and then out to the garden
which is a memorial to Audrey. Each of these locations I used,
in turn, to talk about the giants of Glyndebourne—Christie,
Strasser, Busch, Ebert, and Audrey Christie. We used music
from Glyndebourne recordings of the Mozart operas to bridge
the gaps between one location and the next.

The B.B.C.'s studio managers could of course have reproduced
the acoustic of any of these locations in the studio, but we were
scrupulously honest. I recorded each section of my script in the
very places where I had worked and sung, and had watched
Busch and Ebert at work, over thirty years before and, perhaps
strangely, the authentic quality of the background came over in
transmission. Before Helen and I went down to Glyndebourne
and I showed her round so that she could begin to assess the
technical difficulties of the recording, I took a dive into the

B.B.C. Archive files to dig out the records that I should need. And there I had a nasty shock. They used to say that the first sign of middle age was that you realised policemen looked younger than you did. I found an even more frightening test, in the B.B.C. Archives. There, leering at me from the files, was the name FRANKLIN, DAVID. It is an awesome thing, God wot, to find yourself in anyone's archives, and I began to feel the cold breath of Time down the back of my neck.

Helen and I spent two or three days down there working on the programme—recording my script, listening to a young bass getting hell in the Small Dining Room from Strasser, just as I had done in 1936, making tapes of garden atmosphere and birds singing ('God damn that plane,' we said. 'Better wait until it has gone'), the chorus rehearsing in the distance, the busy-ness of the stage. Helen had not been there before, and was fascinated by the place and by the people she met. I met far more than she did, for everywhere I saw ghosts from the golden days before the war. We were a *company* then, and not just an *ad hoc* collection of singers, hastily assembled for the festival. We were lucky. We were there each year for four months, and we were there continuously.

Then, there were no aeroplanes to whip singers away for a couple of performances in Austria, or Italy, or America, in between shows at Glyndebourne. There were commercial air services, but they were slow and cumbersome, and it still took the best part of a day to fly, say, from Berlin or Vienna. So we all stayed put for the whole of the season, and there was time for the magic of Glyndebourne to work upon us. The place itself was, as always, beautiful, and we were charmed by John and Audrey into feeling that we, too, belonged there. We were hand-picked members of a phenomenally successful theatre and, amongst other singers, we ranked as an élite. So we became a closed community, very conscious of our superiority. It was interesting, and comic too, to watch distinguished foreign singers when they first arrived. Stabile, for instance, was openly amused, almost scornful, when he first walked into the theatre, which then seated around 400. After La Scala, it must have seemed to him like a toy. But when he saw performances, and when he himself began rehearsals, he realised how professional we were, and very quickly he was willingly and enthusiastically absorbed into the Glyndebourne community.

I think it was the work of rehearsals that primarily held us so closely together. Just as Christie was for ever pulling part of the theatre down and putting it up again, so Busch and Ebert broke down the music and the production, and painstakingly put them together, so that the operas ran with brilliant precision and colour. We were absorbed in rehearsals. They held us fascinated. Performances were a nuisance. We did not need the reassurance of applause to tell us how good we were—we already knew. Audiences were an interruption, unwelcome intruders into Glyndebourne. There was a notice on the board in the Green Room that was, I think, significant. I remember that it ran like this:

> Artists must not appear in costume and make-up on the balcony or at the windows of the Green Room, and make themselves the object of the attention of the audience. Nor must artists make individual members of the audience feel that they themselves are subject to the scrutiny of artists in the Green Room.

Deliciously tactful, and characteristic of the care and taste which were applied to every detail of the organisation. On the surface, it meant only that we must not show off in our costumes and make-up in public (but this was quite normal discipline for any theatre), and that we must not put the finger on Noel Coward or Gielgud or Sargent or the Prime Minister as they took their ease on the lawns between the acts. But it went deeper than that. Damn the audience! We lived there, we worked there, and we had the run of the place—until they arrived. We belonged. They had to buy tickets to get in, and now they behaved as if they owned Glyndebourne, and we must hide away in the dressing-room block and the Green Room for all the long interval. During rehearsals, we could lie in the sun and gossip between calls, the men in sports shirts and flannels, and the women in summer frocks (they hadn't started wearing slacks in those days), but now that performances had started, we couldn't go into the gardens even on nights when we weren't singing, unless we were in evening dress.

There was therefore a barrier between the audience and the singers, and this barrier was made stronger and more complete by the Glyndebourne habit of singing everything in the original language. When I began work there, I never questioned this. I suppose my young and flourishing ego was flattered—it was the sign of a superior person to sing in Italian and German. I had heard operas sung in Vienna in German translations from French and Italian and Russian. I had even heard *Cosi* and *Figaro* at Salzburg in German, but all that happened was that my ego took a little more inflation from this. After all, at Glyndebourne, I thought, we did *Cosi* and *Figaro* properly, in Italian. I did not realise—I was blinded by the glamour of Glyndebourne into accepting that everything they did there was right—that hearing operas in German translations in Vienna and Salzburg could be used as an argument for singing them in English in Glyndebourne. It was not until I had sung a couple of seasons in English at the Garden that I began to think differently.

Even in a theatre as vast as the Royal Opera House, using English, you sense the response and the understanding of the audience. At Glyndebourne, friends in the audience, for the most part, were ready to try to persuade you that they didn't like to hear opera in English. 'It sounds . . . *nicer* in Italian,' they said. Even if they knew no Italian? Even then, they said, they preferred it. It seemed more natural, somehow, and, they said, there was the synopsis in the programme. Read that, and you knew where you were. I was never quick enough to be able to learn this sort of thing by heart in a couple of minutes, just before the house lights went down, and to remember it for a whole act, and connect it for an hour and a half with what I saw happening on the stage . . .

ACT III. The Duke's Garden at midnight the same night

Dora has disguised herself in Ferrando's cloak and mask. She imitates his voice, and makes passionate love to his wife, Claudia. Or so she thinks. For suddenly she sees two people walking together in the moonlight. One is the Duke, and the other is—Heavens above, it is Claudia! Then who is it here in her arms? She tears off the mask of the lovely woman, and finds to her astonishment that it is Ferrando! He has been imitating Claudia's voice, and posing as his own wife. Further amusing complications lead to the finale of the Act.

With or without the synopsis in the programme, at Glyndebourne, the audience simply did not understand what was going on. But it didn't matter to them. They had come to worship, and at the end of the act they broke into the ritual cheers, even if they had no idea what it was that they were cheering.

After I left the Garden, I played a couple of seasons as the Haushofmeister in *Ariadne auf Naxos*. It is a brilliantly written comedy part, and I had a wonderful time playing it. During rehearsals, I was extremely funny and stopped the show time and again, with Ebert and the German-speaking cast holding their sides, and throwing themselves round the stage. But on the first night, before a fashionable audience, who mostly didn't understand, and the critics, whose ominiscience in some cases stops short of an understanding of German, I fell quite flat. I gave a biting and witty performance to a silent brick wall. No stopping the show, no belly laughs, not even a titter. There was dead, complete silence. If I had been a young beginner, I should have been bewildered and hurt. But this was 1952 or thereabouts, and by then I had been around. I knew what first night and mid-week audiences were like at Glyndebourne. I knew there is an odd tradition—it is almost that—that at the weekend there are always lots of Germans and Austrians in the house from the refugee colonies in Highgate, and Hampstead, and Maida Vale. Though mid-week I still got no response, on Saturdays and Sundays when they knew what I was saying, I was a riot. I stopped the show every night. Very satisfying.

This has seemed to me for years a complete argument in itself for working in English at Glyndebourne. But there is a second reason. Singing in a language that the audience does not understand has had unfortunate results. They sit in a respectful silence, even at comedies, as if they were listening to a performance of the *St. Matthew Passion*. Harold Rosenthal has a story of a performance of *Cenerentola* at Sadler's Wells at which he found himself in the row behind John Christie. It was sung in English, and brilliantly and amusingly directed, and the audience was having a wonderful evening. They laughed. And laughed. And laughed. Harold saw Christie turn to his companion and heard him say, 'What are they laughing at?' (There was a simple answer to that. It was a comedy.) 'Why are they laughing? Can't hear the music!' Christie himself was the archetype of a Glyndebourne audience, and I believe that the awed reverence which they brought to all Glyndebourne productions had sometimes a wrong effect upon the style of an opera. This has been particularly marked in comedy since the war.

Up until the 1939 season, the repertory consisted of the five major Mozart operas, a tragedy—*Macbeth*, and an Italian comedy—*Don Pasquale*. In Mozart, particularly with Busch at his side, Ebert's work was exquisitely stylish. *Macbeth* had a tremendously dramatic sweep that was quite overwhelming. But *Pasquale* showed, even then, traces of a heavy-handed approach to stage comedy. Ebert was inordinately pleased with an effect that had been prepared for Act II. Ernesto is to be turned out of the house by his uncle, and has an aria to sing before he goes. Instead of singing it in the set—a room in Pasquale's house—Ebert planned that he should sing it in his bedroom, sitting on his trunk that was already packed for leaving. The bedroom was constructed on a rostrum behind one of the flats, faced not with canvas, but with gauze. Lit from the front, it looked a solid part of the walls of the room, but when the front lights were taken down, and other lights behind the gauze were brought up, Ernesto's bedroom magically appeared.

The flat was, I suppose, at the most six feet wide, so it was a very little room, and it was crammed with a tiny bed, a chair, and the trunk, which made it look even more cramped. But Ebert was delighted with it. Borgioli, who was singing Ernesto, strolled on the stage one day when they had just set the scene for the first time and lit it. Ebert said Borgioli must see this marvellous effect, and called out to Charley in the lighting-box to go to Cue 36. The stage lights blacked-out, up came the lights behind the flat, and there was the little room. Ebert beamed with pride, and asked Borgioli what he thought of it. He shrugged. 'Disappointed,' he said. 'There is no toilet roll.' It was, come to think of it, the only possible comment.

Comedy since the war, with the death of Busch and the loss of his judgment, has often suffered from this heaviness of touch, and I have argued that the non-comprehension of the audience is partly to blame for it. Ebert is above all a man of the theatre. His instinct and experience tell him that at this point in the action there must be a laugh. The music expects it. But there is no laugh, because the pointed wit of the libretto, and the humour of the situation cannot reach the audience. So they must contrive a laugh by physical means—and someone kicks a convenient backside, someone shoves a shaving-brush full of lather into a face, slapstick is substituted for elegance, and comedy becomes farce, anything to find some response through the wall of non-communication, anything, that is, short of singing words that the audience can understand.

In any other theatre, its existence might have depended upon the box-office, and the box-office might have had to depend upon the participation of the audience. (Miss Baylis would have found Sadler's Wells even harder to establish, if she had put on performances in foreign languages at the Old Vic. 'Opera in English' was her battle-cry, and it was the foundation stone of the company that she built.) But Christie's private fortune made the theatre independent, and his ingenuity found other sources of income when he could no longer finance it single-handed. So the response of his audiences was not of first importance. In any case, the press notices, from the beginning, told them that Glyndebourne was unequalled and people accepted this verdict, even though they were quite incapable of making a judgment for themselves, or of sharing the pleasures of performances.

There was another important element in Glyndebourne's independence and its closed community. Press criticism disturbed the surface less than in any other theatre that I have worked in. The management had always sold out for the season—why should they worry about critics? Foreign singers didn't worry, either. It is easy to ignore criticism in a foreign language. (In 1939 in a Mozart Festival in Antwerp, I was serenely untroubled by the notices. In *Flemish*—who cares?) The younger English singers were eager to read what the critics had said about them, for it might be professionally of some use to them. The established artists didn't worry, or said they didn't worry. I told Heddle Nash one morning that he had had a very good notice for his performance the night before. 'Critics,' he said, 'the hell with them. I never pay any attention to them. They don't bloody well know. Ignorant, that's what they are. By the way, what did they say about me?' But the general feeling at Glyndebourne was that we knew better than anyone else how good we were; we were above criticism, and we knew it.

From time to time, Christie himself reacted strongly to criticism. In the fifties, he wrote to *The Times* to attack the size of the annual subsidy by the Arts Council to the Royal Opera House. 'Look at us,' he said, in effect, 'the best opera performances in the world, and no subsidy at all.' Harold Rosenthal wrote next day to *The Times*, and pointed out that Glyndebourne's annual programme-book had forty or fifty pages of advertisements by leading firms, who paid high rates, not because their advertisements were worth it commercially, but on a prestige basis. This, said Rosenthal, was a form of hidden subsidy. Christie was furious, and gave orders that Rosenthal should be struck off the list of critics to whom tickets were sent for first nights. In fact, Harold still went, using tickets sent to a paper that Christie didn't know he wrote for, and dodging in and out of the theatre by routes where he could safely avoid a meeting.

The attitude to criticism was an example of the barrier, which was very real, between the singers and their audience. One year, I was rehearsing the part of the Bassa Selim in *Entführung*. I shared performances with Ebert, who of course produced. One morning, he invented a delicate piece of business.

'Would you like to do that, my dear?' he asked.

'Lovely,' I said. 'But look—this is just a tiny effect.'

'Of course.'

'I must just touch it lightly?'

'Natürlich.'

'But, if I do it lightly, the audience will never get it.'

'Quite right.'

'If I press it, throw it out into the house, I shall overdo it.'

'You mustn't do it too heavily.'

'But, if I touch it lightly, and the audience don't get the point, what the hell do I do it for?'

'You and I,' said Ebert, 'we do this for our own enjoyment.'

This, I later realised, was a key sentence in an understanding of Glyndebourne. We did it for our own enjoyment, behind the wall that we had set up, and the audience sat outside.

The important thing in those early days was that behind our wall, there were men whose professional skills made performances of superb quality, even though audiences and critics had little influence upon them. But after the war, when Glyndebourne re-started festivals, there were changes that had their effect upon standards of performance. Somehow, Ebert wasn't the man that he had been while Busch was alive. His judgment had been reinforced and controlled by Busch. Audrey Christie died young; Erede, who had been an outstanding Italian coach, had moved up in the world and become a conductor; Oppenheim had gone before the war to Dartington Hall, and afterwards to Edinburgh; Bing had moved to the Metropolitan, New York. The team had broken up, and only Ebert and Strasser were left of the original management. The development of the aeroplane during the war had led to an enormous growth of airline services, and it was alas all too easy for singers to fly to other houses during the Glyndebourne seasons. The old closed community was much weaker. The first years had been an extraordinary experience, in a unique combination of amateur improvisation and professional direction that had produced the genius of Glyndebourne. Now, the old pros had mostly gone, and the country house atmosphere had given way to a much more commercial operation.

The singers, with one eye on the airline time-tables, had gone commercial, too. They were no longer prepared to stay at Glyndebourne for the whole of the season. There wasn't time for the old magic to work. Even the pattern of the repertory was altered. In the old days, operas *A* and *B* were rehearsed simultaneously for, say, a month before the season opened. *A* and *B* were produced on the first two nights of the season, and rehearsals were begun on *C*. Three weeks later, *C* was added to the repertory, and we started rehearsing *D*. Three weeks of performances of *A*, *B*, *C*, and *D*, while *E* was prepared, and then came into the programme, and all of the five operas took turns at performances until the end of the festival. We were all there all the time, and an ensemble could develop. After the war, for some years operas were rehearsed and performed in pairs; when they had finished their stint, singers had a taxi waiting after their last performance, and hurried to the airport to catch a plane to their next contract. Because of this new ease with which singers could nip around the world Glyndebourne found itself having to compete with foreign houses for the singers they wanted. I heard *Figaro* some years ago, and said bitterly in the long interval that it was the first time I had ever heard a performance of the second finale in which the best voice on the stage was the gardener. What on earth had made them cast that man as the Count? He couldn't sing the part, I said. And the old Glyndebourne friend that I was badgering said that they knew the Count could no longer sing it properly. 'Then, for God's sake, why hire him?' I asked. The answer was, simply, commercial. They had had a very good Count the year before, who

223

had made a great success. They had offered him the part again, but now he wanted twice the money. He had been offered a season in South America, and, flying there and back, he could fit it in between his commitments at his 'home' opera house. So, unless Glyndebourne could match the fee from South America, he was very sorry, but. 'I see all that,' I said, 'but why this awful man you've got?' There was a commercial explanation for that, too. They wanted him for a few performances of a part that he still did well, but there wasn't enough money for him in that part. He wouldn't come, unless he got another part to increase his pay. So their hand was forced, and he was singing the Count in *Figaro*, even though everyone knew that he was awful in it. In my time at Glyndebourne, no one was cast for a part unless they were sure he was the best.

The airlines had damaged the spirit of Glyndebourne, too. In my time, we worked hard, but we were happy. Today, things have changed. Some years ago, I was down at Glyndebourne, and walked into the artists' restaurant for lunch. I found an old friend there, and joined him at his table. 'How are things?' I asked. 'This bloody place,' he said, 'drives you up the wall. Can't wait for the end of the season.' Two minutes later, we were joined by another old friend. I asked him how things were with him. 'Bloody place,' he said, 'drives you up the wall. Can't wait for the end of the season.' I know—these were only two singers in a big company, and I didn't do a research on the attitudes of the rest. But they were both singers whose distinguished careers have owed a lot to Glyndebourne, and I simply cannot remember anyone in the golden years before the war who called it a bloody place. We were happy.

My brief for *Glyndebourne Revisited* had been to build a nostalgic programme. This was not difficult. Being down there made me unhappy about the Glyndebourne I had known that had disappeared, and unhappy, too, about the Glyndebourne that had succeeded it. I liked my Glyndebourne much better than the 1968 model.

NINE

Allegro ma Tranquillo

GLYNDEBOURNE REVISITED was a successful programme, which broke the record in the unit for audience reaction. So the planners asked me to 'Revisit' other places that had been significant in my past. Helen Fry and I made *Covent Garden Revisited*, which scored just one point less than the Glyndebourne programme had done, and *Cambridge Revisited*, which broke the previous record we had just set up. While this book was in preparation, in March 1969, the Writers' Guild of Great Britain gave *Cambridge Revisited* their award for the Best British Radio Features Script of 1968. Then, in the summer of 1968, I was asked to take part in a series called *The Time of My Life*. Harry Rogers was to interview me, and Helen once more produced. It was planned to concentrate on two periods in my life, the chain reaction which took me from a staffroom to the opera house, and the operation on my throat which destroyed my career as a singer and diverted me into other fields.

We all knew that it would be a tricky programme. For me, it would be especially difficult, to talk about a time in my life which had been full of pain and anxiety. Helen wisely ruled out a studio recording. The technical associations of radio would make it no place for an intimate and delicate probing into my professional disaster. Instead, we sat in the familiar comfort of my home, and Harry and I were able to talk, not as interviewer and victim, but as friends. Harry handled me with great tact and discretion, and Helen made a wonderfully professional job of editing the tape. And the broadcast had an extraordinary reaction. I had many letters from listeners who had long wondered why I had suddenly disappeared from singing, and were distressed to discover the reason for it. Many wrote that they had been moved by the story. One man said that he listened to the broadcast in his car, and had driven with tears running down his face. A housewife told me that she was cooking as she listened and cried into the pastry, so that her family had to eat cakes that were oddly salt to the taste.

But I was surprised to find that I was able to talk in the recording quite calmly and without strain. I afterwards realised that I had in fact in the course of a year unwittingly undergone a course of self-psychiatry. The Glyndebourne programme had forced me to dig thirty years into my past, *Covent Garden Revisited* had taken me back twenty years, and *Cambridge Revisited* forty years. These three programmes, and *The Time of My Life*, had disturbed old ghosts, and reawakened old pains—and afterwards, I found that the ghosts no longer frightened me, and that the pains could not now hurt. For years I had been scared of the past, and I couldn't talk about it, even in my own family. I wasn't scared any more—the wounds had been healed.

I realised too that, though the change in my life had been a bit brutal and painful, and at the time had seemed calamitous, it was the best thing that could have happened to me. The life of a singer at the top is short. Out of the company that started at the Garden in 1947 none of my friends among the principals is still before the public. If it hadn't been for my thyroid and the operation to cut it out, I should in any event have finished long before now as a singer. I should have had to find some other way of making a living. I was so distressed at the time that I would not have believed it, if it had been suggested to me that I was lucky to lose my top notes while I was young enough to reorganise. But it is true.

It was true in more ways than one. Singing in opera is exciting, but it forces you to concentrate upon a few qualities. You lead a full life—but doing the same thing over and over again, rehearsing, performing, travelling, rehearsing, performing, travelling. I have been lucky to find myself faced for the last seventeen years with new kinds of work, new techniques to tackle and sometimes to invent, new audiences to handle. Now, at the beginning of my sixties, I am working with a young man's enthusiasm and a young man's enjoyment, and with a consciousness that, now the field of my work has been so broadened, every one of my capabilities, every part of my experience, is working at full stretch.

At the end of the last Glyndebourne season before the war, I went to say goodbye to Ebert at the end-of-season party. 'How have you enjoyed yourself?' he asked me. 'Marvellously,' I said, 'I've learnt more than ever before.' 'That's right,' he said. 'When the artist has no more to learn, he is ready to die.' This made a profound impression on me. It still does. I have had more to learn in the years since I left the Garden than ever I had as a singer. This for me is the real fun of life, having new things to learn. And it still goes on. Every year, there are new problems for me to tackle.

Like writing a book, for instance . . .

Index

ACKNOWLEDGMENTS FOR PHOTOGRAPHS

1a Edward Reeves
1b London News Agency Photos Ltd
2a Picture Features Ltd
2b Priest of Sheffield
3a Edward Mandinian
3b Guy Gravett
4a & 4b Drawn by Milein Cosman
5a Keystone Press Agency
5b Editions Olivier Perrin
6a Staffordshire Advertiser
6b Axel Poignant